RETURN

EILEEN ERICKSON, OIK/L

(~~206~~) ~~232-7182~~

(425) 888-2356

CLINICAL MANAGEMENT OF MEMORY PROBLEMS

Clinical Management of Memory Problems

Edited by Barbara A. Wilson and Nick Moffat

AN ASPEN PUBLICATION ®
Aspen Systems Corporation
Rockville, Maryland

London
1984

Library of Congress Cataloging in Publication Data
Main entry under title:

Clinical management of memory problems.

 "Developed from a conference held at Nottingham
University in 1982"–Introd.
 "An Aspen publication."
 Bibliography: p. 212
 Includes index.
 1. Memory, Disorders of–Patients–Rehabilitation–
Congresses.   2. Brain–Wounds and injuries–Complications
and sequelae–Congresses.   3. Brain damage–Complications
and sequelae–Congresses.   I. Wilson, Barbara.
II. Moffatt, Nick.
RD594.C6   1984   616.8   84-378

ISBN 0-89443-308-3

Printed and bound in Great Britain

CONTENTS

TABLES, FIGURES AND PLATES

Tables

Figures

Plates

LIST OF CONTRIBUTORS

Alan D. Baddeley, Director, Medical Research Council Applied Psychology Unit, 15 Chaucer Road, Cambridge CB2 2EF.

Neil Brooks, Senior Lecturer in Clinical Psychology, University of Glasgow, Department of Psychological Medicine, 6 Whittinghame Gardens, Great Western Road, Glasgow.

Steven J. Cooper, Lecturer, Department of Psychology, University of Birmingham, PO Box 363, Birmingham B15 2TT.

John Harris, Senior Consultant in Human Factors, Scicon Ltd, 49 Berners Street, London W1P 4AQ.

Nadina B. Lincoln, Research Clinical Psychologist, Department of Health Care of the Elderly, Sherwood Hospital, Hucknall Road, Nottingham NG5 1PD.

Nick Moffat, Senior Clinical Psychologist, East Dorset Health Authority District Psychology Service, Branksome Clinic, Layton Road, Parkstone, Poole, Dorset BH12 2BJ.

Clive Skilbeck, Principal Clinical Psychologist, Neurological/Stroke Rehabilitation Unit, Frenchay Hospital, Bristol BS16 1LE.

Barbara Wilson, Senior Clinical Psychologist, Rivermead Rehabilitation Centre, Abingdon Road, Oxford OX1 4XD.

Rodger Llewellyn Wood, Consultant Neuropsychologist, St Andrew's Hospital, Northampton NN1 5DG.

ACKNOWLEDGEMENTS

We would like to express our thanks to Mick Wilson who helped us in the final stages of this book. We are grateful to him for his enthusiastic readings of the chapters, his advice at the redrafting stage, and for undertaking much of the typing of the final script. Thanks are also due to Grace Leung Moffat who worked so hard to ensure that indexing details were accurately collated and processed.

INTRODUCTION

Memory impairments are frequently associated with such conditions as severe head injury, cerebral tumour, intracranial infection, progressive degenerative disease, brain surgery, nutritional disorder and cerebral vascular accident. When memory problems occur in people suffering from such conditions they and their families are likely to experience great difficulty in obtaining treatment or advice that will help them to come to terms with the problematic changes that take place in their lives. Yet such assistance is desperately needed in order that memory-impaired people and their families can eventually assemble strategies that will to some extent alleviate their problems.

The commonly observed advertisements in the press offering to improve memory are of no practical use whatsoever for the great majority of brain-damaged people, who need a protective environment and assistance from professionally competent workers in the field of rehabilitation. However, up until this point in time speech therapists, occupational therapists, clinical psychologists, social workers, doctors, nurses, teachers and physiotherapists have been given little guidance as to what methods are available or which methods are suitable for helping individual patients to cope with their memory problems. Therapists involved in the treatment of the memory impaired who turn to previous publications on memory are unlikely to obtain much in the way of relevant or practically useful information. Although an enormous number of papers have been published on memory, few of these deal with the remediation or amelioration of memory deficits. Those few papers which do address this problem tend to be concerned with the teaching of lists of words or paired associates in experimental situations and are not, therefore, particularly relevant to the everyday problems which are experienced by the memory impaired.

This book aims to provide that guidance which up until now has been unavailable: it seeks to enable those people working with the memory impaired, in whatever capacity, to recognise and to some extent overcome the real-life, practical problems that are encountered. It does not provide magical solutions, easy answers or make promises about restoring memory, but it does attempt to give a better understanding of the difficulties faced by the memory impaired, and offers suggestions as to how to handle, bypass or reduce their memory problems.

As explained in Chapter 1, the book developed from a conference held at Nottingham University in 1982, when a group of professional workers involved in improving the state of memory rehabilitation met to share their knowledge and ideas and to learn from each other. The structure of the book is built upon the papers presented at the Nottingham conference, with a few deletions and additions.

Alan Baddeley's chapter serves as an important foundation for the rest of the book in that it describes the fundamental relationship between theory and practice as far as memory and memory therapy are concerned. A clear account of the psychological structure of human memory is provided by the author who himself has done more than anybody else to ensure that there is a thriving two-way communication between theory and therapy in the field of memory rehabilitation.

Before beginning any remediation of memory impairment an assessment of the nature and extent of the damage is required. In Chapter 2, Neil Brooks and Nadina Lincoln describe procedures for carrying out such an assessment. The emphasis is on assessment for rehabilitation rather than for research purposes or routine administration of tests. The chapter indicates that assessment for rehabilitation is inseparable from treatment and that in order to evaluate the effectiveness of treatment it is necessary to carry out assessment of the treatment outcome. The chapter discusses reasons why assessment should occur, who should assess and when assessments should be made.

In Chapter 3 John Harris describes those methods for improving memory that are available to us at the present time. Comprehensive coverage of the main categories of existing ways of improving memory is provided, including internal strategies, repetitive practice, physical treatments and external aids. Explanations of ways in which these methods seem to work are given, together with the author's views on their respective strengths and weaknesses.

Nick Moffat begins Chapter 4 with a consideration of variables which may affect memory performance, and then discusses the organisation of memory therapy. Several of the methods of improving memory previously described by Harris are examined within the context of the rehabilitation of the memory impaired. Moffat goes on to explain in detail the application of reality orientation training before ending his chapter with a discussion of the issues relating to the possible restitution of memory. He concludes by suggesting that current evidence does not support attempts to retrain memory processes and that therapists might be best advised to circumvent specific memory impairments by encouraging the use of other intact skills to aid remembering.

In Chapter 5, after providing three case descriptions of different types of memory impairment, Barbara Wilson goes on to discuss precise ways of identifying memory problems. The selection of the most appropriate treatment strategies for individual patients is considered and methods for teaching these strategies are examined. Arguments for a behavioural approach to memory rehabilitation are presented and an example of a detailed behavioural programme is supplied. The chapter finishes with descriptions of a range of possibly appropriate strategies from behavioural psychology such as shaping, chaining, prompting and modelling.

No book published today, claiming to speak with some authority to professional workers in such fields as academic research, medicine, education or rehabilitation, can omit discussion of the present and future role of the microcomputer. In Chapter 6 Clive Skilbeck offers the reader a comprehensive historical review of the role of the microcomputer in clinical psychology. He describes the advantages of the microcomputer in terms of savings in time and cost, pointing out further advantages relating to controlled testing, flexibility and ease of data collection and analysis. Application of the microcomputer to the management of memory improvement and its involvement in retraining procedures are discussed fully. The chapter highlights the tremendous potential of the microcomputer in memory rehabilitation.

Steven Cooper's chapter begins by outlining the extent of our current knowledge of some of the events that occur in the brain which correspond in some way to the formation of memories. He discusses the effects of certain drugs which seem to stimulate or inhibit remembering and refers to experiments that have registered significant results. These suggest that 'memory processes may be affected by drug-induced manipulations of cholinergic activity in normal volunteer subjects'. Cooper provides a description of Alzheimer's disease, senile dementia, and notes that it appears to be accompanied by a drastic and selective degeneration of cholinergic neurones in the brain. He refers the reader to a number of studies which explore the possibility that it may be possible to alleviate certain memory impairments to some degree by attempting to raise cholinergic activity in the brain through the administration of drugs.

After brain injury many skills which the normal person takes for granted may be impaired. Among these are skills connected with attention and speed of information-processing. In Chapter 8 Rodger Wood considers disorders of attention, alertness, selectivity, effort and memory. He refers the reader to several studies which attempt to identify the processes involved in the operation of these skills. During rehabilitation a patient will have to revert to a more conscious and controlled form of information-processing, and the second half of the chapter concentrates on various ideas, suggestions and useful tasks for developing attentional training programmes.

Memory impaired people may benefit from interactions with others sharing similar disabilities. In Chapter 9 Wilson and Moffat discuss several possible advantages to be gained by treating the memory impaired in groups. The chapter continues with detailed journal accounts of two memory group programmes. The reader is taken through the activities of each 15-session course and, in the process, is presented with a broad range of group activities and tasks that have been organised by the authors for their patients. Memory therapy groups for the elderly are discussed and the authors advocate reality orientation as a possibly effective approach to the treatment of the confused elderly. The chapter ends with sections on the organisation and evaluation of memory groups.

In the final chapter Nadina Lincoln reflects upon many of the issues raised in the book and provides a general view of the current situation in which workers in memory rehabilitation find themselves. She questions many of the assumptions that are made within this relatively new field, and considers possible changes and improvements which may develop in the future.

1 MEMORY THEORY AND MEMORY THERAPY

Alan D. Baddeley

The present chapter, like most of the volume that follows, began life as a paper presented at a workshop on memory retraining held at the University of Nottingham in Spring 1982. The workshop sprang from discussions between research workers primarily concerned with the theoretical understanding of human memory, and practical clinicians concerned with the task of helping particular patients cope with their memory problems. Given such origins, it seemed sensible to begin with a consideration of current theories of memory, and then go on to discuss their application in practice — and I agreed to give the theoretical introduction. I did so, presenting an overview of current approaches to human memory. Having given it, I had very mixed feelings. On the one hand I felt I had made a reasonably competent attempt at the difficult job of surveying the vast amount of research that has gone on in the area of human memory over the last decade. I believe this to be an intrinsically interesting area, and one which is at least of background relevance to anyone working with patients suffering from memory problems. On the other hand, I felt that I had completely fudged the issue of how and why such theoretical research is relevant to the therapist trying to help an individual patient.

The task I avoided was a difficult one, not least because I knew so little of the characteristics of the audience I was addressing, or of the practical problems of memory therapy. Even with the benefit of hindsight, writing about the relationship between theory and practice in an area as new and diverse as this presents substantial problems. I do however believe that it is extremely important to maintain strong and healthy links between theory and practice. What follows attempts to explain why.

Theory and Practice

It is sometimes claimed that 'there is nothing so practical as a good theory', a comforting adage for the academic, but is it justified?

There is no doubt that in some situations a really good theory can be

5

extremely useful. Let us take a very obvious case such as the role of Newtonian mechanics in structural engineering. It is inconceivable that a structural engineer's education these days would not include an understanding of mechanics. So much so that it is easy to forget that the concepts underlying this are essentially theoretical in nature. A theory is like a map that can help you understand where you are and help you get from one place to another. Scientific theories can be helpful but are not essential; one can find one's way across country without recourse to a map given enough experience, and people were of course building bridges using techniques that were consistent with Newtonian mechanics long before Newton produced his theory.

Like a map, a theory can be useful but requires intelligent interpretation. A theory is not like a recipe giving you a list of things to do in order to achieve a particular aim, although recipe books may in time develop from a theoretical understanding of the field. To go back to our bridge-building, a treatise on mechanics would not tell you how to build a bridge, although it might contain a great deal of extremely useful material if properly applied.

What then can the practising clinician expect to get from theories of memory? I would suggest three things: a general orientation and understanding, suggestions as to particular therapeutic techniques, and finally methodological help in evaluating such techniques.

A Theoretical Overview

While a good therapist will always be aware of the particular characteristics of each individual patient, if he or she is to learn from experience, then it is essential to be aware of what different cases have in common. A good theory, like a map, provides suitable landmarks for identifying where you are at present and helping you to reach a specified goal. Consider for example the question of diagnosis; one of the clearest cases of global amnesia due to brain damage that I myself have encountered was a woman who had attempted suicide through coal-gas poisoning. She had the classic amnesia combination of normal immediate memory coupled with a grossly impaired ability to learn new material. She was for some time categorised as a hysteric amnesic simply because her particular pattern of symptoms was inconsistent with her psychiatrist's totally incorrect concept of the structure and breakdown of human memory. In the absence of explicit theory, we all tend to apply our own implicit theories, which can be all the more dangerous for being applied unthinkingly.

Theories and Strategies

A second way in which theoretical work can be useful is in suggesting new approaches to practical problems. The whole area of behaviour modification in clinical psychology is an offshoot of theoretical approaches to the study of learning, initially in animals. Although the area of memory therapy is still in its infancy, there are already many obvious examples of borrowing techniques devised, or at least explored in the laboratory. These will be discussed in more detail subsequently (see Chapters 4 and 5), but examples include distribution of practice, and the manipulation of coding during learning by such strategies as the use of visual imagery and encouraging deep rather than shallow processing.

Evaluation of Techniques

In the case of memory therapy, this is an area of future importance rather than current achievement. Until techniques are developed and explored, they are obviously not suitable for evaluation. It is however essential that such evaluation does take place. Brain-damaged patients tend to recover spontaneously, and the observation that patients enjoy a particular therapeutic procedure and appear to improve is not by any means an adequate justification for continuing that procedure. The appropriate question is whether such improvement would have occurred anyhow, and if not whether the amount and generality of the improvement is sufficient to justify that degree of expenditure of therapists' and patients' time.

Evaluating the success of memory therapy is likely to prove diffi-cult since it is of course important not to assume that the improvement of patients on laboratory tests of memory will necessarily generalise to everyday memory tasks. However, academic psychologists are increasingly aware of the need to study memory outside the laboratory, and should provide potentially useful allies in tackling this difficult problem.

Most laboratory studies of memory use procedures in which a com-parison is made between two or more large groups of similar subjects. The therapist on the other hand is often confronted with the problem of evaluating a technique based on a relatively small number of subjects with widely differing problems. It seems probable that the single case approach to the evaluation of therapy will prove most useful here. The technique, which was originally developed in the animal laboratory by psychologists influenced by the techniques of B.F. Skinner, has been subsequently applied most effectively to the evaluation of treatment methods in connection with behaviour modification (Hersen and Barlow, 1976).

In this chapter I will be primarily concerned with the first two applications of memory theory, namely the provision of an overview together with the suggestion of possible strategies, although these will not be described in any detail since they are covered in Chapters 3, 4 and 5. It goes without saying, however, that if the field is to develop, then the application of new strategies should go hand-in-hand with their evaluation.

An Overview of Human Memory

Suppose a therapist were to accept what I have just argued, and attempt to obtain an overview of current theories of memory, what should he or she do? Start reading current memory journals perhaps? This would be, I suspect, a puzzling and rather dispiriting experience. Journals, and indeed often textbooks are primarily concerned with points of disagreement and tend to give the bewildering view of any field that it comprises far more controversy than agreement. The reason for this is obvious; people do not write papers about what everyone agrees about, and what is already established does not require further experimentation. However, beneath the controversies and disagreements there is a surprisingly large amount of common ground. The present section will attempt to summarise this and link it to the specific problem of memory therapy. Any overview as brief as this however is inevitably fragmentary. A more extensive account of current views of memory for the non-specialist is given in Baddeley (1982a).

How Many Kinds of Memory?

This is a question that has preoccupied psychologists quite extensively over the last 20 years. It has been, and remains an area of controversy. The non-specialist attempting to understand this area is likely to be puzzled not only by theoretical differences between different authorities, but also by a wide range of different terms often used to refer to very similar concepts. However, since I myself would regard the conceptual distinctions underlying this controversial area as being very important in evaluating and understanding memory breakdown, I shall discuss the area in some detail.

In talking about remembering or forgetting, we tend to refer to 'my memory', as if it were a single organ like the heart or liver. Over the last

20 years, however, it has become increasingly obvious that memory does not represent a single system, but is rather a complex combination of memory subsystems. The available evidence argues very strongly against the idea of a single unitary organ. Some psychologists still argue for what they describe as a unitary system, but when looked at in detail it is a system of such complexity that it could equally well be described as a multiple memory system. To revert to our analogy of theories as maps, it is as if early cartographers were arguing about whether Europe, Asia and Africa should be regarded as one continent or several. What follows represents a simplification of some complex issues. However, although I am sure my colleagues would disagree in detail, there would I think be broad agreement on the functional distinctions underlying the classification system described.

I shall begin by dividing memory into three categories, broadly based on the length of time for which they store information. The division was probably expressed most clearly by Atkinson and Shiffrin, and is presented most convincingly for the general reader in their *Scientific American* article (Atkinson and Shiffrin, 1971). They assume a very brief set of sensory stores, followed by a limited capacity short-term store which in turn feeds information into a long-term memory store. In what follows we shall use this as a framework, while pointing out the ways in which the Atkinson and Shiffrin model has proved to be over-simplified.

Sensory Memory

The various sensory systems such as vision, audition and touch are all assumed to be capable of storing sensory information for a brief period of time. The most extensively investigated component of this system is the very short-term visual store sometimes known as *iconic memory*. It is this system that makes cinematography possible. A series of separate and discrete still pictures, each separated by a blank period is perceived as a single moving figure since the information is stored during the blank interval and integrated into a single percept. In the case of the auditory system a very brief sensory store sometimes termed *echoic memory* allows us to perceive speech sounds. In the case of both vision and hearing, the systems are relatively complex, almost certainly involving more than a single sensory memory trace. A breakdown in such a system would however almost certainly manifest itself as a perceptual difficulty rather than a memory problem, and as such is beyond the scope of the present chapter.

Short-term Working Memory

The second system described by Atkinson and Shiffrin is one which they refer to as the short-term store or STS. They assume this system to be responsible for temporarily holding information while learning, reading, reasoning or thinking. They assume a distinction between this and a long-term memory system — the long-term store (LTS) which preserves information for anything ranging from minutes to years.

The distinction between these two systems, LTS and STS evoked a great deal of controversy during the late 1960s and early 1970s. This particularly concerned the question of whether it was necessary to assume a separate temporary or short-term storage system. Anyone attempting to read about this particular controversy should be warned of two pitfalls connected with the term 'short-term memory'. The first of these is to be aware of the fact that experimental psychologists use this term to refer to memory extending typically over a few seconds only. This is potentially very misleading since the public in general, and many medical practitioners tend to use the term to refer to memory extending over minutes, days, weeks or months, reserving the term 'long-term memory' for memory of events happening many years before. The available experimental evidence suggests that the most appropriate temporal distinction occurs between a few seconds and a few minutes. Nevertheless the term short-term memory is clearly potentially highly misleading and hence will not be used subsequently in this chapter. Other terms that have been suggested in place of short-term memory include *primary memory* (with long-term memory being referred to as *secondary memory*), *immediate memory* and *working memory*. I will use the term primary memory to refer to the simple concept of a unitary temporary memory system such as that suggested by Atkinson and Shiffrin, and will employ the term working memory to refer to a subsequent view, namely that we utilise a whole range of interacting temporary storage systems rather than a single primary memory.

We shall begin by briefly considering the evidence for separating primary and secondary memory, then present the evidence for a complex working memory rather than a simple primary memory system before going on to a more detailed consideration of long-term memory. Evidence that prompted people to distinguish primary and secondary memory in the late 1960s included the following:

Tasks with Two Components. A number of memory tests behave as though they are determined by two separate sets of factors. Consider

Figure 1.1: The Effect of Delay on the Free Recall of Words

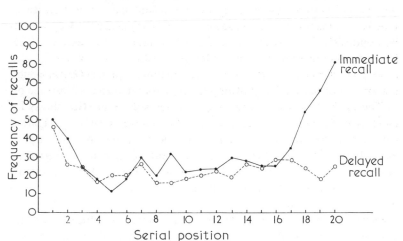

Source: Postman and Phillips, 1965.

for example the task known as *free recall* in which subjects see or hear a list of about 20 unrelated words which they must subsequently try to recall in any order they wish. Figure 1.1 shows the typical performance of a subject on this task; the vertical axis indicates the probability of recalling a particular word and the horizonal axis the order in which the words were presented. Note that when recalled immediately, the first few words are quite well recalled and the last few very well. If instead of allowing the subject to recall straightaway however, one delays him for 15 or 20 seconds, meanwhile preventing him rehearsing the words by giving him another task such as copying letters, one obtains the results shown in the delayed recall curve of Figure 1.1. The advantage previously enjoyed by the last few items, known as the recency effect since these are the most recent items, disappears. In contrast, perform-ance on the earlier time is unaffected.

One way of explaining this result is to suggest that all items are registered in a relatively durable secondary or long-term memory store, but that only the last few items are held in a temporary primary memory system. If recall is delayed, the items in the primary memory system are forgotten leaving only the contents of the more durable secondary store. Other evidence in favour of this distinction comes from the fact that a great many factors that influence the ease of remembering the earlier items have no effect on recency. These include the rate at which the words are presented (slow presentation leads to better recall), the familiarity of the words (familiar words are easier), whether the words are concrete and imageable (imageability helps learning) and so forth. None of these factors influences the recency effect, which is however very sensitive to delay.

If one considers not the material but the people learning the material, then again a clear distinction appears between performance on the recency items and performance on the remainder. This shows up most strikingly in Figure 1.2 which is based on a study comparing globally amnesic patients with control patients having normal memory. Note that performance over the recency part of the curve is equivalent in the two groups, whereas performance on the earlier long-term items is much poorer in the amnesic patients.

Evidence from Amnesia. As Figure 1.2 shows, patients occur who appear to have normal primary memory as measured by the recency effect in free recall, coupled with disastrously poor long-term or secondary memory. This distinction is not limited to free recall. Such patients have normal digit span, that is they can repeat back a sequence of numbers they have just heard just as effectively as could control patients. They may also have intact performance on the short-term forgetting task devised by Peterson and Peterson (1959), although this task is a demanding one which is not always intact in amnesic patients, particularly if they have cognitive deficits that go beyond a pure memory problem (see Baddeley, 1982b for a further discussion of this point).

Not only does one find certain patients who have normal primary memory coupled with impaired long-term or secondary memory, but one also encounters cases where the reverse applies. Shallice and Warrington (1970) describe a patient who shows normal long-term learning coupled with grossly defective primary memory as measured by digit span or by the recency effect in free recall. A number of other cases showing a broadly similar pattern of normal long-term coupled with impaired primary memory have been described and present a strong case for separating the two memory systems (for a further discussion see Baddeley (1982c) and Shallice (1979)).

Coding and Memory. If a subject is given a sequence of unrelated words and required to repeat them back immediately, he will tend to remember them in terms of their sound or articulatory characteristics. If the words are similar along this dimension (for example, *man, cat, mad,*

Figure 1.2: Immediate and Delayed Recall of Words by Amnesic and Control Patients

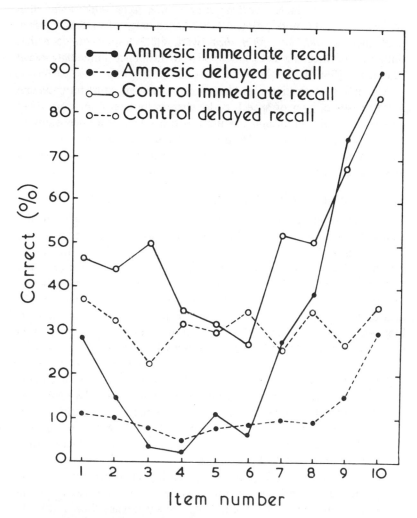

Source: Baddeley and Warrington, 1970.

map, can), the items are liable to become confused in memory leading to more errors than would be found with a dissimilar sequence (e.g. *pen, day, rig, cow, bar*) (Baddeley, 1966a). In contrast, if subjects are required to learn a longer sequence of words, and are prevented from saying them immediately by interposing a delay, other factors become important. Spoken similarity ceases to be a significant variable, but similarity of meaning becomes important. Hence a sequence comprising adjectives of similar meaning such as *big, long, huge, great, tall*, etc. would create more problems than a sequence of dissimilar adjectives such as *old, late, thin, hot, wild*, etc., despite the fact that similarity of meaning does not appear to influence immediate recall (Baddeley, 1966b).

The initial suggestion was that the primary or short-term system relies on some form of speech code whereas long-term memory relies more extensively on meaning. While this proved to be an over-simplification, as we shall see later there is an interesting and important relationship between the manner in which a subject encodes or processes an item and how well it is remembered.

Is Primary Memory a Unitary System?

The original concept of a short-term or primary memory system proposed by Atkinson and Shiffrin treated it as a unitary component. They assumed that information entered the secondary long-term system via the primary short-term store. It was assumed that material was maintained in the temporary storage system, primarily by subvocal rehearsal, and that the longer it was held in the short-term system the greater the chance that it would be transferred to the more durable long-term memory store. However, a number of results emerged that cast doubt on this. These included the following:

(i)   A number of experiments had been carried out in which subjects were required to continually repeat items. The Atkinson and Shiffrin model predicted that the longer the repetition went on, the better the learning. No relationship between rehearsal time and amount learnt was observed in several of these studies (e.g. Craik and Watkins, 1973).

(ii)   If the recency effect in free recall is due to primary memory, and if the primary memory system can only hold a small amount of material, then giving the subject another task to do at the same time as learning should wipe out the recency effect. Baddeley and Hitch (1974) showed that giving a subject a telephone number to remember at the same time as he was hearing unrelated words impaired his long-term learning, but had no effect on recency.

(iii) If the primary memory system is essential for long-term learning, then any patient with a defective primary memory should show grossly impaired long-term learning. As we saw in the case of the patient discussed by Shallice and Warrington (1970) this was not the case.

These and a range of other findings convinced Graham Hitch and I that we should abandon the idea of a single unitary primary memory system and opt instead for the concept of *working memory*. This is assumed to be an alliance of temporary storage systems co-ordinated by an attentional component which we term the *central executive*.

The central executive is assumed to be able to call on a number of subsidiary slave systems. Two such systems have been explored in some detail, namely the articulatory loop and the visuospatial sketch pad. The articulatory loop is a system that utilises subvocal speech and is responsible for the speech-like characteristics of many short-term memory tasks. The visuospatial sketch pad is a temporary system used in creating and manipulating visual images. A more detailed analysis of the type of patient discussed by Shallice and Warrington suggests that the crucial deficit is in the articulatory loop system (Vallar and Baddeley, in press). It seems likely that defects in the visuospatial sketch pad will also be identified, but at present the concept itself is too new to have been widely clinically applied.

Working memory is able to utilise a range of parallel subsidiary systems, and it seems likely that a defect in any one of these will not prove too catastrophic. Hence, the ability of Shallice and Warrington's patient to show normal long-term learning despite grossly impaired primary memory as measured by digit span. In contrast, a failure of the central executive could be likely to limit very severely the patient's ability to process information and to cope with everyday living. Techniques for identifying a defect of the central executive are still in their infancy. However it has been suggested (Rabbitt, 1981; Welford, 1980) that the decrement in performance found with advancing age may reflect a deterioration in working memory. The even more dramatic degradation that occurs in the case of presenile and senile dementia may represent a more serious breakdown in the central executive.

Long-term or Secondary Memory

Most patients referred for treatment of memory problems are likely to be suffering from some form of long-term or secondary memory defect. Such patients are likely to show impaired learning whether this is tested within a few minutes of learning or is delayed for several days or even weeks. As mentioned earlier, the system of memory responsible for retaining information over minutes appears to be broadly the same as that involved in remembering items over a much longer period. However, this does not mean that even the long-term memory constitutes a single unitary system. Two distinctions will be discussed, one a relatively simple division between visual and verbal memory, and the other a more subtle distinction between autobiographical or episodic memory, and semantic memory or memory for knowledge.

Visual and Verbal Memory

If a normal person is shown a series of pictures of easily nameable objects, and subsequently tries to recall them, there is evidence to suggest that his memory will be based on two features of the objects, their visual appearance and their names. This being so, memory tends to be better for such pictures than it would have been purely for their names, since nameable pictures are often represented in two ways, visual and verbal, while words are more likely to be represented in only one. At a common-sense level, it is clear that we can remember both things that we can name and things that we cannot adequately describe verbally, for example, the colour of a particular sunset or the characteristic smile of a friend. This distinction can be very important clinically, since visual and verbal processing tend to be associated with different parts of the brain, and hence one may be disrupted while the other is intact.

From a practical viewpoint this means that it is always important when dealing with a patient with defective memory to test both his verbal and visual capabilities. If one is relatively preserved then this can be used to help him compensate for the defective aspect of memory. For example, if a subject has verbal memory difficulties but has good visual memory, then visual imagery may provide a useful supplement to his normal learning strategies (Jones, 1974; Wilson, 1982). If on the other hand his visual memory is grossly defective, then visual imagery would obviously not be the strategy of choice (see Chapter 5).

Semantic and Episodic Memory

The term *semantic memory* is used to refer to memory for knowledge. Remembering the name of the capital of the USA, the French word for salt or the approximate population of Great Britain would be examples of semantic memory. Typically, one cannot remember the occasion on which a particular item of semantic information was learned, usually because learning has taken place over many and varied occasions. This can be contrasted with *episodic memory* which is much more autobiographical in nature. Remembering what you had for breakfast or recalling an incident that occurred on holiday last year would be examples of episodic memory. Recall in this case typically requires awareness of the specific learning incident rather than access to general knowledge. Clearly, most memory situations have components of semantic and episodic memory. Remembering what you had for breakfast is likely to be at least partially dependent on knowledge of your general breakfast habits as well as recollection of a particular event. It also seems likely that items that are now in semantic memory were first represented as individual episodes. Consider for example the French word for *salt*; this was probably first told to you in a French lesson at school. If you were questioned about it that evening, then attempting to recall it would almost certainly have relied on episodic memory. By now, if you remember it at all, it seems likely that it is as a result of a wide range of subsequent episodes which you can probably no longer recall.

If most situations represent a blend of semantic and episodic memory, is the distinction worth making? It probably is for two reasons; first, because the way in which the two systems appear to be different, and secondly because certain amnesic patients appear to show a breakdown in episodic memory while showing relatively intact semantic memory. Most of the work carried out on learning by psychologists has been concerned with episodic memory since it is much quicker and easier to study than semantic memory. If the distinction between the two is justified, then we should be wary of generalising our results too indiscriminately.

There is no doubt that patients may be densely amnesic, and yet perform normally on tests of semantic memory. However, such tests typically test the retention of information about the language and the world that has been learned very thoroughly, typically, many years prior to the onset of amnesia. There is some evidence to suggest that well-learned episodes of a similar age are also well preserved. Furthermore, adding new material to semantic memory appears to be just as hard for amnesic patients as new episodic learning. Hence, although semantic memory can be well preserved in some patients, the evidence does not argue strongly for neurologically distinct semantic and episodic memory systems (see Baddeley and Wilson, in press, for a more detailed discussion).

There is however evidence that one type of learning, sometimes termed *procedural learning*, may be intact in amnesic patients. Consider in more detail the case of certain amnesic patients, such for example as those suffering from Korsakoff syndrome. This is a condition produced by a vitamin deficiency which in turn results from chronic alcoholism. The patient may show grossly defective memory, being unable to orient himself in time or place, and be quite incapable of recognising for example someone who had just spent several hours working with him. Typically, working memory may be intact, as evidenced by unimpaired recency effects and normal memory span. Ability to learn lists of words however would be grossly defective, as would memory for pictures or events. It has however become increasingly clear in recent years that such patients do show an ability to learn that is relatively intact for certain tasks.

The classic observation of such learning was made many years ago by the Swiss psychiatrist Claparede, who on one occasion, secreted a pin in his hand before shaking hands with a Korsakoff patient on his morning round. Next morning, the patient was reluctant to shake hands, but appeared to have no direct recollection of the actual incident.

Subsequent research has shown that a wide range of learning tasks may be relatively intact in such globally amnesic patients. These include the ability to learn motor skills, perceptual learning tasks such as reading mirror writing, classical conditioning, and the solving of a range of both perceptual and reasoning problems (see Baddeley, 1982b, for a review). What do such tasks have in common? There is growing agreement that their primary characteristic is that they allow the patient to demonstrate his learning without needing to be aware of when or where the learning took place, information which is typically not available to the amnesic patient. If for example he is learning a skill, then the performance of that skill does not require him to remember having been taught it. It is as if the information has been laid down in memory, the skill is there, but any recollection of the process of learning is lost. Since we tend to judge memory in terms of remembered episodes, it is tempting to conclude that such patients have no memory. In fact, certain aspects of their memory are quite normal and such patients therefore could be taught a wide range of skills which they would retain quite effectively, despite a tendency to deny ever having encountered such a skill.

An Overview of the Structure of Human Memory

While controversy about the detailed analysis of human memory continues, it can reasonably be divided into three broad subsystems, a set of sensory memories that are grossly related to the perceptual processes, and which feed into a working memory system. This is itself quite complex but can be regarded as containing an attentional system, the central executive, aided by a number of subsidiary systems such as the articulatory loop, concerned with speech processing, and the visuo-spatial sketch pad, concerned with visual imagery. The working memory system is concerned with the temporary storage of information. As such, it contrasts with the long-term memory system which holds information over much longer periods. Long-term memory in turn can usefully be separated into visual and verbal memory, and into long-term memory, for facts, incidents and events, and procedural learning, the acquisition of mental, and physical skills.

Processing States of Memory

Any memory system, be it a biological system such as the human brain, or an electronic system such as a modern computer, must perform three functions. It must allow information to be fed into the system, the *input* or learning stage; it must be able to maintain information, *storage*; and it must be able to access information when appropriate, the process of *retrieval*. The section that follows will consider each of these in turn, primarily using examples from long-term memory, since this is most relevant to memory therapy. It will become clear however, that although it is relatively easy to make a logical distinction between these three stages, in actual practice they interact, a point that can be most readily illustrated using the analogy that is often drawn between a memory system and a library.

Input

Obviously for something to be remembered it must have been learned in the first place. The manner of the learning is however crucially important if subsequent recall is to be efficient. More specifically, new material must be categorised and organised with respect to what is already known, just as any adequate library must have an organised cataloguing and shelving system. A library that merely accumulated books in random piles would be virtually unusable.

Having decided that cataloguing is necessary, what principles should be used? A librarian could for example catalogue all red books together and all yellow books, or could classify books according to their size. However, while this might be useful if one were simply looking for something to prop up a wobbly table, it would not be a suitable cataloguing system for finding information on a particular subject. If one wishes to access by subject, then obviously items should be coded by subject. The same thing applies in human memory. We typically wish to access information about the world in terms of its meaning, and hence long-term memory tends to categories and work most efficiently on the basis of meaning. However, meaning is by no means the only thing that needs to be stored. If we wish to remember someone's name, then obviously we need to store verbal or phonological information as well as semantic and episodic information about that person. The term coding is used to refer to the processing of information during learning, and has formed perhaps the most active area of research in human memory over the last decade. What factors have proved to be important?

Attention. If the person is to learn something then he or she must attend to it. While this may seem obvious, there are occasional claims to the contrary, as for example in the case of sleep teaching, where it has been claimed that information presented while sleeping is absorbed and retained. Unfortunately, in practice, such short cuts to painless learning simply do not seem to work.

The role of attention in learning is a very central one. If for example a person attempts to split his attention between a learning task and something quite different, such as dealing cards into different suits, then the more difficult the dealing task the less he will remember of the words. A minor exception to this is the recency effect, which seems insensitive to division of attention. At a practical level, this suggests that watching the television with one eye and reading a book with the other might allow you the comforting feeling that you have remembered what you read in the line before, but will nevertheless grossly reduce the amount that you retain subsequently of whatever you read, or watched.

Clearly then, patients who have difficulty in sustaining attention will have difficulty in learning. Hence patients with frontal lobe damage or patients suffering from dementia are likely to show poor learning unless considerable efforts are made to keep their attention on the task in hand.

Intention to Learn. This might appear to be an important variable, but in fact it is not. Experimental studies have shown that provided subjects attend to the material and process it in an appropriate way, it does not matter whether they are trying to learn or not. Similarly trying to learn but performing inappropriate learning strategies will lead to relatively little improvement. What is important is what the patient does and how, but not why he does it.

Organisation. Learning is crucially dependent on organisation of material. Just as the core of a good library is its cataloguing system, so the essence of a good memory is the way in which material is organised during learning. People who are expert in a particular area will already have a rich and well organised cataloguing system which will enable them to acquire new material more easily and more rapidly. Hence an expert chess player can acquire in a single glimpse of a game more information than a novice player can acquire in four or five times as many glimpses. A football enthusiast can hear the results and recall them much more effectively than someone who has a merely passing interest in football, and an electronics expert can 'read' and remember a circuit diagram that would require vastly longer for the amateur to learn. In all these cases, the new material is organised in terms of what already exists, and efficient learning should attempt to take advantage of what is already known in order to graft on new material.

Levels of Processing. As we saw earlier, the immediate recall of lists of words seems to depend heavily on the sound or spoken characteristics of those words, while long-term learning appears to rely more on semantic coding. Craik and Lockhart (1972) generalised this type of finding by suggesting that material can be processed at a range of different 'depths', and that the deeper the processing the better the retention. Suppose I were to present you with a list of words, requiring you to answer questions about each word. For some words I might ask you questions that required only a relatively superficial processing of the word; for example, *Is the word LAMB written in lower case letters or capitals?* Or I might ask a question requiring slightly deeper processing; *Does the word 'dog' rhyme with 'log'?* Or I might ask a question that required yet deeper semantic processing: *Would the word 'pig' be a suitable completion for the sentence 'The farmer went to the market to buy a...'?*

It proves to be the case that the most superficial processing in terms of letter characteristics leads to poorest recall, processing in terms of rhyme somewhat better, while semantic processing leads to the best retention. While the interpretation of this result is still controversial, there is no doubt that as a rule of thumb, deeper encoding does tend to lead to better learning.

What is meant by deeper encoding? This presents a problem, certainly at a theoretical level. However at a practical level the following features appear to characterise efficient deep processing:

(a) Elaboration: working on the detail of material and relating it to what one already knows appears to enhance learning.

(b) Compatibility: material that is consistent with existing knowledge is easier to learn than inconsistent material, and neutral material can be learnt best by attempting to relate it to what is already known.

(c) Self-reference: learners who are asked to judge how material relates to themselves seem to remember it better than if they are required to judge its relevance to other people.

Distribution of Practice in Learning

The principle of a little and often is a good learning precept. This applies at two levels. First, if you are trying to teach over a long period of time, then it is a mistake to try to pack too much into each individual day. A study on learning to type compared training regimes involving one hour a day, two hours a day and four hours a day. Both the learning rate and subsequent retention was best for the one hour a day group and worst for the four hour group.

A similar principle operates at the micro level. Suppose for example you were trying to teach someone the name of a person. If you present this information twice, then presenting it twice in quick succession leads to less learning than presenting it twice with a few minutes delay in between. In learning it is important to keep track of what has been learned by including frequent tests, and if you test recall after a short delay, rather than a long one, the patient is more likely to be able to recall it. A successful recall will have two advantages, one a motivational encouragement, and the other due to the fact that the result itself will function as a second learning trial. Bearing this in mind, the optimal teaching strategy is to begin by presenting and testing after a short delay, but gradually build up the interval as learning proceeds, aiming always to test the item at the longest interval for which the subject is likely to be able to recall it. Such a strategy hence combines early success and encouragement with a gradually increasing distribution of practice. (See Landauer and Bjork, 1978, for a more detailed description of this approach.)

Storage

Once information is registered in memory, then it must be stored until subsequently needed. Forgetting over time may either represent loss of that information or increased difficulty in retrieving it. Reverting to our library analogy, loss of information would presumably represent books either being thrown away, or possibly becoming unreadable due to fading print. The issue of how much forgetting, if any occurs because of loss rather than inaccessibility remains controversial.

The typical form of a forgetting curve was first demonstrated by the German psychologist Hermann Ebbinghaus as long ago as 1885. The function is exponential, with forgetting rapid at first, becoming more and more gradual as time elaspses. In general, rate of forgetting appears to be surprisingly stable across different groups of people. Hence grossly amnesic Korsakoff patients may show very impaired learning, but what they have learnt is remembered just as well as in the case of normals. There is however some preliminary evidence to suggest that patients suffering from closed head injury may forget abnormally rapidly, as do patients who have recently received electroconvulsive therapy for relief of depression (Sunderland, Harris and Baddeley, 1983; Squire, 1981). However, we still know relatively little about forgetting rates for different types of patient and consequently it is probably wise, in dealing with patients who have memory problems, to allow for the possibility that they may forget particularly rapidly, and may need rather more extensive revision at the beginning of each session than would normally be the case.

It is almost certainly the case that memory storage depends on some form of neurochemical change. There is a growing body of evidence to suggest that patients suffering from dementia exhibit both memory problems and deficits in certain potentially important neurotransmitters. This has encouraged the search for drugs that might allow the deficit to be made good, so far with relatively limited success (see Chapter 7 for a more detailed discussion).

Retrieval

Memory systems like libraries can only be regarded as successful if they can both store information and retrieve it on request. There is no doubt that some forgetting occurs, not because the information is lost, but merely because it becomes increasingly difficult to retrieve. An everyday example of this is the tip-of-the-tongue effect in which one tries to remember something, often a name, which one is certain one knows but simply cannot produce at the time. One can often be quite successful in saying how many syllables there are in the name and recall some of its letters, and yet not be able to produce the item. When it is presented, one typically has no difficulty in recognising that it is the correct response.

What determines whether an item can or cannot be retrieved? One factor we have discussed already, namely how it was encoded in the first place. Casual and disorganised encoding tends to lead to unreliable retrieval. However, whatever the manner of encoding, retrieval seems to be best if the encoding situation is reinstated. This aspect of memory has been explored most vigorously by Tulving who has formulated what he terms the *Encoding Specificity Principle*.

Encoding Specificity

As mentioned earlier, this states that retrieval will be optimal when it occurs in the same context as learning. This can be illustrated most simply using the case of environmental context.

Context Dependent Memory

The philosopher Locke describes the case of a young man who took dancing lessons. The lessons occurred in a room containing an old trunk. The young man learnt to dance quite effectively in that room but 'though in that chamber he could dance excellently well, yet it was only while that trunk was there; nor could he perform well in any other place, unless that or some other such trunk had its due position in the room' (Locke, 1960; Everyman's Library Edition [1961] Vol. 1, pp. 339–40).

A similar effect of environmental context was observed by a colleague Duncan Godden and I in the case of deep-sea divers (Godden and Baddeley, 1975). We taught our divers a list of words either on land or underwater, and required them to recall the words in either the same environment or the different one. Our divers learnt a similar amount on land or underwater, but recalled about 40 per cent less when they attempted to remember the words in the opposite environment to that in which they learnt them. However, when instead of requiring them to *recall* the words we used a *recognition* measure in which they had to pick the previously presented words out of a list, our context-dependency effect disappeared (Godden and Baddeley, 1980). They recognised the same number regardless of whether recognition occurred in the same environment as learning or the opposite. This suggests that the words had indeed been stored, and that accessing them was helped by reinstating the learning context. Under recognition conditions, since the words were presented to the subject, access was not a problem; the difficulty lay in deciding whether the accessed word had been presented earlier in the experiment. The contextual effects we observed with recall were particularly large, presumably because the difference between being on land and underwater is particularly dramatic. There is however considerable evidence to suggest that reliable though less marked effects occur with less pronounced environmental changes.

State-dependent Memory

If instead of changing the external environment within which a person is operating, one changes his internal environment by means of drugs, a similar effect occurs. It has for example been observed that alcoholics who hide money and liquor while drunk, may be unable to remember where it was hidden when sober, but recall when drunk again (Goodwin, Powell, Bremer, Hoine and Stern, 1969); what is learned when drunk is apparently best recalled drunk. Again, as with context-dependent memory, when subjects are tested by recognition rather than recall, the effect of state during learning disappears (Eich, 1980).

Encoding Specificity

So far we have talked about the contextual effects in learning provided by the subject's environment, either external or internal. The psychological context in which learning occurs can however have an equally marked effect. An extensive series of studies by Tulving has developed the concept of a *retrieval cue*. Retrieval cues are fragments of the original learning experience which can serve to prompt recall or recognition. They can be used to explore the way in which the original learning took place.

Let us begin with a fairly extreme case. Suppose you are trying to help a patient remember a word so that it can be recalled later on request. Let us begin by supposing that it is a word that has two meanings like *jam* (as in strawberry jam and traffic jam), and that you encourage one of these interpretations during learning. You might for example say 'the next word is *jam*, as in: *They had jam for tea*.' Somewhat later the patient fails to remember it and you give him a hint. If you give him the hint of 'strawberry' or 'something you might have for tea', this will very probably help him. If on the other hand you give him a hint concerned with the other meaning of jam such as 'traffic', then this is likely to actively *reduce* the probability that he will remember the word. Indeed under these circumstances, it is often possible to show him the word and he will deny that it is the one that was presented. What this means is that what he has stored is the *meaning* of the word, not the word itself.

If this effect only occurred when words have two meanings, it would be of theoretical but not great practical importance. However, similar effects occur when different features of a word with only one meaning are stressed. Suppose you had used the word *piano*, and given as an illustrative sentence, *The strong men lifted the piano*. You would find that 'something heavy' was a very effective hint, but that 'something tuneful' was not. What the subject encodes appears to be those aspects of the stimulus that are highlighted by the context. If the retrieval cue emphasises some other feature, then it is unlikely to help and may indeed actively hinder.

These results clearly show that patients are likely to be helped by hints, but that these should be carefully chosen, bearing in mind the context in which the material was learned. The principle underlying them however has a much more general and important implication for therapy. The implication is captured by the term *encoding variability* which is the converse of encoding specificity.

Encoding Variability

A constant problem for therapy of any kind is the question of the extent to which improvements observed in the clinic actually generalise to the patient's everyday life. For example, a recent study of stroke patients showed that the level of performance on activities of daily living which they demonstrated in hospital was substantially greater than the activities they actually accomplished for themselves when they subsequently returned home (Sheikh, Smith, Mead and Brennan, 1978). There are of course many possible reasons for this; but one of them is the phenomenon of encoding specificity; all too often, what is learnt in one specific context does not generalise to others. One way of minimising this danger is to ensure that once a skill has been acquired, it should be utilised and practised in as wide a range of environments as possible. Ideally of course, these should closely resemble the environment in which the skill will be practised outside the hospital, but if this is not possible, a wide range of hospital contexts is better than confining practice to one situation.

Conclusions

Memory theory cannot and will not ever be in a position to provide the therapist with simple recipes for treating memory problems. What theory can do is to provide a broad orientation within which to understand something of the patient's deficit, and suggest possible techniques and strategies for ameliorating these problems. We have in the last decade learnt a good deal about how to enhance learning and memory within the laboratory. To what extent these techniques are applicable in the clinic, and more importantly in the world outside, remains to be seen. There is certainly no guarantee of success; indeed it is by no means certain at this stage whether the retraining of cognitive function in brain-damaged patients will ever be an important and significant component of therapy. It is however certainly a possibility that needs to be explored extensively and evaluated thoroughly and carefully. Such an exploration and evaluation needs the combined skills of both the theorist and the clinician.

2 ASSESSMENT FOR REHABILITATION

Neil Brooks and Nadina B. Lincoln

The role of assessment in rehabilitation varies very much from department to department. In some cases patients are given a series of very structured tasks and on the basis of performance on these tasks a rehabilitation programme is planned and its effectiveness is monitored by repetition of the assessment tasks. In others, the assessment and treatment stages cannot be clearly differentiated and abilities are assessed and treated on the basis of observations made throughout the rehabilitation programme. In the latter case monitoring the effectiveness of treatment is usually based on observation of whether the patient appears to have improved on the activities.

If we are going to separate assessment techniques from intervention strategies then we need first to consider what is meant by assessment. In this chapter, assessment is considered as a structured programme of observations made by the rehabilitation team. These observations may be used to identify the difficulties that a person has, to measure their severity, determine the impact they have on daily life and to monitor any changes in ability that occur, either as a result of spontaneous recovery or in response to treatment. In order to decide which assessment techniques to use we need to consider four basic questions. We need to consider why assessments are being carried out, who is going to do them, when they are going to do them and what functions need to be assessed. The answers to these questions will determine the techniques that are to be used on any given occasion.

Why are Assessments Carried Out?

It is all too easy to carry out an assessment simply because it is the one carried out in the department. Such assessments may be carried out merely to justify the existence of the department: this is not adequate, but is distressingly common nevertheless. If greater consideration is given to why the assessment is being carried out, then this unnecessary routine can be avoided.

One of the main reasons for assessing a patient, particularly in the

28

early stages, is to identify what his or her abilities and deficits are. Such an assessment will include a wide range of practical skills and, when considering patients with memory problems, a wide range of cognitive abilities. These assessments tend to be carried out using standardised procedures, for which there is some indication of how a person of any given age, intelligence level or social background, would be likely to perform. These include standardised tests, rating scales and question-naires. The information gathered can be used to plan the rehabilitation programme because it indicates which skills a person is likely to have lost. Repetition of these procedures will indicate the extent to which the patient has improved either as a result of treatment, spontaneous recovery or increased familiarity with the test materials or test regime.

The second purpose of assessments may be to identify functions hypothesised to underlie observed deficits. This is an important point, as the reasons for failure on a test may be many. The patient who, for example, cannot complete a task in rehabilitation may have a number of deficits ranging from general slowness, to an attentional or concen-tration deficit, to low drive and motivation, to poor arousal. A know-ledge of the underlying deficits will enable rehabilitation staff to plan a treatment programme tailored uniquely to that patient rather than the broad range of patients who come through the department.

Although the purpose may be to identify and assess cognitive deficits after brain damage much of the research work has been of an atheoretical and rather *ad hoc* nature; the measures used are often related only peripherally, if at all, to current cognitive theorising, and this inevitably means that it is very difficult to specify exactly why a given patient has a given cognitive deficit. There are exceptions to this general rule, for example, the use of a short- and long-term memory model (Brooks, 1975; Parker and Serrats, 1976; Wilson, Brooks and Phillips, 1982). Other exceptions would include the excellent work of Van Zomeren and his colleagues on attention deficits (Van Zomeren, Brouwer and Deelman, 1983), and Levin's use of a hemispheric dis-connection model in assessing deficits after head injury (Levin, Gross-man, Sarwar and Meyers, 1981). With these exceptions, however, clinical assessment of cognitive functions, particularly after head injury, has proceeded almost entirely independently of current theoretical views about cognition. The assessment of more focal lesions has not been atheoretical to the same extent, as the excellent work carried out by Warrington and her colleagues (Warrington, 1971; Warrington, 1974; Warrington and James, 1967) illustrates.

While *ad hoc* clinical tests will undoubtedly identify major deficits, the tests are often too multifactorial to allow any informed judgement about precisely why a patient fails on the test. A 'frontal' patient and one with a left temporal lesion may both fail the same verbal learning test, with apparently identical severities of deficit. The underlying reasons for failure, however, may be very varied indeed, demanding entirely different procedures for their further elucidation, and different approaches to rehabilitation and management.

The third reason for assessing a patient is to identify the effect any deficits observed have on his everyday life. The skills required in the outside world are very different from those required in a hospital. Some patients may cope much better in the familiar surroundings of their own homes than in the occupational therapy department, surrounded by other people with an unfamiliar arrangement of household equipment. In other cases, patients may be able to carry out routine daily activities in the company of others simply because they get necessary clues from what others are doing. However, on their own at home such clues may not be available and the person may be unable to cope with simple routine self-care activities. Alternatively, the patient may fail to cope because those looking after him at home may prefer to do things for him rather than waiting for the completion of a slow and inaccurate performance. Andrews and Stewart (1979) investigated this in a series of stroke patients, and found that performance in activities of daily living in the clinic was better than in the patient's own home. Indeed, whereas there were a number of ADL areas in which the patient performed better in the clinic than at home, the reverse was not observed. It is therefore necessary to assess people's performance in the environment in which their skills will be needed as well as in the rehabilitation department. This applies to many social skills as well as simple daily activities. Can the person cope with a noisy office, a crowded works canteen, climbing three flights of stairs to his flat when the lifts are not working, and asking for a pint of beer in a pub with an unfamiliar landlord?

Discrepancies between performance on standard tasks in a hospital setting and performance in the outside world have recently received considerable attention. Sunderland, Harris and Baddeley (1983) carried out a study to investigate whether laboratory tests predict everyday memory. They took three groups of patients. Two of the groups consisted of patients who had received severe head injury (assessed within a few months of injury in one group and between two and eight years after injury in the other). The third group consisted of accident victims who had suffered recent orthopaedic injuries, but claimed never to have been knocked unconscious. The three groups were similar in terms of type of accident, socio-economic status and age. All patients were tested on an objective test battery and were asked to complete a questionnaire to assess the incidence of memory failures. In addition, a relative or close friend of each patient was interviewed and asked to estimate the frequency of memory failures using the same questionnaire items. Both the patient and the relative were given a check-list at the end of the interview to complete on seven consecutive days following the interview indicating whether that form of memory failure had happened to the patient each day. Performance on the objective tests correlated significantly with scores on the relatives' questionnaire for the non-head injured and the long-term head injured group, but not for the recently head injured subjects who had yet to reach a stable state. The authors report that correlations between test performance and questionnaire were higher for tests involving prose recall and paired associate learning than for tests of visual memory, and they suggest that the lower correlations with visual memory tests may have been due to the low salience of visual errors in everyday life. In addition, the patients' questionnaires showed the least agreement with the check-lists and the objective tests illustrating the problem of validity of self-report with these patients. Further evidence comes from Brooks (1979) who used a simpler version of the Sunderland questionnaire, and found no association between clinical memory test performance and questionnaire score, at three months after injury, but significant correlations between questionnaire and both verbal and non-verbal memory measures at six months after injury.

The fourth reason for assessment is to identify the goals of the rehabilitation programme. It is not enough merely to assess the patient in the laboratory or clinic, to identify the nature of the deficit and the effects it has on everyday life, and to monitor progress. It is also necessary to identify which skills need to be acquired and in what order. Some deficits may be relatively trivial in terms of their impact on actual abilities, yet put considerable emotional strain on the relatives of the patient. It may be necessary to treat these before the more obvious practical deficits. For example, a patient who repeatedly asks the same question or tells the same story may impose far more emotional strain on relatives due to this reiteration rather than to his inability to carry out activities unsupervised. Priorities need to be established both from the patients' and the relatives' points of view when deciding the overall treatment plan. Social circumstances may change during rehabilitation so that the goals identified at the beginning may become secondary to others which have subsequently assumed importance. So, not only do the initial goals need to be specified, but they also need to be reviewed from time to time to check that they are still appropriate.

Who Makes Assessments?

Initially assessments are made by the team most closely involved with the patient's rehabilitation. This will include the physicians, surgeons, nurses, rehabilitation therapists, psychologists and social workers. Each member of the team will consider specific aspects of the patient's abilities which would not necessarily be considered by other members of the team, although in a good, well-integrated team, overlap will (and should) occur. So, for example, the psychologist may be concerned with assessing the nature of the memory deficit (whether the problems are predominantly verbal or visual), the strategy used by the patient to solve a particular task, and the duration of retention of information. The rehabilitation therapists are likely to be more directly concerned with the impact of the memory deficit on the person's life. The occupational therapist may assess whether memory problems affect the patient's ability to carry out routine domestic chores. For example Mrs AW had difficulty following a recipe because, between reading the instructions in the recipe book and going to pick up the item from the shelf, she forgot what she was supposed to be doing next. The speech therapist may assess the effect of a deficit on communication skills. For example, the problems encountered by the patient who is unable to understand a short passage in the newspaper because he forgets earlier information as he reads through the paper. The physiotherapist may find the patient is unable to practise a series of exercises on his own because, even though the exercises have been demonstrated many times before, the sequence is either too long or too complex for the patient to recall more than the first few stages. Nurses may observe that the patient has problems with following through a sequence of activities such as getting up, washing, dressing and going to breakfast, because he loses track of what he has done, and what has yet to be done.

The role of the family as suppliers of information should not be neglected and family members can fill in simple ratings and check lists about behaviours outside the rehabilitation setting. This is important because some things never or rarely happen in a hospital setting, yet observation of how the patient copes with unusual problems at home may provide valuable insight into the nature of the difficulties. Unexpected callers at the house, a changed appointment time or a diversion on a shopping route because of a burst water-main may disrupt a person's routine to the extent that difficulties which had hitherto been unnoticed become very apparent. Similarly, if the patient had been employed at the time of the injury, then information from the employer may be particularly valuable, not only in giving further information about the patient's strengths and weaknesses in employment-related areas, but also, as rehabilitation progresses, in assessing the patient's acquisition of the skills necessary for return to work.

It is important to note that there may be great discrepancies in the information supplied by different people, and the likely sources of these discrepancies need to be identified. One possibility is that a discrepancy is due simply to an unreliable rating scale, and this is unfortunately a very common feature of scales used in rehabilitation departments, in which the questions are often ambiguous and open to widely divergent interpretation by different members of the team. Furthermore, if the patient and relative are both used as direct sources of information about the patient's functioning, discrepancies may be particularly large in areas representing behavioural and psychological functions (McKinlay and Brooks, in press). However, in some instances there may also be quite marked discrepancies in patients' reported physical abilities in activities of daily living and those of relatives (Lincoln, 1979). Such discrepancies as these not only highlight areas of particular concern for different people in contact with the patient but they may also indicate the extent to which the patient is aware of his own difficulties.

When Should Assessments Be Carried Out?

Assessments should be made initially as near as possible to the beginning of the rehabilitation process. This allows for an assessment of the effectiveness of rehabilitation, or of spontaneous recovery, but the earlier the assessment is made then the more difficult it is to make very specific predictions about the patient's likely progress. Very early after a lesion only gross and short-term predictions can be made, but as time progresses the accuracy and uniqueness of the prediction increases as the patient comes nearer to his final level. However, as the patient nears this level the less change is likely and the less useful the assessment. There is no easy answer here.

The timing of the assessment is to some extent determined by the purpose of the assessment. In the early stages one is more likely to be concerned with identifying abilities and deficits and functions assumed to be underlying the deficits. The recovery of these will then be monitored. As time progresses this type of assessment becomes less important and greater emphasis is placed on the effect the deficits have on daily life. Later still, assessments will be more specifically directed towards planning the future, such as deciding whether a patient has the skills necessary to return to his former employment or whether some alternative form of employment is appropriate.

The frequency of assessment depends on the function being assessed and the time after the lesion. The earlier the assessments are begun, the more rapid is change likely to be in all areas of functioning. However, some functions do change at different rates from others and this must be taken into account in timing assessments. Gross motor functions and the gross aspects of language may recover quickly to an adequate, though incomplete, level in many patients. This is not the case with memory functions which typically improve more slowly and to a less adequate level (Brooks, 1983; Brooks and Aughton, 1979).

The frequency of reassessment also depends on the type of measure being used. Clearly when familiarity or practice effects are likely to affect performance then the assessment cannot be repeated very often. In contrast, if behavioural observation is being used, the actual assessment procedure is unlikely to affect the patient's performance and so can be repeated as often as desired. Different assessments will be repeated at different stages. It is fairly typical for standardised psychological tests to be carried out at 1, 3, 6 and 12 months post-injury, activities of daily living to be assessed at 4 or 6 weekly intervals and observational rating scales to be carried out daily.

What Functions Need to be Assessed?

The aim of this section is to describe some of the functions which need to be assessed (a totally comprehensive list is clearly beyond the scope of this chapter) and also to illustrate some of the techniques which are currently available. At a very general level, the assessment should encompass the full range of functions known to be important in achieving competent activities of daily living and adequate interpersonal cognitive or vocational performance in the outside world. Many functions likely to be important can be specified from clinical experience or simply from common sense. For example, memory, perceptual deficits, language, speed of performance, dexterity, motor power and sensory loss can all be seen to have direct implications for adequate performance in the outside world.

This list can be supplemented by those which are known directly to contribute to vocational failure. These have been studied in some detail by Lewinsohn and Graf (1973) who found that failure of occupational placement after various kinds of disability, was predicted by disturbances in locomotion, social immaturity, inadequacy, lack of emotional support at home, suspicion, poor motivation, poor attention span, depression and unrealistic goals. Interestingly, in addition to these deficits, there were a number of problems or items which occurred frequently in patients with brain damage, but were *not* found to be significant in predicting vocational success, or predicted only weakly. These were deficits in speech, reading and writing and also rigidity, anxiety, being easily upset, being too slow and having motor incoordination. On factor analysis, various factors were found to be predictive of vocational outcome. Behaviour disorders and cognitive difficulties accounted for the largest proportion of the variability. Other factors accounting for slightly less of the variability in outcome were environmental problems, motor control, age, neuroticism and personal appearance. A number of these areas are easy to assess in the clinic. For example, some may be measured by means of standardised questionnaires (neuroticism), behavioural observation (personal appearance), careful history (environmental problems, age) and physical examination (motor control). The remaining areas, cognitive disturbance and behaviour disorders, which together account for the largest proportions of variance are less easy to assess, but worth considering in more detail. The emphasis will be placed on the assessment of memory problems since this is the central focus of this book. However, it must be borne in mind that memory problems should always be assessed in conjunction with other cognitive deficits and many of the limitations of the techniques used apply equally to other areas of cognitive disturbance.

Practical Assessment of Memory Functions

The problem of assessing any cognitive function is to know the areas which can safely be left out. Brain damage of different aetiologies, different velocities, different sites and occurring at different ages can have markedly different effects on cognitive functions. Memory and learning are two functions which are most commonly affected and therefore it is likely that any neurophysiological assessment for rehabilitation will incorporate some assessment of these functions. In addition, their effect on daily life, employment and interpersonal relationships must be considered.

The first stage of memory assessment is to identify which aspects of memory are affected and which are relatively intact. This is usually done using psychological tests or at least tests developed by psychologists. There is a myth that only psychologists may use many of the standard test procedures. While it does hold some truth in relation to restricted circulation tests such as the Wechsler Adult Intelligence Scale (WAIS) (Wechsler, 1955), many of the psychological tests used in clinical practices could be administered by other members of the rehabilitation team provided they have the necessary training to enable them to interpret the results obtained.

Memory has to be evaluated in relation to a patient's general level of intellectual functioning, particularly his premorbid level. In most cases assessment of IQ does not contribute anything materially to the information gained from assessing individual cognitive functions. However, it does provide a baseline against which other functions may be compared. Tests used for this purpose include the WAIS (Wechsler, 1955), Progressive Matrices and Mill Hill Vocabulary (Raven, 1958). Another which may help provide an indication of premorbid intellectual level is a measure of reading ability (Nelson and O'Connell, 1978).

Once the likely premorbid intelligence level has been established it is possible to consider whether different aspects of memory functioning are impaired relative to this level. The ideal would be to have a battery of memory tests tapping different aspects of memory functioning. Although some batteries are available, none is entirely satisfactory and for this reason many clinicians use a selection of different tests. The selection of measures is largely a matter of personal preference but some of the more commonly used procedures will be described.

The most widely used battery of memory tests is the Wechsler Memory Scale (WMS) (Wechsler, 1945). This consists of seven subtests: Personal and Current Information, Orientation, Mental Control, Logical Memory, Memory Span, Visual Reproduction and Associate Learning. These together provide a summary score of memory functioning, the memory quotient. Despite many criticisms about its validity (for a review see Erickson and Scott, 1977) it provides a relatively short screening assessment which can be used to detect memory impairment in many patients (Brooks, 1976). It is least sensitive to impairments of memory for visual material and for this reason additional visual memory tests are often carried out in conjunction with the WMS.

Another battery of memory tests is the Williams Scale for the Measurement of Memory (Williams, 1968). This includes tests of immediate recall, non-verbal learning (Rey-Davis test), verbal learning (a modified version of Walton and Black's (1957) test), delayed recall and memory for past personal events. This is also open to criticisms about its reliability and validity and has not gained popularity as a clinical tool. A further memory battery is being developed by Warrington and this will include some of the tests which have already been used clinically to measure specific features of memory functioning (see below).

The alternative approach to using a memory battery is to select a range of different tests to measure particular aspects of memory functioning. This has the advantage that the 'best' tests can be used to assess particular memory functions but because of differences in method of construction and normative samples, comparisons between tests often cannot be made. Some of the most commonly used tests are shown in Table 2.1. It can be seen that some of these tests are also included in the memory batteries mentioned above. These are used as individual tests and not necessarily given as part of the full test battery.

Table 2.1: Table of Memory Tests used in Clinical Practice

Recall	Nature of Material	
	Verbal	Visual
Immediate Short-term	Digit span	Corsi non-verbal digit span
	Wechsler Logical Memory	Benton Visual Retention
	Forced Choice Words	Forced Choice Faces
	Paired Associate Learning	Wechsler Visual Reproduction
		Rey-Davis Test
Delayed	Wechsler Logical Memory	Delayed recall of Rey-Davis
		Osterreith figure
	Williams Delayed Recall	Williams Delayed Recall

The first criterion used in selecting a range of memory tests is whether memory for verbal or non-verbal visual material is being assessed. Although, following cerebral trauma, clearly lateralised cognitive dysfunctions are less common than with stroke, some relative strengths and weaknesses may be observed which assist in the selection of treatment strategy (see Chapter 5). The second aspect to be considered in selecting tests is the time interval between the presentation of material and recall. Most examiners include measures of short-term memory, in which recall is directly after the material has been presented and a delayed recall in which material has to be recalled after a delay of ten minutes or more.

The most widely used assessment of verbal memory is the Logical Recall Subtest of the Wechsler Memory Scale (Wechsler, 1945). Two stories are read to the patient, and then recalled immediately afterwards: in addition most examiners now retest after a time delay, usually a half-hour. Normative data are available for different age groups of subjects, although the data are rather limited. This test has the advantage of high 'face validity', in that its purpose is fairly obvious to the patient who does not feel he is being asked to carry out an obscure or inappropriate task. It also seems to be relatively highly correlated with performance in everyday life (Brooks, 1979; Sunderland *et al.*, 1983). Although the original version of the test did not incorporate the delayed recall of the stories, introduction of this makes the test more sensitive to minor problems in verbal memory and has been shown to be sensitive to the deficits in head-injured patients (Brooks, 1972, 1976, 1983; Brooks *et al.*, 1980).

There are various forms of paired-associate learning tasks which are used to measure verbal learning ability. One of these is derived from the Wechsler battery (1945) but there are others which vary in terms of the number of word pairs and the degree of association between words in the pairs (Inglis, 1957; Walton and Black, 1957; Brooks and Baddeley, 1976). In all these tasks pairs of words are read to the patient and then one word of the pair is given and the patient asked to recall the word which went with it. The tests differ in the number of times the task is repeated and the scoring method.

Both paired associate tasks and the Wechsler Logical Memory require intelligible speech from the patient. One which does not have this requirement is the Forced Choice Words test (Warrington, 1974). Words are shown to the patient one at a time on cards. The patient is then presented with a list of pairs of words, one word of each pair being from the series shown to the patient. The task of the patient is to select which word of each pair he has just seen. This task is relatively quick and easy to give and also has high face validity.

Delayed recall of verbal material is usually assessed on the Logical Memory test, but an alternative is to use the delayed recall test from the Williams battery. A card with nine pictures is shown to the patient, who is asked to name each picture. After a ten minute delay the patient is asked to recall the pictures, and for those items which he fails he is then given cues. If the patient fails to recall all the pictures after the cues he is then shown a card with 15 pictures and asked to select from these which ones were on the original card. It is not clear to what extent the test measures visual or verbal recall, since the patient both looks at the pictures and names them. However, the test does provide a measure of delayed recall suitable for patients with poor speech, which makes the delayed Logical Memory difficult, or with poor manual dexterity, which makes drawing tasks difficult.

Visual memory tests usually involve the patient drawing geometric shapes from memory, either immediately after having been shown the design or after a delay. The Wechsler Memory Scale includes the Visual Reproduction Subtest for this purpose but it is relatively insensitive to milder problems. A more complex version of this task is the Benton Visual Retention test (Benton, 1974). This consists of a series of ten designs of increasing complexity which are shown to the patient one at a time and who is required to reproduce each from memory. There is also a forced choice version of the test which removes the need for adequate manual dexterity to draw (Benton, 1950), but the normative data for this version are rather limited.

Another assessment of non-verbal memory which does not require the patient to draw is the Forced Choice Faces test (Warrington, 1974). This task is similar to the Forced Choice Words test described earlier, but instead of words the material consists of photographs of people's faces. A less widely used task is the continuous recognition task devised by Kimura (1963). Subjects are shown a series of abstract patterns. They are then shown a longer series which includes some of the original designs which recur in the series. The subject's task is to say which pattern he has seen before.

Procedures for assessing delayed recall of visual material are few. The Williams delayed recall has already been mentioned and there is a delayed recall version of the Benton Visual Retention test (Benton, 1962). One other procedure is delayed recall of the Rey–Osterreith figure (Rey, 1959). In this task the patient first has to copy a complex pattern; after a delay, usually a half-hour, he is required to draw the pattern again from memory. Normative data for both this task and the other delayed visual recall tasks are very limited, and again it has the problem that sufficient manual dexterity is required for the patient to be able to draw.

The advantage of these memory tasks is that there are some normative data available, though rarely as much as would be considered ideal. They have also been found to be sensitive to deficits in memory. However, they do not relate closely to some of the difficulties exhibited by patients in daily life. An alternative is to devise tasks which measure the specific deficit of clinical concern. For example, recalling people's names is frequently reported to be difficult. One could obtain photographs of ten faces and tell the patient the name of each person depicted, for example, this is Ann Jones and this is Peter Black, etc. Indeed this precise procedure has been used to assess recovery after head injury in children (Chadwick, Rutter, Schaffer and Shrout, 1981) and it proved to be a very sensitive indicator of impairment. Recall could be tested immediately after presentation and after a delay. Retesting on such a task might be carried out after a few weeks to assess the effect of spontaneous recovery, or after a specific training programme to teach the patient strategies for the recall of people's names. It should be stressed that interpretation of results of such tests requires considerable caution. An improvement in test score does not necessarily mean that recovery of the underlying ability has occurred, as there may be an effect of practice to be accounted for. However, if prior to a treatment programme a patient scored 0 or 1 out of 10 on the test on four consecutive trials at daily intervals and after a training programme that patient scored more than 6 out of 10 on each of four trials, it would be reasonable to consider that the change in score might be related to the effect of the treatment programme. Similar procedures may be devised for learning a route between A and B; recalling a newspaper article; or recalling where in the kitchen items of cutlery and crockery should be put away after washing up. The advantage of this type of procedure is that tasks can be designed to assess the precise problems of an individual patient rather than those found in general in many individuals. Provided that adequate single case experimental designs are used they may also be incorporated into the evaluation of specific treatment techniques (Gianutsos and Gianutsos, 1979; Glasgow, Zeiss, Barrera and Lewinsohn, 1977; Wilson, 1982), and can then be very powerful research tools.

In order to assess the effect of memory problems in daily life rating scales, questionnaires and behavioural observations must all be considered. Some published questionnaires are already available, for example, the Subjective Memory Questionnaire (Bennett-Levy and Powell, 1980) and the Inventory of Memory Experiences (Herrman and Neisser, 1978). The questionnaire by Sunderland *et al.* (1983) consists of 35 different types of everyday error. Items were included if they tapped the types of errors that subjects had an opportunity to make in their daily lives. They included cognitive difficulties which pilot work had suggested were prevalent after head injury and included as wide a range of memory failures as possible. The 35 examples were rated for frequency of occurrence 'over the past few weeks', and

Table 2.2: Diary of a Patient with Memory Problems

20 April 1982		List of Items Forgotten 20th April–22nd April 1982
12.30 pm	6	Realised I hadn't put the washing out before leaving home.
1.15 pm	7	Had to check up washing symbols.
3.30 pm	8	Remembered that I should have ordered bread for Friday.
4.10 pm	9	The Asda list was missing from its usual place.
4.35 pm	10	Rang to order bread but couldn't remember 'wholemeal'.
5.50 pm	11	Remembered that I should have collected items to be dry cleaned from my sister's.
5.10 pm	12	Realised tomorrow is our wedding anniversary only when received card from sister.
5.25 pm	13	Found I hadn't put the oven on earlier as I'd intended to do.
7.35 pm	14	When helping husband to fill in a form, couldn't remember car number, whereabouts of passport and NAS card.
8.30 pm	15	Realised I'd forgotten to take Bakewell tart to Mum and Dad's.
11.30 pm	16	Had to get out of bed to check I'd locked the front door and put the milk bottles out. Remembered I hadn't yet cancelled cream order.

answers were classified on a five point scale ranging from 'on every occasion' to 'never'. However, as previously pointed out, inaccuracies of self-report may occur and it is always useful to include observational assessments by other people as well as self-report by the patient. Tasks may be devised to measure more specific aspects of memory function with individual patients. One way of deciding what to assess in detail is to ask the patient to keep a diary for a week of all the occasions when he was aware of forgetting things or when other people point out that he had forgotten something. An example of such a diary is shown in Table 2.2. This shows up problem areas that can be assessed in more detail. Sometimes this may simply involve systematic recording of what a person does. For example, a patient would turn up at the wrong department at the wrong time for treatment sessions, usually because he forgot to look at his programme card or got distracted *en route* and went to a different place from where he intended to go. Recording of each time he arrived in a treatment room, and whether it was the correct place to be, provided a baseline assessment of the number of times he went to the wrong place and the number of minutes he was late in arriving at the correct place.

Behavioural observations and ratings are useful for identifying prob-lems and evaluating progress with treatment. They may not enable one to predict, with any accuracy greater than that derived from common sense, the likely outcome of rehabilitation or the time course over which improvement may be expected to continue. Attempts have been made to use some of the standardised tests for this purpose but even then predictions tend to be of broad categories of independence and not specific enough to make concrete recommendations for clinical management of individual patients. These predictive indices are also limited by how little we know about the extent to which rehabilitation actually influences outcome. At present we are not really in a position to predict the extent to which memory deficits will respond to treatment or the restrictions that memory deficits are likely to impose on daily life in even the short-term future. One unfortunate exception to this is the amnesic syndrome which inevitably imposes major and often complete limitations on daily life.

Assessment of Related Functions

Memory assessment cannot be considered in isolation and many other cognitive functions will affect performance on memory tasks and the ability of a patient to cope with memory deficits in daily life.

Perceptual functions are more often assessed in stroke patients than in head-injured patients, but even in the latter group, deficits quite often occur, particularly early after injury. If a person's perceptual abilities are impaired then this is likely to affect memory for visual material and ability to use visually based strategies to cope with memory problems. Various techniques are available for assessing perceptual problems, such as copying the Rey–Osterreith complex figure (Rey, 1959), Unusual Views (Warrington and Taylor, 1973), Cube Counting (Ratcliff, 1970), Gollin incomplete Pictures (Gollin, 1960) and there is one which has been designed specifically for use by occupational therapists, the Rivermead Perceptual Assessment (Whiting, Cockburn, Bhavnani and Lincoln, 1984). These tests may be used to identify problems but may need to be supplemented by behavioural observation of, for example, dressing, manoeuvring a wheelchair through a door and face recognition.

Language abilities will similarly affect patients' ability to succeed on verbal memory tasks and on daily life activities involving verbal memory. The patient's ability to communicate functionally should therefore be assessed. It is all too easy for the psychologist or speech therapist to get carried away with the minutiae of speech and language assessment in patients who have 'interesting' dysphasic conditions, whereas what matters clinically is the adequacy of the patient's ability to comprehend auditory and visual verbal instructions, and to communicate with other people. A wide range of aphasia batteries is available in this area, together with additional tests of specific language function. Functional communication skills may be assessed by measures such as the Functional Communication Profile (Sarno, 1969), The Communication Activities in Daily Living Scale (Holland, 1980) and the Speech Questionnaire (Lincoln, 1982). These, rather than the more specific language tests or aphasia batteries, may provide assessments of the effects of language and verbal memory deficits in daily life.

Other aspects of cognitive function which need consideration are speed, attention, reasoning and the ability to inhibit responses. Simple assessments of speed can be made during activities in occupational therapy. For example, the time taken to sort different size sticks, to put pegs in a board or to join dots can easily be recorded. Rating scales can be used to assess whether the patient falls in the average, above or below category and this may be supplemented by more specific assessments of psychomotor reaction time. As a general rule latency measures may show the effects of recovery or treatment long after accuracy measures have stabilised.

Tests of 'frontal lobe' functions may provide valuable information in the context of rehabilitation. Patients with difficulty in initiating or inhibiting responses have in effect a dual deficit which makes their ability to cope with other deficits, such as memory problems, far less than would otherwise be the case. Indeed, such patients often fail on memory and other tests because they fail to carry out an initial analysis of the demands of the situation, and respond, impulsively and in-appropriately, and are then unable to shift from the inappropriate to more appropriate responses.

Another crucial predictor of rehabilitation success is the extent to which the patient has any awareness of the nature and severity of his deficit. This may need to be assessed continually throughout the rehabiliation process, and it is here that discrepancies of the patient's assessment of his problem and that of those around him becomes of particular significance. When discrepancies arise, a judicial use of behavioural treatments, individually or group based, and directive counselling with clear behavioural targets may be particularly useful. A group setting in which patients report their assessment of each other may well carry more weight to the patient than the therapist reporting. The group setting may be particularly appropriate for dealing with problems of awareness of deficit.

Cognitive deficits are striking after acute brain damage, but they comprise only part of the total picture of deficits which include physical as well as affective/behavioural changes. Physical deficits may impose limitations on cognitive ability by reducing the opportunity for

Figure 2.1: Personality Profile and Presence of Personality Change in 55 Cases, Six Months after Severe Head Injury

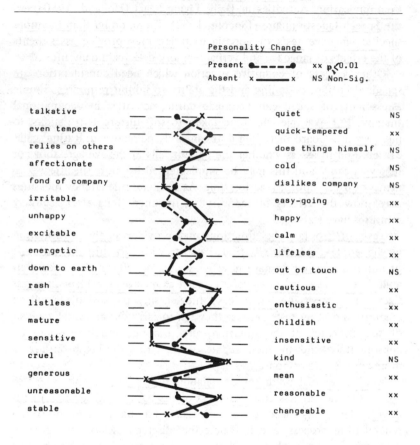

interaction with other people, but emotional, behavioural and personality changes may have an even greater impact on the patient's ability to identify and process information in an appropriate way (McKinlay, Brooks, Bond, Martinage and Marshall, 1981; Brooks and McKinlay, 1983). The behavioural and personality changes should therefore be examined as a routine part of the assessment, often using simple and purpose-built tests. An example of such a test is shown in Figure 2.1 which comprises a list of bipolar adjectives used in the identification and assessment of personality changes after severe head injury (Brooks and McKinlay, 1983).

Conclusions

Assessment for rehabilitation is more than simply applying a series of standardised tests. Some of the functions which are known to predict rehabilitation and vocational success cannot conveniently be assessed by means of readily available standard measures and the assessment procedure has to be adapted to the problems encountered by the patient and to the different environments in which the patient may find himself. Assessment should include behavioural and interpersonal functioning as well as cognitive and psychomotor functions. All the members of the rehabilitation team should be involved in the assessment of patients and should meet regularly, perhaps weekly, to pool their information. They can then use this pooled information to structure and plan each patient's rehabilitation programme. The programme for each patient should be individually tailored, with short- and long-term goals, which are clearly operationally identified and known to the patient and staff. A rehabilitation regime that simply fits patients into a regular 'unit regime', common to all patients is likely to be less successful than one that institutes a regime derived from a detailed assessment of the particular problems of each patient, and which evaluates the extent to which the goals of the regime have been reached.

3 METHODS OF IMPROVING MEMORY*

John Harris

Introduction

Several recent books and papers on memory have noted that memory research is now about 100 years old, taking 1885 as the starting date when Ebbinghaus published his experimental studies of memory. The study of memory has continued on a large scale and in recent times hundreds of research papers have been published annually. One might have expected that with all this research sophisticated ways of improving memory would be available or at least under the final stages of development. However, most of the work has been on how things are forgotten; very little has been connected with methods of improving memory. This is partly due to the limited number of techniques that seemed to be available, and it is also partly due to the way these techniques have been used for sensational entertainments, and also the crude commercialism that is so often associated with selling ways to improve your memory. You may have seen advertisements in the press headed 'Is memory your problem?' or 'Develop a super-power memory'. Academic psychologists, with their scientific aspirations, have often preferred pure to applied research, and they definitely wish to avoid being associated with this sort of sensational commercialism.

So this chapter does not catalogue a series of super new mnemonics that are being developed in psychological laboratories, rather its main purpose is to explain the broad categories of existing ways of improving memory as shown in Figure 3.1.

Internal Strategies

Naturally Learned Internal Strategies

I shall start with the naturally learned strategies, because they are rather different from the others; they are strategies most of us use quite naturally, often without realising it. Imagine that you are asked to

---

* This is an updated and extended version of a paper written by the same author when he was working at the Medical Research Council Applied Psychology Unit, Cambridge (Harris, 1980b).

Figure 3.1: Ways of Improving Memory Performance that are Differentiated and Described in this Chapter.

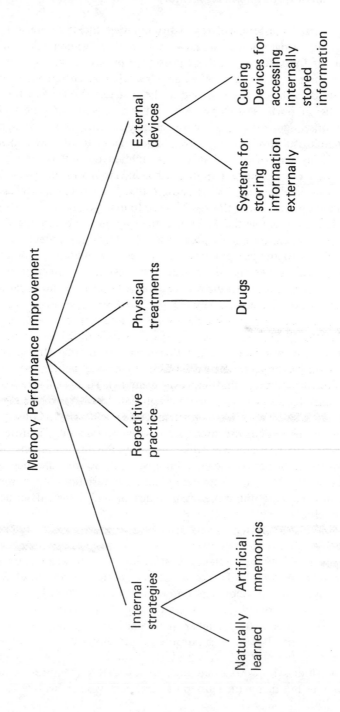

memorise 20 historical dates in five minutes; then you are tested and get, say, 14 right. If you are now given another five minutes to improve your performance as much as possible, how would you split up your time among the 20 dates? Most adults would concentrate more time on those dates they had got wrong in the first test. You might think that this is an obvious strategy. After all it is a waste of time trying to memorise something you have already learnt. But developmental psychologists investigating how children learn to use their memories efficiently have shown that young children do not use this type of strategy. For example, a study at the University of Minnesota (Masur, McIntyre and Flavell, 1973) showed that this particular strategy does not appear until about the age of seven to nine years.

Another example that is familiar to experimental psychologists is the strategy, often used in the free recall of a randomly ordered word list, that leads to the last presented items being recalled first. We all use a multitude of these natural memory strategies, but they are not normally thought of as memory *aids*, because they are so much part of our normal memory skills.

Artificial Mnemonics

Now I shall move on to the other group of internal strategies. They often go by the name 'mnemonics' (though some people use this term to describe anything that improves memory). These skills are similar to the ones I have just described, except that they have to be consciously learned and used, often requiring considerable effort. Consequently, most of us seldom use them, even when we are fully mature adults (Harris, 1980a). However, they do form the main content of most books and courses on memory improvement. So what are they, and do they work? Most of these techniques are variations on a very few themes, perhaps not more than a dozen, and I shall describe some examples.

One technique that can be used to remember a random sequence of words, maintaining the correct order, is to make up a story connecting them. You can then retell the story to yourself when you need to remember the words. This technique has been shown to be effective in the psychological laboratory (Bower and Clark, 1969), but how often do you want to remember a list of words? You may reply that you frequently want to remember the names of the things to buy on a shopping trip. But for this purpose people prefer to use external aids, such as a shopping list. This preference came out very clearly in interview studies I have carried out, first with Southampton University students and then with a group of Cambridge women, who were mainly housewives (Harris, 1980a).

Another mnemonic helps you to recognise people's faces and to remember their names. First of all you study the person's face to find an unusual feature. Next you change their name into something meaningful, and finally you associate the two. For example, red-bearded Mr Hiles could be imagined with hills growing out of his beard.

Even if this works in the laboratory, how useful is it in the real world? One could argue that on meeting people for the first time we are usually expected to strike up a conversation with them. This does not leave much time for finding unusual features of their faces or even meaningful aspects of their names. Anyway most people do not have convenient red beards! This and similar techniques may, however, be of some use in helping people with certain types of memory problem to learn the names, for example, of their workmates or rehabilitation staff, when the problem may be learning the names at all rather than learning them on the first meeting (see Wilson and Moffat, 1984).

A third type of mnemonic is exemplified by the sentence 'Richard Of York Gained Battles in Vain'. The first letters of the words in this sentence are also the first letters of the colours of the rainbow, and they are in order: Red, Orange, Yellow, Green, Blue, Indigo, Violet. Just as with the story method, first letter mnemonics are mainly useful when you need to remember things in their correct order and then only when you do not prefer to write them down. I can only think of two types of such occasions. The first type is when both the items and the order they occur in are permanent, and when you may want to refer to them, in order, from time to time. The order of the colours of the rainbow, or of the cranial nerves are good examples. This is also true of rhymes that we use to help us remember facts, such as the one that starts 'Thirty days hath September . . . ' The facts are also permanent. More typical of the things we have to remember in everyday life are the items on a shopping list, which may vary from one shopping trip to another, so that it is hardly worth learning a new mnemonic on each occasion. For the patient with memory deficits, however, it may be that most fundamental difficulties are associated with retaining relatively stable information such as common routes, addresses, names of colleagues or hospital staff, and various types of sequences. In such cases mnemonics may help.

The second situation in which these first letter and rhyme mnemonics are useful is when written reminders are not available. In examinations written reminders are normally forbidden and they are usually regarded as a form of cheating. Learned mnemonics, on the other hand, are usually acceptable, and anyway the invigilator cannot see them. Certainly many students do use mnemonics, particularly of the first letter and rhyme varieties (though, according to my study (Harris, 1980a), even students use these mnemonics much less often than they use many external aids, such as diaries, memos, shopping lists and asking someone for a reminder). A similar situation occurs for patients with memory problems when they do not wish to be seen to be using external aids, such as written reminders, because it might mark them out as handicapped.

For those readers that want to find out more about mnemonics, I suggest they consult Higbee (1977), Lorayne and Lucas (1975), Morris (1977) and Yates (1966).

Repetitive Practice

In an earlier version of this chapter (Harris, 1980b), I did not mention one potential method that I now realise should be considered because its use appears to be widespread in rehabilitation units. This potential method is the use of repeated practice on memory games, such as Kim's game, or on laboratory tasks, such as paired-associate learning. A recent survey of the management of memory disorders in Britain (Harris and Sunderland, 1981) showed that such techniques are in use. However, it is not at all clear how effective they are. If the practice is applied to a task that the patient needs to learn, then it can clearly be of benefit, but the tasks are often artificial or based on games. Their use appears to be

> based on the assumption that memory responds like a 'mental muscle', and that exercising it on one task will strengthen it for use on other tasks, so that any improvement on artificial games will generalize to the requirements of everyday life. Such a view seems too simple and over-optimistic. Current theoretical views about memory, although diverse, tend to agree that memory represents a far more complicated set of interacting cognitive skills and abilities than any idea of a mental muscle seems to imply. More damaging is the evidence that memory skills acquired with practice on very specific tasks may not generalize even to apparently similar tasks. For example, Ericsson, Chase and Falcon (1980) trained a student on conventional digit span tests. Over 20 months his digit span increased from about 7 to 80 digits; however, the effect of the

practice did not even generalize to memory span for consonants, which remained at only about 6 when digit span had already increased substantially.

However, there are also arguments in support of repetitive practice on games or laboratory tests. First, it may be good for the patient's morale, because he knows something is being done to help his memory problems, and he will also be aware of his improvements on the tasks he is practising. This may encourage him that it is possible to improve his performance, so that he feels it is worth making an effect with everyday memory tasks. Second, there is some evidence from animal studies, of neural regeneration following brain injury (Wall, 1975), and also that early intervention with physical exercise promotes recovery after motor cortex damage better than later intervention (Black, Markowitz and Cianci, 1975). It is at least possible that mental exercise during a critical period of neural regeneration may in some way enhance the regeneration. (Harris and Sunderland, 1981, p. 208)

If this turns out to be the case, it throws into question the common practice of waiting for a stable baseline before intervening with memory training, a practice that derives from the need for assessment rather than the prime objective of rehabilitation.

Physical Treatments

By physical treatments I mean ways of manipulating the basic biological and chemical processes on which memory depends or that represent memory at a physiological level. Certainly these processes can be influenced, as studies of the effects of drugs on memory have shown, and first-hand knowledge of the effect that alcohol can have on memory is not confined to psychologists and scientists!

Most of the experimental work has been done on drugs that, like alcohol, decrease memory performance and it has been done with animals, but research is now being done on humans, and with memory enhancing drugs such as Piracetam. There are also drugs such as Cyclanderlate and Hydergine that are marketed to aid mental functioning of all sorts in the elderly, including, of course, their memories. The topic of memory and drugs (particularly those affecting cholinergic neurotransmitters) is covered in detail in Chapter 7 by Steven Cooper, so I shall move on to the next type of aid.

External Aids

The last main category is external memory aids, such as the traditional knotted handkerchief. The spontaneous use of external aids develops during childhood, just as the use of internal aids does.

In one study Kreutzer, Leonard and Flavell (1975) questioned children about various aspects of memory; for example, they asked them how many ways they could think of to be sure they would take their skates to school the next day. The children gave more external methods than internal ones, such as putting their skates by the front door, putting them in their satchels, or asking someone to remind them. This was true for all four age groups, whose ages ranged from six to eleven years, but the older groups had much richer repertoires of external methods than did the younger ones.

The researchers found a similar result with another question about methods of remembering a friend's birthday party, and one about a friend trying to work out the age of his dog, which was about what he could do to help him remember which Christmas he had received the dog as a puppy. Again all the groups of children gave many more external methods than internal ones, and the older children had richer repertoires.

External Information Storage

External aids can be divided into two groups. One group is made up of those aids that we use to store information externally. We may use them either because they are more accurate or complete than internal storage, or because internal storage mechanisms may be overloaded. Sometimes it involves storing small amounts of information over short periods of time, such as jotting down intermediate results during mental calculations; or it may involve storage of large quantities of information over much longer periods. Examples of this are the information stored in documents, filing systems, books, libraries and, of course, computers.

Professor Hunter (1979) of Keele University referred to these systems as 'communal memory stores' and he noted that their functions include the passing of knowledge from generation to generation, in effect a form of cultural memory. (He also pointed out that the technology and culture of non-literate societies are remembered with such aids as rituals. The example he quoted from Dr Bronowski was a ritual that ensures that the different stages of making a sword are all performed correctly and in the right order. Chanting and recitation can also be used as cultural memory aids, the younger individuals slowly learning the chants and words, and gradually becoming able to join in or take over.)

The latest form of external memory store is provided by computers. In fact, it is in this role that computers have had the biggest impact on most people. Details of their bank accounts, car registrations and mortgages are all likely to be stored away in computer files. This concept of storing vast quantities of organised information that can be accessed very rapidly is familiar to most of us, but for personal use, except possibly in our jobs, these aids are only now becoming available, with systems such as Prestel giving us access to vast communal memory aids. (Prestel is a system that links your television to a remote computer via your telephone. The main service offered by Prestel is access to enormous amounts of information stored in the computer.)

External storage in the form of written information, such as timetables, lists, plans, sketchmaps and diagrams can be a very cheap and effective way of helping people with memory deficits. Although this may be seen as a 'crutch' rather than a method of memorising the information, it can overcome the practical difficulties and allow the patient to lead a more normal life. Also, in some cases, repeated use of such an aid is likely to lead to some of the information being internalised.

Some written aids, such as shopping lists, only store relatively small amounts of information, acting as cues for actions that also require the use of internally stored information. The next subsection covers such cueing aids.

Cueing Devices

This section on cueing devices is longer than the others, firstly, because remembering to do things is a personal interest of mine (Harris, 1984; Harris and Wilkins, 1982), and secondly because, unlike the case of mnemonics, I do not know of any general descriptions to which to refer the reader. The requirement for aids that provide memory cues is very different from mere external storage of information. For example, the words 'wedding anniversary' in a diary are usually sufficient (if they are read at the appropriate time), because you are quite capable of retrieving from your own memory the information that you should buy some flowers or take what ever action is appropriate. What you need is a *cue* for a particular action, not a detailed description of the action itself.

You can further classify cueing devices according to the cue they provide. An alarm cooking-timer provides an *active* reminder, while a shopping list provides *specific* information about which items to buy. This type of classification led me to look at the criteria for the effectiveness of cueing devices and of the cues they provide.

For a cue to be maximally effective it needs to have certain properties. First, it should be given as close as possible before the time when the action is required – it may be no good reminding people as they leave home in the morning to buy some bread on the way home from work. Secondly, it would be active rather than passive – a passive reminder in a diary may fail if you forget to consult it. Thirdly, it should be a specific reminder for the particular action that is required – a knotted handkerchief may only remind you that something must be remembered, but not what that something is.

While some currently available memory aids provide cues that rate well on one or two of these criteria, few rate well on all three. In certain situations a cooking timer with a bell or buzzer rates particularly well. As regards temporal proximity, it is set to ring at the time when the action is required (such as taking a cake out of the oven). As regards being active, the bell rings so that you do not have to remember independently to consult it. As regards specificity, the cooking timer's bell is usually distinct from the door bell or that of the telephone. But it is not perfect in this respect as people often cook more than one thing at a time. An elderly person might well interpret the timer's bell as relevant to the saucepan which is visible rather than to the cake in the oven which is not.

Because they provide active and timely cues, some people use portable alarms and cooking timers for other purposes, such as to remind them to turn on the TV for a certain programme. However, the more purposes for which a bell timer is used, the less specific are the cues that the bell provides. The Esselte 'Electronic Diary' shown in Figure 3.2 overcomes this problem. The Electronic Diary consists of an alarm clock and a pad of paper. Each page is divided into quarter of an hour sections, opposite which you can write a *specific* reminder message. Then you use the same ordinary lead pencil to join two lines of conducting ink, opposite the time you require the reminder. The graphite in the pencil mark completes the circuit and the alarm rings at the time indicated. When this happens, you find out the current time by looking at the clock, and you can then tell what you are supposed to be doing by reading what is written opposite this time on the pad.

This a very neat idea and should work well in an office or laboratory, provided that the action being cued can be performed straight away at the quarter-hour times at which the alarm can be set. You only

Figure 3.2: Esselte 'Electronic Diary'

need a few minutes, or sometimes seconds, to forget. I once set an Esselte alarm for 2.45 to remind me of a meeting ten minutes later. To fill this ten minute wait I picked up an article to read. Fifteen minutes later I was still reading the article! More recently a colleague and I have found that people can forget to do things in ten seconds or less or if they are distracted by, say, watching an exciting film (Harris and Wilkins, 1982).

Some electronic calculators with extra functions have alarms that can be set to the minute, and on some of them an attempt has been made to deal with specificity. Typically four different signals can be set independently. Each alarm consists of a group of 'pips', so that one goes 'pip . . . pip . . . pip', the second goes 'pip pip . . . pip pip . . . pip pip', and so on. At first, it seems that this is a neat way to provide specificity, but the problem with it is that you have to remember the specific relevance of each signal, or you have to write it down somewhere.

An additional problem with conventional bell timers is that they can only be set to ring at one particular time. A further setting can be made only when the first one has been reached. Also they can often only be set to ring up to one hour in advance. These limits have been raised considerably by a sophisticated clock system called Time Trac, as illustrated in Figure 3.3. Up to 30 alarms can be set, not only for a

Figure 3.3: 'Time Trac' Alarm Clock/Calendar

particular time but also for a particular date up to a year in advance. But imagine setting such a device to ring at three o'clock on a day ten months from now. Would you remember then why you had set it?

The final limitation of conventional bell timers is that they restrict the way of choosing the time for the bell to ring. With conventional cooking alarms you usually set the *length of time* until the bell rings; that is the time-elapsed method. Whereas with alarm clocks you set the *actual time* when you want it to ring. Ideally you need both methods available.

Multi-function digital watches often include alarm facilities, and these are gradually becoming more sophisticated. Some can be set by either the time-elapsed or the absolute time method. Although, as far as I know, they have not overcome the problem of specificity, they do have two distinct advantages. Firstly, the alarm watch is very portable and, secondly, it has another, more frequent use — it tells the time. As a result it is normally carried around, so you do not have to remember separately to take it with you when you want to use it.

So, in addition to the criteria I have already mentioned for judging the effectiveness of cues, there are at least eight additional ones that apply to the memory aids that provide the cues.

Firstly, the aid should obviously be as portable as possible. Next, it should be of use in as wide a range of situations as is feasible – so that you bother to carry it around with you, and so that you develop the habit of using it every time you want to remember something you might otherwise forget. It should be able to store as many cues as possible, and have as large a time range as possible – so that you are able to set cues to be given at any time from the present up to at least a year in the future. Ideally cues entered so far in advance must be reviewable at times between when they are entered and when they are activated. The time settings should be possible as both actual time and time elapsed. These time settings should be accurate to the minute, and lastly, the memory aid should be easy to use, and not dependent on other instruments, such as the pencil of the Esselte electronic diary.

The total of eleven criteria for cues and for the instruments that provide them are not always completely compatible. For example, portability demands smallness whereas some of the sophistication I have argued for would inevitably mean an increase in size. However, it is still possible to use the criteria to set about improving memory aids of this type or developing new ones.

For example, several years ago I drew up the general specifications needed for the type of memory aid shown in Figure 3.4. At its most simple, paired times like '12.45 p.m.', and spoken reminder messages, such as 'Phone John Smith', are entered together. The time is entered on to the display using a calculatory type keyboard, and the reminder message is recorded via a microphone. The reminder is played back at the time with which it was originally entered.

A portable device like this should be effective because it provides cues that are active, specific and timely. Although the one shown in the illustration is rather crude, it could be developed to meet most of the device criteria I have mentioned.

Nothing like this is available yet, as far as I know – the National Research and Development Corporation were unable to adopt it, because they considered that any patient would not have been strong enough to meet their strict rules. Something that comes close to it is called the Mind Reader, and is shown in Figure 3.5.

It consists of a microprocessor preprogrammed to store messages that you enter using a touch sensitive keyboard, and they are displayed on what the manufacturers call a 'Times Square' moving display, which allows messages of considerable length to be read as they repeatedly flow across it. The active cue is a 'beep', which is emitted at the time when the message is displayed. It is very easy to use, considering its

Figure 3.4: Early Version of Author's 'Mema' Memory Aid

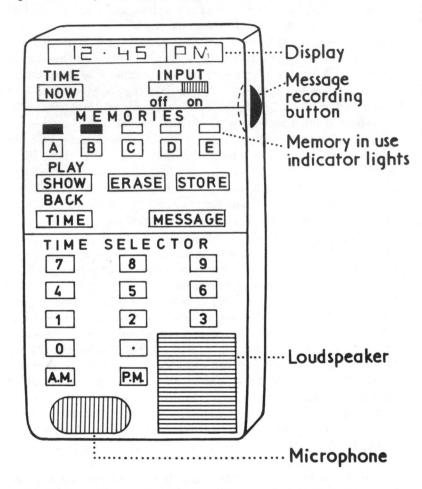

sophistication, because it makes good use of default options and prompts for the information required. Its main drawbacks are its lack of portability (on account of its being mains-powered and rather large), and its price of well over £100. At the cost of being rather more difficult to use, some other aids do roughly the same job for rather less money and are very much more portable. These are the Toshiba Memo Note II (Figure 3.6) which weighs under four ounces, and the Sharp E6200 (Figure 3.7) which, although larger, is still easily portable. The similar (British designed) Biztek Pad (Figure 3.8) offers an appointment list and a separate alarm. Barbara Wilson (Wilson and

Figure 3.5: 'Mind Reader' Memory Aid

Moffat, 1983) has used the Toshiba Memo Note 60 with patients (it is similar to the Memo Note II in operation but is somewhat larger). It takes even normal people a while to remember how to enter the reminders into these machines and Wilson found that this was a great problem for those with memory impairment. Even if this is done for them, some patients cannot even remember simple steps such as how to clear the display. She considers that existing machines are only really useful for patients who sometimes refuse to use notebooks, such as some who have frontal lobe involvement. However, with an appropriate design, I believe they would be of much wider use. What is needed is a machine as portable as the Memo Note II, but one that asks for the information it wants in a similar way to the Mind Reader. Indeed the ideal aid may be expected to remind the user how to use it!

Recently I have heard from Rodger Wood (1983, personal communication) of success in using a wrist-watch alarm together with a diary, with two severely head-injured patients (PTAs of several months). Initially the diary had been used with external cues provided by rehabilitation staff, but this proved unpopular and alarm wristwatches were then used instead, initially ringing every 15 minutes. Surprisingly (at least to me!), this proved more popular, and the patients eventually learned to check their diaries regularly and even to write in extra items. For at least one of the patients it also gave her

Figure 3.6: Toshiba 'Memo Note II' Memory Aid/Calculator

Figure 3.7: Sharp EL-6200 Schedule Planner/Calculator

Figure 3.8: Domicrest 'Biztek Pad' Memory Aid/Calculator

greater confidence in dealing with day to day events. (In both cases more conventional types of memory training had not been successful.) This approach may be more appropriate in many cases than an aid with an electronic display. It is easier to remember how to use diaries. There is, for example, no screen to remember how to clear. In many cases it may prove possible gradually to reduce the active reminders to a point at which the patients are left simply using normal duties, aids that do not even mark them out as being handicapped.

To finish with, it is worth noting that without spending any money at all, most of us could make far more effective use of active, specific and timely memory cues. Remember the skates left by the front door? They are likely the catch the child's attention at the time they need to be remembered and their specific significance is clear. While most of us are quite capable of devising such schemes, it is difficult to predict those occasions when we shall need an active reminder. So it is safer to develop a habit of assuming a reminder is necessary whenever there is a penalty attached to forgetting. I do try to use these methods myself, usually notes left in strategic places, but my frequent lapses are a constant source of amusement to my family, colleagues and friends, who gently remind me to practise what I preach!

4 STRATEGIES OF MEMORY THERAPY

Nick Moffat

Introduction

The previous chapter discussed methods of improving memory and provided a conceptual framework for their categorisation. The present chapter examines these and other memory strategies in more detail, with particular reference to the rehabilitation of the brain-injured. It is emphasised that although a given memory strategy may be beneficial to one individual it may be of no value to another, and indeed in some cases may actually prove to be detrimental. Varying responses to treatment will be largely dependent upon the nature and extent of a person's brain damage. As the process of selecting the most appropriate memory training strategies for a given individual will be described in the next chapter it will not be discussed further here.

This chapter begins with a consideration of variables which may affect memory performance, and then discusses the organisation of memory therapy. This is followed by a description of various visual imagery and verbal learning strategies, and the use of self-instructions and external memory aids. The penultimate section describes reality orientation training, and the chapter concludes by considering the issue of the restitution of memory.

Variables Which May Affect Memory

The range of brain structures implicated in memory and the diversity of processes involved in remembering may explain why memory performance is readily disrupted by brain damage. However, memory performance and memory complaints may also be influenced by affective states (Kahn, Zarit, Hilbert and Niederehe, 1975), and by other cognitive variables, such as the speed of responding. Thus, the investigation of the interrelationships between memory problems and other additional variables will be important because factors bearing upon amnesia may need to be dealt with before the true memory loss can be elucidated.

Reactions to the Onset of Memory Loss

The initial experience of brain damage may sensitise a patient, the family and possibly the staff to memory problems. Thus, in the case of the head-injured there may be a period of retrograde (RA) and post-traumatic (PTA) amnesia surrounding the circumstances of the trauma, which in themselves may form a focus of concern. Furthermore, anxiety about memory loss may be heightened by staff regularly probing memory for ongoing events as an index of the severity of brain damage (Russell and Smith, 1961).

Although PTA and some aspects of memory functioning may recover with time, it cannot be assumed that the patient's beliefs about memory performance, or those of others, are necessarily commensurate with the potential level of functioning. Thus, the author has seen some head-injured patients who showed concern about their memory abilities which was not confirmed by standard memory testing. Feedback to these patients of their test results, together with reassurance that only some severely head-injured patients suffer persistent memory problems, appeared to reduce anxiety about memory performance, and encouraged greater success in coping with everyday remembering. The same principles can be applied to the non-confused elderly who may incorrectly attribute occasional absent-mindedness to age-related decline in memory abilities. Thus, as discussed more fully in Chapter 9, those elderly who evidence memory complaints without impairment on memory tests may benefit from participation in a memory group. Even when there is evidence of impaired memory the reduction of excessive anxiety and the delineation of the person's assets and deficits may be helpful to the amnesic and the family. However, the personal distress that can accompany problems of remembering, and the burden of living with someone who, for example, regularly repeats the same question should not be underestimated.

Where there is an acute onset to the memory loss the process of dealing with memory failures may be adversely affected by social factors. Thus, in the acute recovery stage the patient may have few demands placed upon him or her, with work and other responsibilities involving remembering being carried out by others. There is a danger that this system of acute care may lag behind the progress the patient is capable of. This may be an inadvertant process since the rate of recovery is not understood, or there may be maintaining factors which prolong the over-protection.

In order to delineate the psychological aspects of acute versus chronic care of amnesia the operant model developed by Fordyce (1976) with regard to chronic pain will be used as a framework for exposition.

Operant Analysis of Forgetting Behaviour

The first question to be asked is whether forgetting behaviour is, in fact, being reinforced positively. Is the patient being given attention for complaining of being unable to remember what to do? For instance, the occupational therapy staff of one unit had attributed the poor learning of a young head-injured patient to his poor concentration. From the behavioural analysis of his behaviour it emerged that he received considerable staff attention for asking to be reminded what to do, but if he carried on working he was given less attention since the staff then worked with other patients. During a period of retraining the staff contingencies were reversed so that he received attention following increasing periods of time spent carrying out activities without asking for further assistance. This system increased the time spent working and also enabled staff to devise additional tasks for him.

Positive reinforcement of forgetting behaviour may also occur when the repeated questions or statements made by some memory impaired patients receive responses from others. An alternative approach is to define certain repeated items and consistently ignore their occurrence. This was accomplished with a severely memory impaired man who repeated themes about his pre-injury employment, or his recovery. These themes were interfering with memory therapy sessions, being mentioned on average seven times during each hour-long session. During the intervention stage the themes were completely ignored and the therapy tasks continued. This resulted in the reduction of the number of themes to an average of less than two per session, and their timing changed so that instead of interrupting the tasks they only occurred at the end of the session. Unfortunately, there was no generalisation of this improvement to other settings. Indeed, when another therapist conducted one of the sessions he recorded 16 themes in the hour. However, improvements were maintained for the two original therapists across the one, three and six month follow-up sessions.

Negative reinforcement of forgetting may occur when a patient avoids an unpleasant task by a convenient lapse of memory. Training to overcome this should aim to set tasks which are within the ability level of the patient, and the requirements should gradually be increased to correspond with and maximise progress. This issue will be discussed more fully in a later section.

It needs to be stated here, however, that a further question in operant analysis relates to reinforcement of *appropriate* remembering behaviour. Just as inappropriate behaviour may be reinforced so might appropriate behaviour be ignored. Further problems may arise when memory impaired people are over-protected by their families or by staff working with them, and as a result any residual memory skills may be under-used. (With the more recently brain damaged the aim may be to avoid the development of such under-utilisation.)

In an attempt to increase the expectations of memory among nursing-home residents, Langer, Rodin, Beck, Weinman and Spitzer (1979) provided tokens for correctly answering questions which required the residents to find out information by the time of the next visit. The demands made upon the residents were gradually increased over time, and tokens exchanged for a gift at the end of the three-week period. It was found that the number of correct answers increased across the interviews, with the contingent token group supplying the correct information in a shorter period of time than those in the control conditions. Furthermore, there was generalisation of improved memory to tests of immediate and remote memory among the contingent token group. The authors suggest that it may be worthwhile maintaining demands upon the memory of the elderly since in the first part of their study the no-treatment and minimal treatment groups showed a significant decline in memory over a six-week period, whereas the experimental group showed a significant increase in short-term memory.

The operant analysis of forgetting behaviour outlined above is only intended to provide an understanding of certain aspects of the complaints of forgetting. For example, it throws no light on the relationship between everyday memory functioning and test performance. With many amnesic patients additional aspects of memory therapy may be necessary, as discussed below.

Organisation of Memory Therapy

In order to devise a memory therapy programme it is necessary to assess the assets and deficits of the person, establish the priorities for therapy and then select the most appropriate training strategies. This is obviously an important and involved process, and further discussion will be confined to the selection and design of suitable training tasks, since the other considerations are dealt with elsewhere in this book, particularly in the next chapter.

Golden (1978) suggests that there are four important ingredients in the design of a rehabilitation task:

(1) It should include the impaired skill that one is trying to re-formulate. All other skill requirements in the task should be in areas with which the subject has little or no trouble.

(2) The therapist should be able to vary the task in difficulty from a level which would be simple for the patient to a level representing normal performance.

(3) The number of errors made by the patient should be controlled.

(4) The task should be quantifiable so that progress may be objectively stated.

The first requirement mentioned above implies that, with regard to memory therapy, remembering will be required at some stage during the therapy. This is obviously essential but, as discussed at the end of this chapter, memory therapy is not intended to consist of simply practising remembering, since memory is not considered to be like a 'mental muscle' (Higbee, 1977, Harris and Sunderland, 1981). What may be required instead is that the person's assets will be utilised to overcome a problem (see Chapter 5).

The second and third requirements outlined by Golden (1978) involve varying the difficulty of the task. This can be achieved by altering the amount or complexity of information to be learned, the provision of learning strategies, the duration of retention expected, and the cues offered at the retrieval stage. Many of these features will be peculiar to the material or the strategy being taught, but the general aim is to set the requirements at a level which ensures a reasonable degree of success. The precision teaching technique (Raybould and Solity, 1982) which has been applied in special education may prove to be particularly beneficial in aiding memory therapy to continually match the level of complexity of the task to the ability of the amnesic. This method is particularly suitable for computer applications in memory therapy since the computer programme can be designed to continually adjust the duration of retention, or any other specified variable, according to the level of performance over the preceding trials.

An additional consideration in establishing the level of difficulty during training is that in order to avoid the apparently common problem of an early error being repeated thereafter, the errorless learning technique can be applied. This involves the provision of the task in such a way that the person cannot fail to provide the correct answer. For example, in teaching a blind and deaf head-injured man to use the manual alphabet as a means of communication, one letter was taken at a time and presented repeatedly. The errorless approach can be taken too far, as occurred in the early stages of training with this man, who retorted, 'Not another . . . X'. Subsequent training sessions were modified to embed the new letter in words he already knew, which made the task more interesting and acceptable.

The final two requirements mentioned by Golden (1978) involve the quantification of results and the provision of feedback about performance. These features are important for the amnesic and the therapist, since progress in memory therapy may be slow at times and may require careful graphing in order to be noticed. It may be valuable to provide standardised prompts if the information to be learned is not freely recalled during training sessions, since this may reveal learning taking place before this is detected in measures of free recall (Moffat and Coward, 1983).

An additional consideration in the organisation of memory therapy is the specification of the number, frequency and duration of training sessions. As Baddeley (Chapter 1) has already discussed, it is generally preferable to space out the learning and provide short sessions, since if training is pursued too intensively this may be counter-productive and may reduce interest on the part of the patient and therapist (Johnson, 1979). During training sessions involving rehearsal the aim should be to handle an immediate test of recall rather than encourage rapid repetition of the material. This is both more effective as a learning strategy, and offers an ongoing monitoring of and involvement by the patient.

It is obviously difficult to determine the appropriate number of sessions before beginning memory therapy. Therefore, it may be more expedient to specify criteria to determine the termination of treatment. This will need to include lack of progress as well as the achievement of a specific aim. As mentioned earlier, progress may be slow and once achieved may not be maintained. Therefore, it may be worthwhile offering over-learning practice once a task has been learned in order to help maintain progress, and to provide regular follow-up with booster sessions if necessary.

Having established some of the ways in which the therapist might organise the conditions for carrying out memory therapy, attention can be turned to the memory strategies that the client could be taught in order to overcome specific memory complaints. The strategies outlined below are generally aimed at finding alternative means of remembering information, and may be considered to be ways of ameliorating a memory problem rather than restoring or retraining a memory deficit.

External Memory Aids

It has already been mentioned that the mere provision of external memory aids, such as signposts, may not be sufficient to ensure their use. Thus, although there is a good range of potential external memory aids (Harris, 1978), their incorporation in a memory therapy programme may require careful planning. Part of the problem is the limitation of existing memory cueing devices, as discussed by Harris (Chapter 3). However, the Automatic Memorandum Clock (Shenton, 1975) which was available almost a century ago possessed many of the requirements of a good cueing device, and yet it proved a financial disaster!

Obviously in order to be beneficial a memory aid must be fully utilised. The difficulty of proper use was demonstrated in a pilot project with a Korsakoff syndrome patient (Davies and Binks, 1983). He was given certain commands to remember, and other commands he wrote in a book. It was found that at the pre-arranged signal he had forgotten its significance and did not complete any of the actions. However, once he was prompted to use the book the written commands were obeyed, but not those previously committed to memory. This kind of system was successfully employed with a patient with early Alzheimer's disease who used a digital alarm watch which 'beeped' every hour to remind him to look at his daily programme and attend his appointments (Kurlychek, 1983).

External memory aids may not only be valuable for the amnesic, but may also prove a suitable *aide mémoire* for those relating to the amnesic. Thus, in the Davies and Binks study the prompt card was designed to be shown to others so that they interacted appropriately with Mr F, the amnesic. The prompt card provided specific guidelines (for example, noted important dates and addresses for him and got him to check them). Mr F was also given role play training at how to ask someone to jot something down in his book. In this way the use of the aid became fully established in his daily routine, and was still in use at a one year follow-up.

Following the successful maintenance of this programme, some of the internal memory strategies of the type described below were taught.

Visual Imagery

There are a number of memory strategies described below which make use of the formation of a mental picture of information to aid remembering.

Memory for Names

In learning a person's name, such as Angela Webster, a mental image can be constructed involving an Angel, Web and a Star. This system has been successfully applied to learning the names of staff and patients by amnesic individuals attending rehabilitation centres (Moffat and Coward, 1983; Wilson, 1981). In order for this procedure to be effective it may be necessary to provide the mental image for the person, perhaps as a drawing. It appears that the simpler the method of constructing the mental image the better: whilst the more elaborate face-name association technique may be possible for normal subjects (McCarty, 1980), it appears to be impractical for many brain-damaged individuals (Glasgow, Zeiss, Barrera and Lewinsohn, 1977; and Wilson, 1981).

The face–name association method involves linking a distinctive feature of a person with the name, which is transformed into an imaginable form as outlined above. For example, if the distinctive feature of Angela Webster was her hair, the image might be of an angel and a star caught in a web, made out of her hair. The advantage of this system is that it provides a unique link between the person's name and their face, which is in keeping with the finding that the images should be interacting but need not be bizarre (Wollen, Weber and Lowry, 1972). However, it appears that the small number of names taught to the brain-injured, and the way in which practice can be spaced out by using the multiple baseline design (Hersen and Barlow, 1976) may reduce any confusion between the names to be learned and the respective faces.

The visual imagery method for learning names may not only enhance initial learning compared with a rehearsal condition, but the names may be better retained over at least a three- to six-month period (Moffat and Coward, 1983).

Peg-type Mnemonics

The various peg-type mnemonics all involve the learning of a set of standard peg words to which are associated further items which are to be remembered. The mnemonics only vary in terms of the set of peg words, with the other requirements remaining very similar. Thus, for example, research using peg mnemonics, and related work on paired-associate learning, have all emphasised the need to form strong visual and interacting images between the peg word and the item to be remembered. This requirement helps to focus attention at both the encoding and retrieval stages, although it may actually take less time to learn the information using the peg-type mnemonic than if no mnemonic had been provided (Groninger, 1971). It appears that the interactive images can be provided by the trainer without impairing recall, although the learner should ideally be encouraged to generate his own visual images.

An additional feature of the peg-type mnemonics is that the peg words offer a partial retrieval cue about the information which was originally encoded, and unlike some other mnemonics (for example, the link method) recall of a given item is not dependent upon the successful recall of others.

There are three major variants of the peg mnemonic, namely the rhyming peg method; the phonetic system (sometimes also referred to as the hook or digit-sound method); and the loci method. These mnemonics will be described in turn, together with the additional use of the phonetic system to encode numbers into a visual or verbal system to aid remembering of digit strings, such as telephone numbers.

For simplicity the examples given below only describe the learning of a few items. However, in practice many items can be remembered using these mnemonics.

Rhyming Peg Method

The peg list is formed by choosing words that possess a rhyming relationship to the respective number, as illustrated in the following list:

One	bun	Six	sticks
Two	shoe	Seven	heaven
Three	tree	Eight	gate
Four	door	Nine	wine
Five	hive	Ten	hen

Once this list is adequately learned, then items to be remembered can be associated with the peg word by forming a visual image of the peg word interacting with the particular item. An example of the application of this method with an amnesic is given in Evans (1981), and is provided below:

Peg Word	Item to be Remembered	Possible Pictorial Image
1 Sun	Get up	Sun shining on person waking up
2 Shoe	Have breakfast	Eating breakfast whilst sat in a large shoe
3 Tree	Collect clothes	Clothes hanging on a tree
4 Door	Go into bathroom	Open door with pictures of activities to be completed in bathroom, e.g. brush teeth
5 Dive	Come out of bathroom dressed	Diving out of bathroom fully dressed
6 Sticks	Do hair	Hair standing on end like sticks

In the example cited above the rhyming peg method was used to remind the person to carry out future actions (prospective memory). However, the more typical experimental application has been to recall material previously learned using this technique (retrospective memory). This has included word lists, although second language learning (Paivio and Desrochers, 1979) and prose learning (Krebs, Snowman and Smith, 1978) have also been taught.

The rhyming peg method has proved an effective mnemonic with normal subjects (e.g. Morris and Reid, 1970), but has generally been unsuccessful with the elderly (Mason and Smith, 1977; Smith, 1975), particularly when retention is tested over more than a few minutes (Hellebusch, 1976). This may be because the elderly are generally less able to use visual imagery, although this is not a sufficient explanation since the elderly do benefit from use of the method of loci (see below).

The sparse experience of using the rhyming peg method with the brain-injured suggests that although some mildly head-injured patients may benefit, those with more pronounced unilateral damage of either hemisphere may not (Wilson and Moffat, 1984). This may be due to either a failure to retrieve the word associated with a peg word, or difficulty recalling the actual peg words.

A general problem of the rhyming peg mnemonic is the difficulty of generating pegs for numbers greater than ten. This limits the amount of information that the system can successfully encode, although it may be possible to remember more than one set of items at a time using the peg method (Bower and Reitman, 1972). Furthermore, it appears that the same peg items (that is, one is a bun, etc.) can be used over and over again since the learning of a new set of items to be associated with the peg list successfully displaces the previously learned list (retroactive without proactive interference). This enables the repeated use of the peg method to remember information which may be altered after a relatively short period of time, such as things to do, despite the fact that it is not suited for remembering more than ten items of information.

The Phonetic System

The phonetic system has gradually evolved over the past 300 years to its present form which relies on a relationship between numbers and consonant sounds. All of the consonant sounds are included in the phonetic system, except sounds associated with w, h and y (easily remembered as 'why'). It is the sound which is important rather than the constituent letters. This allows the grouping together of similar sounds (for example, sh, ch, and a soft 'g'). These groups of consonant sounds are then associated with the numbers nought to nine using a rather complex and mixed set of criteria, as outlined below. The sounds associated with each number can then be used to form words by the addition of vowels. For example, 021 could be encoded as SuNDay.

Number	Consonant-sounds	Rationale
0	z (s, soft 'c')	'z' is first sound of the word 'zero'
1	t, d or th	the letter 't' and 'd' each have *one* downstroke
2	n	'n' has *two* downstrokes
3	m	'm' has *three* downstrokes
4	r	last sound of the word 'four'
5	l	Roman number for '50' is 'L'
6	j (sh, ch, soft 'g')	the letter j turned around resembles a 6
7	k (hard 'c' or 'g')	a K can be formed by using two 7's
8	f (v, ph)	written f and 8 both have two loops, one above the other
9	p (b)	P is like a reversed 9

Using the consonant-sounds to form words, an additional mnemonic can be formed to remember the phonetic system, namely, '0123456789' becomes 'Satan may relish coffee pie'.

The sounds associated with each number offer a range of possible keywords, but it is probably preferable to select high imagery concrete words, for example, 'inn' rather than 'now' for number two. Examples of suitable keywords for the numbers up to 20 are given below, with alternative words, and additional keywords for higher numbers being available in various texts (for example, Buzan, 1977; Furst, 1972; Lorayne, 1979).

1	Tie	6	Shoe	11	Teeth	16	Dish
2	Noah	7	Key	12	Tin	17	Duck
3	May	8	Ivy	13	Tomb	18	Dove
4	Ray	9	Pie	14	Tyre	19	Tape
5	Law	10	Toes	15	Doll	20	Nose

Once the keywords have been learned it is then possible to form visual images with other items to be remembered, as illustrated above with the rhyming peg method. Thus, for example, to remember to go to the bank, and then buy some fruit and a birthday card, visual images can be formed between tie and bank (e.g. a giant tie with the name of the bank on it flying on a flagpole above the bank), Noah and fruit (e.g. fruit rather than animals being directed on to Noah's ark), and between May and birthday card (e.g. a maypole with birthday cards fluttering at the ends of the coloured ribbons). The advantage of the phonetic method over the rhyming pegs is the ease of generating keywords for numbers beyond ten, enabling more than ten items to be easily encoded. A further advantage of this method is the facility to encode strings of digits, such as telephone or cash card numbers into visual and/ or verbal images which may be easier to remember than the original digit strings. For example, to remember Mr Welham's telephone number (6941), the word 'shepherd' may be substituted for the digits. The association between Mr Welham and shepherd may be further enhanced by transforming his name into a visual image, such as wool man, which sound similar to Welham and helps to associate his name with the corresponding image of him as a shepherd (see section on memory for names for further details).

Patten (1972) used this method with patients suffering from severe verbal memory deficits, and claimed that four of the seven cases benefited both on experimental material and in remembering practical information. It appeared that those who were unable to master this system were not aware of their memory deficit and were unable to form clear visual images. Patten found that even those who did benefit took up to four weeks to learn the mnemonic. However, a number of the exponents of the phonetic mnemonic claim that the effort expended in learning the technique is repaid by the benefits that can be accrued, since the mnemonic may help remember specific appointments, or important information containing numbers (for example, 454 grammes equals 1 pound weight can be remembered as 'ruler').

Method of Loci

For those who have a problem remembering the peg words involved in the rhyming peg or phonetic mnemonics, the items to be learned can be linked with familiar locations, such as rooms in a familiar house, buildings in a well-known street, or parts of the body. Thus, for example, to remember items on a shopping list (tomatoes, sausages, etc.) the rooms in a person's house can be used as the peg locations. In this way a visual image may be formed of a large tomato sitting in a chair in the dining room, and a giant sausage taking a bath, etc. When recall of the items is required the person imagines each room in the house in turn, and recalls the image, and hence the items originally encoded.

This technique has been used successfully with the elderly (Robertson-Tchabo, Hausman and Arenberg, 1976), and may be appropriate for some memory impaired individuals (Wilson and Moffat, 1984), although the ability of this method to assist everyday memory has yet to be demonstrated with subjects other than experts in mnemonics (Higbee, 1977).

The use of natural and well-learned locations is not only helpful in simplying the learning of the peg words, but may also act as additional cues to the use of the mnemonic. Thus, if a particular errand has to be remembered when returing home (e.g. feed the fish), a visual image can be built up involving the front door and the fish (e.g. as you open the door water comes pouring out together with large fish). Upon returning home and entering the front door the image may be spontaneously recalled, or if the method has been used routinely a moment's hesitation and mental search may reveal whether anything has been associated with the front door.

An often quoted example of the early use of the method of loci is provided by Yates (1966), who described how Simonides of Thessaly remembered who had been present at a banquet by recalling where each guest had been seated. However, Simonides was presumably only using location as a retrieval cue, since he probably did not deliberately visually encode where each person was sitting before he left the banquet. Therefore, this retrieval-only process might be more characteristic of the strategy of the mental retracing of events than of the method of loci.

Mental Retracing of Events

This strategy involves mentally retracing a sequence of past events to assist the recall of something that has happened and the approximate time of its occurrence. This retrieval process is likely to apply only to information that is already established in memory and may be less suitable for recalling recently lost intentions, since Reason and Mycielska (1982) suggest that this kind of information may only be remembered for a brief period of time.

Although this technique has been advocated for remembering when and where a misplaced item may be recovered, Furst (1972) suggests that the item is less likely to be lost in the first place if a visual image is formed linking the item with its location. Thus, if a pair of scissors are left on the dining-room table a visual image of a large pair of scissors cutting through the dining table may be formed before responding to any distraction (for example, answering the doorbell). It is suggested that later on this image may be recalled in order to retrace the whereabouts of the scissors. No systematic study of this method has been reported, but as with other forms of visual imagery training the time and effort required to form the initial image may be beneficial to later retrieval.

Motor Coding

It has already been mentioned that severely amnesic patients may be able to learn motor skills (Brooks and Baddeley, 1976). Powell (1981) has proposed that this ability might be used to assist impaired verbal memory. Thus, a name such as Mr Bird might be learned by associating the person with an appropriate action symbolising that name. Utilising this suggestion, a severely head-injured amnesic learned to recall the name Anita to the cue of the person, or in fact anyone, shaking their hair, since the name had originally been learned as *A neater* way of doing her hair, accompanied by the person shaking her hair (Wilson and Moffat, 1984).

A more controlled trial of the motor coding technique was attempted by asking a severely head-injured amnesic to learn two lists of eight words; one list using the motor coding method, and the other list by providing an equivalent amount of time for rehearsal. The motor coded words were learned as a sequence of actions associated with each word. For example, the word 'baby' was symbolised by the action of rocking the two arms as if holding a baby. The training was followed by an increasing interval before retention was tested. It was found that there was a considerable advantage in using the motor coding technique (mean recall = 7.58 words) compared with the rehearsal condition (mean recall = 3.17 words). These results do not establish the efficacy *per se* since the novelty of this method appealed to this patient, which presumably assisted his performance (Jackson and Moffat, 1982). However, hitherto motor coding appears to have been neglected and thus may warrant further investigation as a possible memory strategy and as an experimental variable, since the relationship with other variables, such as concreteness and imagery, has yet to be established.

Conclusions about Visual Imagery Procedures

Inevitably, there are limitations to the practical benefits that may be accrued from the visual imagery procedures mentioned above. This has been admitted by some of the authors of memory enhancement books, notably Cermak (1980) who found few personal benefits from visual imagery. However, it may be inappropriate to judge the merits of a technique by the benefits to a healthy person, since the amnesic may be deprived of the normal channels of remembering. Further details of the application of visual imagery with the brain-damaged may be found in the next chapter and in Wilson and Moffat (1984).

Discussion will now turn to verbal mnemonics which Cermak (1980) found more useful in aiding his memory, and which have undergone some investigation with clinical populations.

Verbal Strategies

A number of variables have been found to influence the amount of verbal information recalled by either normal or amnesic subjects. This has included the organising of words in categories, according to their meaning or the sound of the words (Baddeley and Warrington, 1973).

Alternatively, a verbal link, such as hand, has been used to associate a pair of words (for example, clock–glove) and hence reduce the number of trials required to learn the word pairs (Cermak, 1976).

A further strategy has been to form a story linking the items to be remembered (Gianutsos and Gianutsos, 1979). This task has proved difficult for some amnesics (Crovitz, Harvey and Horn, 1979) and in many respects can be considered a visual imagery procedure since the linking of each item in the list with the next may be achieved using a visual image.

The value of these mnemonics have generally been confined to experimental tasks.

Study Method

A common difficulty for amnesics is remembering written prose such as newspaper articles. Various techniques have been proposed to help study this type of material, using a series of stages.

Perhaps the most widely known application of a study technique with the brain-injured was carried out by Glasgow, Zeiss, Barrera and Lewinsohn (1977). They used the following steps to assist the verbal memory disorder of a young severely head-injured woman:

Preview: Establish the general order of the text.
Question: Think of the main questions about the material.
Read: Read the text carefully.
State: Repeat the information that has been read.
Test: Check that the test has been understood and the questions which were posed were satisfactorily answered.

Using selected passages the PQRST method resulted in superior recall compared with a rehearsal condition and the subject's own pre-intervention strategy. However, part of the benefit of the PQRST method was presumably derived from the extra time taken to apply the PQRST method. During the second phase of the study the PQRST training successfully generalised to the remembering of newspaper articles.

Haffey (1983) has demonstrated how a severely headed injured male increased his memory for texts by 30-40 per cent using a much modified version of the study technique, together with additional training for related problems.

The study technique has also been applied to the repeated questions of an amnesic (see Chapter 5).

Rhymes

Gardner (1977) has demonstrated that a very severely and globally amnesic patient was able to learn a short paragraph containing salient personal details by incorporating the words as lyrics in a song. Thus, the patient learned the following information during six daily sessions of only ten minutes duration; except for the last line, which required additional training:

Henry's my name; Memory's the game; I'm in the VA in Jamaica

Plain; My bed's on 7D; The year is '73; Every day I make a little gain.

The patient progressed from initially requiring verbal prompts in order to recall the lyrics; then was able to sing the words without musical accompaniment, and finally could recite the words on their own. At a three-month follow-up he was able to produce the song complete with lyrics with little difficulty, thereby showing excellent retention of this skill. Thus, the use of melody may be an important component at the learning stage, but could become redundant once this is achieved.

Gardner's patient was presumably helped by being an accomplished pianist, although patients without previous musical skills may also be able to use this technique; rhymes are easier to learn than normal prose (Bower and Bolton, 1969). This appears to be due to the rhyming format restricting the possibilities for a given response, and also providing a structure which may enable the person to know the location of certain words, and when he has reached the end of his recall. Nevertheless, it appears that there is nothing especially unique about the use of rhymes as a learning strategy, since it is no more effective than other methods which restrict the selection of correct answers.

Alphabetical Cueing and First Letter Mnemonics

Sometimes when attempting to recall particular words (for example, a person's name) one may think of the first letter of other properties of the word before or even without being able to recall the correct word. Furthermore, it has been demonstrated that the provision of the first letter, or first three letters of a word (for example, lea for learn) during attempted recall of a word list may significantly improve recall. This effect has been noted most strongly with pre-senile dementia (Miller, 1975) and mild to moderate senile dementia patients (Morris, Wheatley and Britton, 1983), who performed as well as their respective control groups under the cued recall condition despite a significant impairment on the free recall and recognition procedures. The implications of this finding for memory therapy with the confused elderly have only just been recognised (Morris *et al.*, 1983), although the practical benefits of first letter cueing during the learning of names has been demonstrated with a Korsakoff patient (Jaffe and Katz, 1975) and with head-injured subjects (Moffat and Coward, 1983).

The first letter cues can be available at the retrieval stage either by the provision of the correct first letters (for example, PM for Paul

Matthews) or the encouragement to search through the alphabet to select the appropriate first letters. For one head-injured patient the alphabet was written down on a cue card which he carried with him. His wife then directed him to use this card to help retrieve friends' names when he could not recall them spontaneously. To assist his recall the first letters of the majority of his friends and relatives' names were identified by the use of large size print. In cases where a new name is being learned emphasis can be placed on the first letter of the name at the encoding ('my name is John Farr, remember the initials J.F.') and retrieval stages ('my name is John F., F. for . . .'). This exercise may become redundant once the name has been learned, but it might have been an important stepping stone to this achievement.

A further illustration of the use of first letter mnemonics is in the remembering of items of information, particularly in a set order. This may involve taking the first letter of each word to be remembered, and forming an acronym, which may be a new word (for example, 'RADAR' for Royal Association for Disability and Rehabilitation). These kinds of abbreviations are obviously in widespread use, and have been the subject of specialised dictionaries (Pugh, 1970; White, 1971). An extension of this abbreviation method is the use of the first letters of the words to be remembered to form new words which may be strung together into a sentence. For example, Higbee (1977) described how one woman used the sentence 'Shirley Shouldn't Eat Fresh Mushrooms' to remember the correct sequence in cooking (sugar, shortening, eggs, flour, and then milk). This type of mnemonic has also been compiled into a dictionary form (*Dictionary of Mnemonics*, 1972; Smith 1969).

Obviously the mnemonics contained in the various specialised dictionaries have a specific function; and as Harris (see Chapter 3) and others have commented, there is a limited need to remember items in a set order. However, the enterprising memory therapist may recognise selected applications for this type of mnemonic, such as in teaching the correct sequence in an assembly task.

Self-instructions

An alternative to the use of artificial mnemonics to learn a task is the selection of a statement or set of statements to tackle the problem. For example, Hussian (1981) taught an elderly forgetful woman to use statements such as 'I'll go into one of the shops along the way whenever I forget all five of the items which I came for and refer to my list.' This approach enabled her to resume shopping independently.

I have used self-instructions to improve the work performance of a young head-injured employee. A task analysis of his behaviour revealed a range of frequent mistakes (for example, forgetting to connect a vital pipe in the machine), and the absence of certain desired behaviours (for example, establishing the sequence of individual tasks). Then, self-instructions such as 'check this task, and then start the next one' were introduced which resulted in a rapid increase in identified positive achievements. There was also gradual change from the baseline of no 'good days' at work per week to a rating of each day being a 'good day' at work by the seventh week of training. This progress was maintained at a five month follow-up.

A more broad and perhaps ambitious use of self-instructions might be to help the amnesic to decide how best to use his residual memory. This might be in order to overcome excessive caution (for example, 'Go on have a guess, you're usually right'). On the other hand the person may require reminding about which strategy would be most appropriate for him to remember something (for example, a person's name). Furthermore, he may remember having learned a task by using a memory strategy, but be unable to recall the technique used. Naturally, this kind of questioning is only likely to come from someone who is a graduate of a comprehensive memory therapy programme. However, there are an increasing number of such people, and interest must also be directed to continued use of memory strategies after the person is discharged from treatment.

Perhaps self-instructional statements of a problem-solving nature may be appropriate for some of these people (for example, remember to use clear and interactive mental pictures). However, there may emerge a set of mnemonics to help select the appropriate mnemonic to use, such as:

Pegs are the key to my memory
Numbers make sounds and
Names I can see
I can PQRST stories
and say my ABC

As explained in the next chapter, the selection of a memory strategy to learn a particular task has to be based upon the particular memory skills and deficits of that individual and therefore each set of guidelines has to be personalised.

Reality Orientation[1]

Reality Orientation (RO) aims to maintain or retrain a person's awareness of time, place and current events by incorporating this information
in staff interactions with the patient. This structured conversation
may be assisted by classroom sessions, the use of external aids, repetition and possibly by specific behavioural training. This continual use
of RO procedures in every interaction with the patient is known as
24-hour RO.

    RO classes were originally intended as a supplement to the 24-hour
approach, but sometimes have been used in isolation. These sessions
are generally held daily for half-an-hour to an hour, with three to six
patients and one or two therapists, depending upon the level of
confusion of the members. The type of activities usually carried out in
an RO session are described more fully in Chapter 9.

    The basic format of reality orientation, whether 24-hour or class-
room sessions include reminding the patient who they are, who is
speaking to them, providing information about time and place, and a
commentary about what is going on. It is suggested that the therapist
speaks clearly, keeping statements specific and brief. The patient is
encouraged to rehearse the information provided and to converse with
the staff and patients. The staff member requires some knowledge of
the patient's family and personal history, since it is important to be
able to verify information provided by the patient. References by the
patient to the past should be responded to accordingly (for example,
'Yes, you used to live in Basingstoke').

    A central tenet of RO is that the patient should be respected as an
individual, and that dignity and choice should be maintained at all
times. Therefore, RO training tries to avoid a teacher–pupil relationship, and aims to create an enjoyable experience for the patient. Thus,
RO training can be considered as a positive and humanitarian approach
to working with the confused person. In keeping with this intention,
staff involvement in RO has resulted in increased positive attitudes
towards the elderly (Smith and Barker, 1972).

    In assessing the benefits of RO for altering patients' behaviour, it
needs to be stated that the baseline for the confused elderly may be a
declining one, and therefore an effective treatment may be one which
slows down or arrests this decline rather than producing improvements.
Therefore, it is encouraging that classroom RO has proved effective in

1. Also referred to as Reality Orientation Therapy (ROT) in later chapters.

improving patients' verbal orientation (Citrin and Dixon, 1977; Hanley, McGuire and Boyd, 1981; Harris and Ivory, 1976; Johnson, 1979; Woods, 1979). Unfortunately, as some of the authors admit, although the gains achieved are generally statistically significant, the percentage increase in scores may be of limited clinical value (Hanley, McGuire and Boyd, 1981).

The generalisation of training to other cognitive variables has been noted, but this has been confined to memory tests (Woods, 1979), which may not directly relate to everyday performance (Sunderland, Harris and Baddeley, 1983). Thus, RO training did not generalise to other verbal orientation items which were not taught in the sessions (Goldstein, Turner, Holzman, Kanagy, Elmore and Barry, 1982).

In considering the generalisation of RO training to social behaviour, again there are mixed results. There have been some reports of improved behaviour following RO training (Cornbleth and Cornbleth, 1979; Holden and Sinebruchow, 1979; Merchant and Saxby, 1981; and Woodward, 1979). However, there has also been a series of negative results covering self-care skills (Harris and Ivory, 1976); ratings on a behaviour scale (Hanley *et al.*, 1981; Woods, 1979); direct observation of behaviour (Goldstein *et al.*, 1982; Johnson, 1979); relatives' ratings of the patient's behaviour (Greene, Nicol and Jamieson, 1979); and self-report by patients of their life satisfaction (MacDonald and Settin, 1978).

There appear to be several reasons why RO has not produced consistent improvements in behaviour. Firstly, RO is primarily a method for improving verbal orientation and has less to offer in the direct management of withdrawn or anti-social behaviour.

Secondly, many of the studies have used classroom RO without a concomitant 24-hour approach; and behaviour change was originally intended only as an accompaniment to the 24-hour approach. Therefore, it would have been fortuitous if behaviour change had been demonstrated, but not unduly unexpected if it were not.

Thirdly, although there may be a change in staff behaviour during classroom RO (Woods *et al.*, 1980), there is no available evidence of this being maintained outside of RO sessions, nor has this always been intended.

Fourthly, in those studies employing the 24-hour approach, there may have been a problem of staff compliance. Thus, Hanley (1980) found that following the introduction of 24-hour RO there was no change in the number of staff interactions with patients, nor any change in the use of verbal reality-based statements by the staff in these interactions. This finding was contrary to the more optimistic estimates given by the staff of their own behaviour.

Perhaps staff compliance and also the efficacy of RO can be increased by setting more specific initial objectives. Thus, Hanley, McGuire and Boyd (1981) found significant improvements in ward orientation following training in this one aspect of functioning. Furthermore, in this way selected aspects of RO can be evaluated, for example, that signposts were not sufficient to improve patients' orientation in the ward (Hanley, 1981).

By gradually incorporating additional behaviours the efficacy of RO training for each behaviour can be established using a multiple baseline single case experimental design (Kazdin, 1982; Woods, 1983).

The author has favoured this approach for staff as well as patient training, since this progressively builds up staff skills in assessment, training and evaluation. The staff training begins with a general introduction, making use of a tape/slide package, video tapes, handouts, and role play (see Appendix I for details of RO training materials). This is followed by the selection of particular patients by members of staff who are then responsible for their assessment and training (where increased experimental control is required, other staff may carry out the assessments on behalf of that staff member). For each behaviour that is targeted for training there is a somewhat similar process of assessment; preparing the aids and materials required; determining the processes of training, and maximising opportunities for generalisation of the behaviour to various settings, and for the maintenance of any behaviour change.

The training of a particular behaviour of a patient may initially be carried out by all staff at all times, which is in keeping with the original 24-hour approach to RO (Folsom, 1968). However, as intended, this may be supplemented by classroom or additional individual sessions. It is not necessary, nor even desirable, for a patient to be included in more than one RO session per day (Johnson, 1979), since this may lead to boredom for all concerned. Furthermore, ten minutes of individual time with a patient may be more effective and labour-saving than a group session, particularly for the more severely impaired patient (Johnson, 1979).

It is important to be able to provide a flexible and varied training programme, since there may be marked individual differences in response to RO. Thus, whilst some patients may benefit from RO, others may be made worse, either cognitively (Goldstein *et al.*, 1982) or behaviourally (Johnson, 1979).

In order to have regard to a patient's capabilities, three levels of classroom RO have been suggested (Holden and Woods, 1982). These are also discussed further in Chapter 9.

As well as being adaptable for different levels of functioning of the confused elderly, RO may also be appropriate for other client groups, such as those recovering from a severe head injury, a toxic confusional state, or suffering from a severe amnesia, such as Korsakoff's psychosis. Furthermore, RO can be used in settings other than a ward, including day hospitals (Greene, Smith and Gardiner, 1980); and may be appropriate for relatives to learn and implement.

Perhaps future developments of RO procedures will tackle what may be one of the weakest features of RO from a learning point of view, namely the reliance upon rehearsal. Much of the repetition that is practised appears to be best described as maintenance rehearsal, rather than elaborate rehearsal (Craik and Watkins, 1973). It has already been demonstrated that this type of rehearsal is not an effective learning strategy for severe amnesics (Brooks and Baddeley, 1976; Milner, Corkin and Teuber, 1968).

Although there is scope for improving RO techniques, there is sufficient evidence for the efficacy of RO to warrant more widespread use. The implementation of RO does not require expensive equipment, or highly qualified or elaborately trained staff. However, as has already been discussed, staff training is an important factor in the success of RO. There are a range of suitable training materials already available (see Appendix I), and additional training programmes are in preparation for this increasingly popular approach to working mainly with the confused elderly.

Restitution of Memory

The memory strategies above are generally aimed at circumventing a specific memory impairment by using other intact skills to aid remembering. An alternative goal is the attempt to retrain the memory process itself, which might have the benefit of improving a wide range of functions related to the original memory loss. In order to investigate the possibility of the restitution of function the normal recovery of memory functions will be examined.

If the memory impairment has been due to a reversible condition such as a toxic confusional state, or alcohol abuse over a relatively short time, then recovery of function may occur once the basic cause has been removed, and appropriate restorative measures undertaken.

If, on the other hand, the memory impairment is more directly associated with brain damage, then the recovery process may be slow and only partial. Thus, with the severely head-injured, immediate memory span tends to be least affected by brain injury, and may recover slowly to a normal level by three years post-injury (Lezak, 1979; Van Zomeren, 1981). However, during this time period few head-injured patients show any improvement in verbal memory, or verbal learning (Brooks, 1976; Lezak, 1979). Furthermore, in the Lezak, and other longitudinal studies, there was a marked deterioration on the more complex immediate memory and retention tasks approximately two years post-injury. This 'secondary regression' has also been reported for intellectual tasks (Vigoroux *et al.*, 1971) and late-onset epilepsy (Jennett, 1976).

Therefore, it appears that there may be some later changes in tissues or metabolic processes which are counter-productive to recovery. This is in keeping with the comments by Devor (1982), that 'the brain was designed to avoid injury, not to recover from it', and that the changes which occur 'are probably not designed to foster behavioural recovery of function . . . and in fact they may often be detrimental'.

Thus, although dendritic and axonal sprouting may occur in the central nervous system and may be related to restitution of function (Glees and Cole, 1950), this is often restricted by the formation of scar tissue, which cannot be controlled by drug treatments. Therefore, direct regrowth appears to suffer from an inherent limitation. Another problem is that sprouting may take place from intact cells to a denervated or partially denervated region, which may cause unexpected and unpleasant effects, including spasticity (McCough, Austin, Liu and Liu, 1958).

An alternative explanation for early improvements in functioning is that a large proportion of the pathways in the adult central nervous system may be 'relatively ineffective' (Wall, 1977), but be uncovered or strengthened following the loss of a primary input. It is too early to state whether this process can mediate recovery of function, or be of significance in long-term rehabilitation; particularly since Wall suggests that these 'silent' synapses respond rapidly following the brain lesion.

Denervation Super-sensitivity

Another possible explanation for recovery of function following reduced input to an area is increased sensitivity of the post-synaptic membrane. This principle can only apply where destruction of inputs into an area has occurred, leaving receptive neurons intact. There has been some support for this explanation of recovery (Glick and Greenstein, 1973) with the super-sensitivity response assumed to occur within one month of the experimental lesion. Again, the value of this process for rehabilitation is not understood at this time.

Thus, generally there do not appear to be any established guidelines about how rehabilitation techniques can foster direct neuronal growth. However, it is worth speculating about the possible benefits of repeated practice, since a number of therapists use this method to help improve memory (Harris and Sunderland, 1981).

Where attempts to retrain or improve memory functioning by repeated practice have been tried the results have been disappointing, both for normal subjects (Ericsson, Chase and Falcon, 1980), and amnesics (Milner, Corkin and Teuber, 1968; Brooks and Baddeley, 1976).

Therefore, there may be no support for such commonly used memory exercises as Kim's Game, which after all owes its origin to a story by Rudyard Kipling rather than being an experimentally validated technique. Furthermore, memory is a complex process which is unlikely to respond as a 'mental muscle' (Sunderland and Harris, 1981).

An alternative to direct retraining is the possibility that other areas of the brain may take over the function previously carried out by the damaged areas. Thus, in the case of recovery from severe dysfluency following unilateral left hemisphere damage, the right hemisphere has been shown to acquire language function (Cummings, Benson, Walsh and Levine, 1979). This process occurs in the more severely impaired non-fluent aphasics, whilst the less severely language impaired tended to retain language dominance in the left hemisphere (Castro–Caldas and Botelho, 1980). It might be assumed that a similar process could occur with memory functions; for example, the gradual emergence of verbal memory in the non-dominant hemisphere. This would seem unlikely for several reasons. Firstly, whilst there was a gradual recovery of language functioning over a two-year period, the same has not been demonstrated for verbal memory. In fact, at the time when this process is considered to be occurring for language, memory ability may actually deteriorate. Secondly, since the transfer of language to the non-dominant hemisphere only occurred in the non-fluent aphasics, it would be difficult to test verbal memory in such patients, particularly since they may show evidence of dysfluency and amnesia (Thomsen, 1977).

The third limitation is that memory for everyday information may not be as specifically localised as language functioning. Thus, memory for a particular event, for example a visit to a relative, may rely upon memory for that particular occasion as well as knowledge about the person constructed over many years; all of which may be composed of visual, verbal and perhaps other aspects of memory. If one feature of memory is rendered deficient, it may be more viable to utilise the remaining memory abilities, rather than make demands upon a deficient attribute. Therefore, as demonstrated in this and the next chapter, learning a person's name may be achieved by recoding the name into a visual image. This represents an alternative strategy to be used by the amnesic, rather than a reorganisation of the memory structures. This method applies not only to specific retraining, but also to recovery of function, since Gazzaniga (1978) stated that 'in general, it is our belief that recovery almost invariably is the product of an alternative behavioural strategy being brought into play, with a patient in a sense solving a behavioural task by taking a different "route to Rome" '

The conclusion of this review of the plasticity of the central nervous system with regard to memory functioning is that the current evidence does not support attempts to retrain memory processes. Perhaps intensive investigations of amnesics over a long period of time may reveal later improvements in functioning, and if appropriately conducted may provide suggestions about retraining techniques. Few investigations of direct retraining have been reported to date, and it is possible that some fruitful results may be forthcoming. However, for the therapist seeking ways of helping the memory-impaired, the strategies described above provide the most appropriate choice available, although there is considerable scope for innovation since memory therapy has only recently started to develop and be evaluated.

5 MEMORY THERAPY IN PRACTICE

Barbara Wilson

Introduction

The reader of this chapter will want to know how memory therapy works in practice. Before considering this major question, and the numerous subsidiary questions arising from the complicated processes involved in memory rehabilitation, it will perhaps be helpful for the reader if I describe some of the patients who come to us at Rivermead Rehabilitation Centre requiring treatment for memory impairment. The following are three case studies which, in their different ways, represent a series of problems the therapist is likely to encounter across a whole spectrum of patients, each of whom will have his or her own unique pattern of difficulties.

Patient KJ is a 59-year-old man who developed meningitis 18 months ago. At first he was ataxic and dysphasic but he is now physically well and shows no sign of a language disorder. Indeed, there is nothing wrong with him at all apart from a severe and global amnesia. Superficially it is hard to believe there is *anything* wrong with KJ. He is intelligent and polite, and looks perfectly normal. However, within any conversation that aims to penetrate beneath the shallow surface of normal politeness KJ's amnesia becomes apparent. He repeats information he has previously volunteered. He may ask about something that is worrying him, be reassured by an explanation, yet repeat the same question within two or three minutes. He does not know what month or day it is or, if not at home, even where he is. He cannot remember how to find his way from one place to another unless it is a very familiar route. In order to reach a destination within the grounds of the rehabilitation centre he has to constantly refer to written instructions in his notebook. It is impossible for him to undertake any journey further afield unless he is accompanied. His memory for events in the past is more reliable than for those which have recently occurred. However, even in the former there are gaps and mistakes. For example, he thinks his daughter still lives in the town she moved from ten years ago. He

89

says that the present president of the United States is Jimmy Carter and the previous one was Ronald Reagan. These are examples of an episodic memory deficit described in Chapter 1.

One of KJ's strengths, however, is that he makes extensive use of a diary and a notebook, recording information which he thinks might be useful or important. He came to Rivermead for an assessment of his memory difficulties and to obtain advice on what steps could be taken to ameliorate them. Both he and his wife accept that he will never be able to work again and that his memory will never return to normal. They believe that any gains from memory therapy, however small, which will enable him to be more independent or help him to learn new information more efficiently will be worthwhile.

KJ, then, is a person with a classic amnesic syndrome. He has a reasonable understanding of his problems and realistic expectations of what memory therapy has to offer. Together with his wife he has already worked out several ways to reduce the effects of his disability.

Patient DE is a 38-year-old woman who had a subarachnoid haemorrhage eight months ago. The haemorrhage followed a ruptured aneurysm on the anterior communicating artery. A left frontal cranitomy was performed to clip the aneurysm and DE was left with memory problems. Prior to the haemorrhage she had been employed as a shop assistant. She is now friendly and talkative but anxious about her inability to remember ongoing events or conversations. She is more orientated in time than KJ and can almost always give the correct month and day of the week. She rarely knows the correct date, however. Her memory for names is poor but she can learn new names if she has regular and frequent contact with the individuals concerned. She learned my name, for example, after four days during which I had seen her for an hour each day and told her my name on about a dozen occasions.

Her performance on most memory tests is extremely poor. She is able to repeat back only two digits in the digit-span task, and nothing at all of a prose passage from the Wechsler Memory Scale. She is not aphasic however and her reading is apparently normal. Unlike KJ she can find her way about the rehabilitation centre with little trouble and has no difficulty remembering faces, i.e. she knows immediately if she has met the person before. (Again, this is unlike KJ who does not remember people's faces and walks past therapists he sees for two or three hours a day unless they smile and talk to him first.)

DE has been given a notebook but she rarely uses it, saying she does not want to depend on that and wants her memory to get better. She frequently asks 'Will I ever get better?' but does not repeat other questions or anecdotes as KJ does. DE wants to return to work but this is unlikely as she will not be able to remember customers' requests long enough to fulfil their orders. Both she and her family want the staff at Rivermead to give her back her memory.

DE, then, is less severely amnesic than KJ, she has fewer problems with non-verbal material (for example, faces and routes) and she is able to learn new information if it is repeated to her often enough. On the other hand, she makes almost no attempt to bypass her problems with external aids. In this respect she is like many other patients with ruptured anterior communicating artery aneurysms who are reluctant to write down information despite the fact that they have no defects in motor skills, language, reading or writing. DE is also less realistic about the future. She believes – or claims to believe – that her memory will improve in time and that she will be able to manage at work.

Patient MC is a 27-year-old man who received a severe head injury two and a half years ago. He suffered a depressed fracture of the right temporo-parietal bone necessitating removal of part of the bone. He had a bone flap inserted but this became infected and was removed. Some months later another bone flap was inserted. In addition to an extremely dense amnesia MC has perceptual problems including difficulties with face-matching tasks and some degree of unilateral neglect. MC is also unable to walk and is confined to a wheelchair. There is no language disorder however and he is a charming and polite person who is always cheerful. He has become fairly skilful at masking the extent of his difficulties. For example, if he hears someone saying 'Good morning, Sue' he also says 'Good morning, Sue'. He greets everyone in a friendly manner so people are usually unaware that he does not recognise them. MC believes his accident occurred a few months ago. He says he received brain damage and has some difficulty with his memory. He also says photographs of faces are confusing – to him they are just pictures which do not really mean anything. He does not appear to be distressed by the handicap and in this respect he is similar to many people who have had a stroke in the right temporo-parietal area in that they are often indifferent to their handicaps. At one time he showed a tendency to repeat the same question many times over but rarely does this now. His repetition is restricted to making the same responses to certain questions. For example, if he is asked 'Are you ready?' he always replies, 'Ready, willing and disabled'. If he is asked, 'What month is it now?' he always replies 'February'.

MC pushes himself round in his wheelchair competently but he is continuously lost: he is to be seen trying to get into doors that are locked or going into rooms that he need not enter. If asked directly what he thinks will happen in the future MC says that he will get back to normal and return to work. His parents, however, are realistic about the nature and extent of his handicap. They never stop trying to help MC and they register genuine pleasure at any step forward, however minimal.

MC, then, is not a pure amnesic, his memory deficits are compounded by perceptual problems and thus he finds greatest difficulty with non-verbal information such as faces and routes. Nevertheless, his memory for any kind of information is extremely poor. Although he is able to read and write he does not use external aids to any significant degree. Reasons for the lack of usage of such aids include the fact that he is so handicapped that he can do very little for himself; his unilateral neglect slows him down (writing is time-consuming); and, of course, he *forgets* to use the aids.

These three case studies illustrate the problems that will be familiar to many readers of this book. However, there are also numerous memory impaired people who do not resemble any of the cases described above, all of whom have particularly severe problems. There are countless brain-damaged people with far milder memory deficits whose needs will be different from the patients described above and who should be easier to help. Still others will have a more widespread intellectual deterioration like that found in patients with pre-senile dementia. Therapists will meet and want to help a wide variety of memory impaired people ranging from those with an almost normal absent-mindedness through to the severely demented geriatric patient. Although this chapter advocates memory therapy it would be wrong to think that we can actually restore the lost memory function of our patients. There may be exceptions among those patients whose deficits are very mild but our concern in this chapter is with those patients with severe and permanent organic memory deficits. For these there is no easy solution and the therapist who attempts to improve the memory functioning of these people is almost certain to fail. On the other hand if the therapist's aim is to reduce the everyday memory problems such as those experienced by the patients described above then some degree of success is more likely.

As was pointed out in Chapter 1, memory is not one unified skill or ability. It consists of a complicated range of 'sub-systems'. For this reason no single solution can be found to help all people with memory difficulties. Neither can we expect one strategy or technique to solve all the memory problems faced by one individual patient. Different solutions will probably be needed for different aspects of the memory deficit. Implicit in the argument so far is support for an approach to treatment which aims to reduce the severity of the numerous problems faced by memory impaired people so that the quality of their daily lives will be improved. The first stage in this process is to identify these problems.

Identifying Problems for Treatment

The therapist who recognises that the initial stage in treatment must be identification of a patient's problems will receive little help from the published accounts of attempts to improve the recall of brain-damaged people. Most research in this area has concentrated on teaching lists of words or paired associates rather than seeking to identify or treat practical problems faced by memory impaired people. There are of course exceptions. For example, Sunderland, Harris and Baddeley (1983) gave a questionnaire to head-injured people and their relatives in order to discover the kinds of memory problems the head-injured faced. As far as treatment is concerned Wilson (1982) described methods for treating a number of specifically identified problems. As there are signs that more researchers are beginning to concentrate on practical issues it is hoped that therapists will gain considerably more help from the literature in the future than they have in the past.

More immediately, of course, the therapist can obtain most information from interviewing the patient and the patient's family. In their daily lives the memory impaired need to remember vital things such as what happened a few hours ago, or where they left their belongings, or the names of their relatives and friends. In certain cases the patients themselves will be able to specify their particular difficulties. One of my patients, for example, is very good at describing his main problems. He says that he is unable to remember people's names, or what day of the week it is. He has to look in his notebook when he is on the bus in order to recall his destination. He is a keen gardener but in order to retain some piece of information about gardening he has to read the same paragraph over and over again and even then he is likely to get the details confused. With this man it is reasonably straightforward to decide areas on which to work. Other patients, however, refuse to admit they have any difficulties. They forget how forgetful they are. Others know they have problems but are unable to be specific when attempting to describe them. Many say something like, 'It's everything . . . I just can't remember anything.' When this happens it is possible to go through a check-list or questionnaire. Several have been developed, for example, Bennett–Levy and Powell (1980) and Herrman and Neisser (1978). Probably one of the most useful questionnaires is that (described earlier) by Sunderland, Harris and Baddeley (1983). However, as the authors point out, filling in such a questionnaire is in itself a memory task so some memory impaired people are not likely to be very accurate.

It is usually better to ask the relatives or other staff closely involved with the patient to fill in the questionnaire or check-list. Sunderland *et al.* (1983) and Sunderland, Harris and Gleave (in press) have used both questionnaire and check-list with head-injured patients and their relatives in an attempt to see how often everyday memory problems occur and whether or not findings correlate with performance on standardised tests. The check-lists are filled in each evening for seven days. Those that have been produced by Sunderland *et al.* have been modified and adapted for therapists to use at Rivermead Rehabilitation Centre. Therapists fill in the list at the end of each session (there are five sessions a day) for each patient for a two-week period. This sounds very time-consuming and disruptive but in practice therapists find the task easy and much useful information has been gathered in this way. A sample of the 28-item check-list is illustrated in Table 5.1.

In addition to asking the patient, the relatives and the staff, the memory therapist should try to observe the patient in a variety of settings to see the kind of problems which may occur. In the case of out-patients this might be difficult but in a hospital or rehabilitation unit one might be able to observe in occupational therapy, physiotherapy, in a memory group, or even at lunchtime. The observer should ask such questions as: 'Does the patient keep repeating the same story, question or joke? Does the patient forget instructions? Does the patient get lost on the way to the canteen?'

A further very important consideration for the therapist when

Table 5.1: A Sample Page of the 28-item Checklist

Date: ——— Day: ———

	Session					
	9.00–10.30	10.45–12.00	1.30–2.30	2.30–3.00	3.15–4.30	

1. Did X forget where s/he put something? Did s/he lose things around the department?

2. Did s/he forget a change in her/his daily routine? For example, a change in the place where something is kept? Or a change in the time that something happens? Or follow an old routine by mistake?

3. Did s/he have to go back to check whether s/he had done something that s/he meant to do?

4. Did s/he forget when something happened? For example, whether it was yesterday or last week?

5. Did s/he forget to take things with her/him, or leave things behind and have to go back for them?

6. Did s/he forget that s/he was told something yesterday or a few days ago, and have to be reminded of it?

7. Did s/he ramble and speak about unimportant or irrelevant things?

8. Did s/he fail to recognise, by sight, close relatives or friends that s/he meets often?

9. Did s/he have difficulty in picking up a new skill. For example, in learning a new game or in working a new gadget after s/he had practised once or twice?

10. Did s/he find that a word was 'on the tip of her/his tongue' and knew what it was but couldn't find it?

11. Did s/he forget to do things s/he said s/he would do?

Source: With permission from Alan Sunderland

selecting problems for treatment is the future vocation and destination of the patient once therapy has finished. The aims of treatment will be very different for someone who is hoping to take up a university place or return to a high-powered job than they will be for someone going to sheltered accommodation or into long-term care. Treatment goals will be influenced by information from all the sources outlined above. In addition direct assessment of the patient's memory may prove useful. Chapter 2 gives a detailed discussion of memory assessment but it is worth emphasising here that both standardised and behavioural assessments are desirable in ascertaining what problems to tackle. Standardised tests can help answer some of the following questions: Is the memory deficit due to functional or organic causes? Is there a specific memory deficit or is there general intellectual impairment? Is the memory deficit global or restricted to certain material or modalities? How well can the patient acquire new information? How well is this information retained? What changes occur over time?

Fuller discussion of standardised memory testing can be found in Erikson and Scott (1977). Schacter and Crovitz (1977) also give useful and detailed discussion of memory impairment after closed head injury. Results from standardised tests, however, do not provide much information on everyday memory problems. They have some limited usefulness in predicting whether or not everyday problems are likely to occur (Sunderland *et al.*, 1983) but only at a very gross level of accuracy. They do not specify which particular problems memory impaired people are likely to face nor do they quantify the frequency or severity of such problems. The material in the tests also tends to be irrelevant to the patients' particular needs, interests and life style — so motivation to do the tests may be lacking. Memory questionnaires have been used in an attempt to overcome these difficulties and to some extent they have been successful in identifying everyday memory problems (Sunderland, Harris and Gleave, in press). It must be noted, however, that these questionnaires are unable to provide sufficiently detailed information about types of problems, their frequency or their severity. Questionnaires, then, are not an adequate substitute for direct measurement.

In addition to standardised tests and questionnaires some kind of behavioural assessment is necessary in order to (a) identify the particular problems faced by the patient; (b) measure the frequency and/or severity of these problems and (c) evaluate the effectiveness or otherwise of an intervention programme. For those readers who are not familiar with the procedure of behavioural assessment Keefe, Kopel and

Gordon (1978) is recommended as a simple introduction. Basically, a behavioural assessment should (a) Identify the problem as unambiguously as possible. ('Memory difficulty', for example, would not be an appropriate definition as it lacks specificity. 'Difficulty finding the way from the ward to physiotherapy' on the other hand would be an appropriate description.) (b) Measure the deficit, that is, assess how often the problem occurs or how often the behaviour fails to occur, thus establishing a baseline against which the effects of treatment can be compared. (c) Set a target or goal, for example, teach the way from the ward to physiotherapy. (d) Select the most appropriate treatment. (e) Assess the ongoing treatment. (f) Evaluate therapy. Most of these points will be discussed in the last sections of this chapter.

A behavioural memory test is currently being validated at Rivermead. This test requires patients to remember to carry out some simple everyday tasks and to retain some information similar to that required for adequate everyday functioning. Preliminary analysis of the data from the first 20 memory impaired patients can be seen in Table 5.2. Whilst this kind of assessment will not identify all the problems it should delineate areas where practical everyday memory problems are likely to occur and it may offer guidelines for treatment.

The next question the therapist may ask is: 'How many problems should be tackled at any one time?' There is no easy answer to this question. Circumstances will probably dictate what actually happens. The most intensive memory therapy I have undertaken was with Mr B, a 51-year-old-man (whose treatment is described in detail elsewhere; see Wilson, 1982). Mr B had suffered a bilateral stroke which left him with a classic amnesic syndrome, that is he had no physical, language or intellectual problems except with tasks involving memory. He received general memory stimulation five days a week for a period of six weeks. In addition four specific memory problems were treated. These involved remembering his daily timetable, people's names, a shopping list and routes around the unit. Three of these were reduced by memory training strategies (different strategies being needed for each problem). The fourth, remembering short routes, remained resistant to all the approaches tried. Concurrently with this programme Mr B was making extensive use of his notebook which contained details of his stroke, the consequences of this, what was happening at home and so forth. Notebooks are, of course, external aids and provide valuable help in reducing everyday problems. In effect, many of Mr B's problems were being dealt with simultaneously.

At the other extreme there are patients who are so impaired that

Table 5.2: Summary of Results on the Rivermead Behavioural Memory Test Items[a] (based on first 20 memory impaired patients)

PATIENT	1.	2.	3.	4.	5.	6.	7.	8.	9.	10.	11.	TOTALS
1.					✓	✓				✓	✓	4
2.			✓	✓		✓	✓					4
3.									✓			1
4.		✓		✓	✓	✓	✓			✓	✓	7
5.	✓			✓	✓	✓	✓	✓	✓		✓	8
6.												0
7.												0
8.		✓	✓	✓	✓	✓	✓	✓	✓			8
9.				✓	✓	✓			✓	✓		5
10.												0
11.												0
12.				✓	✓			✓				3
13.		✓		✓		✓						3
14.	✓						✓	✓	✓		✓	5
15.				✓	✓	✓		✓		✓		5
16.				✓	✓	✓		✓				4
17.				✓		✓		✓			✓	4
18.		✓	✓	✓	✓	✓		✓	✓		✓	8
19.												0
20.		✓				✓	✓	✓	✓		✓	6
Totals	2	3	3	11	10	11	6	10	7	5	7	

Note: a. Key Items —
1. Remembering one new name.
2. Remembering to ask for a personal belonging that had been hidden.
3. Remembering to do something when alarm sounds.
4. Remembering a new route (immediate recall).
5. Remembering a new route (delayed recall).
6. Remembering to deliver message.
7. Learning new skill.
8. Orientation (year, month, day of week, place).
9. Date (separate from other orientation questions as correlation between 8 and 9 is not high).
10. Face recognition (five faces to be recalled from ten after five minutes delay).
11. Picture recognition (10 pictures to be recalled from 20 after five minutes delay).

almost everything is done for them. They are taken from one place to another and they may be unable to use external aids because of physical limitations, reading difficulties or sensory deficits. In these cases it is probably wiser to begin with one problem area, see what can be done, and extend the range of problems tackled when it is feasible.

With yet another group of patients it may be quite clear what the memory therapist is required to do. For example, helping a patient to remember how to transfer from a wheelchair to an ordinary chair or stopping a patient from repeating the same question over and over again. Other well defined problems I have dealt with at Rivermead include an inability to remember two things at once, failure to learn a task in the workshop and refusal to use a notebook.

In this section I have attempted to show therapists ways of identifying problems for treatment. The next stage in memory therapy is to consider how to select the most appropriate treatment strategies for individual patients.

Suiting Strategy to Patient

The strategies available to memory therapists have already been described in Chapter 4. It is not intended to describe the strategies again in this chapter but rather to suggest ways in which a therapist might arrive at a decision as to which strategies to use with different patients. With the exception of Wilson and Moffat (1984) there is little guidance in the published literature as to how to choose the appropriate strategy for a particular patient. Factors which influence whether or not anyone can use a certain technique depend, among other things, on the cause and site of brain damage, and the individual patient's style and preference.

The flow chart in Figure 5.1 offers one plan of action therapists might wish to follow in selecting a treatment strategy. Although I would not expect this plan to work every time for all patients and all problems it should be useful as a starting point. It may help therapists to clarify their own thoughts and trigger off further ideas.

For patients with general intellectual impairment therapists may find the best they can do is to make certain changes in the environment to enable patients to cope better with their handicap. Such changes include labelling doors, painting lines from one place to another or repositioning written material or objects so they will be more easily seen. Colour cues may also be used to provide extra information. Harris (1980a), for example, describes how painting the lavatory doors a different colour from all the other doors reduced incontinence in one geriatric unit. Wilson (1981a) describes how coloured dots on visual symbol cards enabled one severely aphasic man to discriminate between confusing symbols.

Reality Orientation Therapy is another approach which can be considered (see Chapters 4 and 9 for a more detailed analysis of Reality Orientation Therapy). As head-injured patients still in post-traumatic amnesia resemble to some extent the demented geriatric patients for

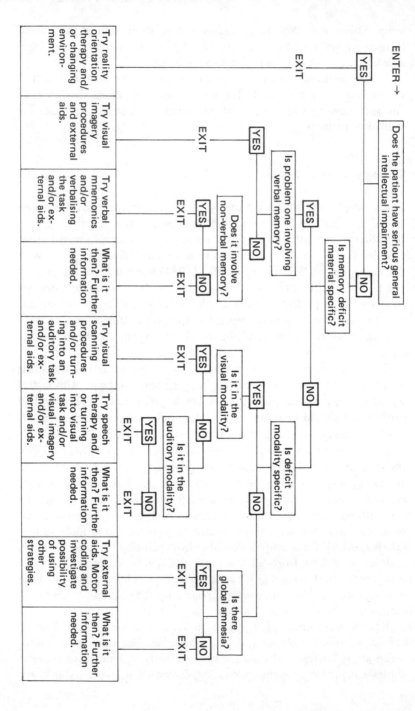

Figure 5.1: Deciding on a Treatment Strategy for a Memory Impaired Patient

whom Reality Orientation Therapy was initially developed, it might be advisable to attempt ROT with the former group. Complete success cannot be guaranteed, however! At Rivermead I once tried ROT with a young head-injured man still in post-traumatic amnesia. Before treatment I asked him where he thought he was and he replied, 'It's Brackley School, isn't it?' He then went on to point out the English, Mathematics and Science departments. This was followed by three weeks of daily ROT. At the end of this time I asked him where he thought he was now and he replied, 'Rivermead Rehabilitation Centre. But it's really Brackley School'!

As far as external aids are concerned some may be helpful for those with general intellectual deterioration. The people who will benefit most from such aids, however, are those whose intellectual functioning is adequate but who have a specific memory deficit or a global amnesia. For these people external aids would appear to have a crucially important role to play in the rehabilitation of memory. Problems arise because it is not always easy to convince memory impaired patients themselves of the importance of such aids. They may be unaware of the severity of their difficulties. They may see such aids as signs of weakness and argue that their memories will not improve if they rely upon notebooks. Alternatively, they may simply forget to write down information or forget to check whether something is recorded. Counselling or instruction in the use of aids may be necessary in these cases. Sometimes it may be possible to change from one kind of aid to another. Take, for example, the case of a patient who refuses or is unable to remember to use a notebook. He or she may benefit from the provision of an electronic aid which has both an auditory signal (to act as a reminder to look at the aid) and a written message describing what has to be done.

Success may be achieved by replacing a written aid with a pictorial aid for an aphasic patient who is no longer able to read. One such aid was devised at Rivermead for an aphasic woman who could not learn how to transfer from her wheelchair to her bed. (Figure 5.2 illustrates the aid.) The patient kept this pictorial representation with her and referred to it when transferring. The problem was not completely solved as she still needed observation during transfer. However, she transferred less dangerously than before and required less help from others.

No single external aid is likely to solve all the problems faced by a memory impaired person. Different aids may be necessary for different tasks. For example, a wall calendar may tell a memory impaired person the date of his next dental appointment but it is unlikely to

Figure 5.2: A Pictorial Memory Aid to Help an Aphasic Patient
Remember How to Transfer

TRANSFER

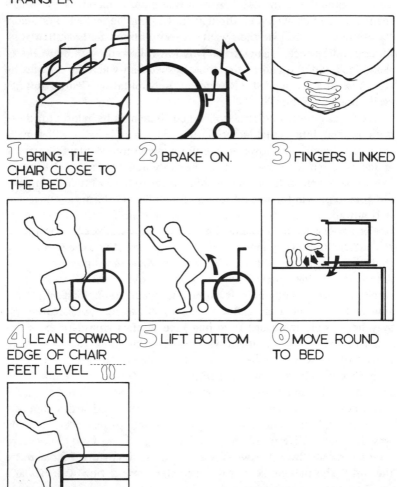

1 BRING THE CHAIR CLOSE TO THE BED

2 BRAKE ON.

3 FINGERS LINKED

4 LEAN FORWARD EDGE OF CHAIR FEET LEVEL

5 LIFT BOTTOM

6 MOVE ROUND TO BED

7 LOWER BOTTOM DOWN SLOWLY

contain information about how to get to the dentist's surgery. Given the importance of external aids there are surprisingly few published accounts of such aids being used with memory impaired people. Fowler, Hart and Sheehan (1972) used a small portable timer with a head-injured man. The man set the timer to remind himself to look at his timetable of daily events and move from one scheduled activity to another. The timer was gradually faded out. Klein and Fowler (1981) used a calculator with a built-in timer (the Casio PW.80) to remind paraplegics to lift from their wheelchairs regularly in order to prevent pressure sores. Wilson and Moffat (1984) used the same timer to remind a dysarthric patient to swallow saliva regularly.

In addition to the treatments described above there has also been some discussion by other interested parties concerning the potential use of electronic external aids with the brain-damaged. For example, Jones and Adam (1979) suggested using a microcomputer as a pros- thetic memory. A small tape recorder would be included, containing instructions as to what to do. Harris (1978, 1980b), and Chapter 3 of this book, give detailed accounts of the kinds of aids available (see also Chapter 6).

Unfortunately, all the electronic aids available up to this present time have serious disadvantages for the memory impaired. In the first place they are expensive. It is impossible for many patients to learn how to programme them and even when the machines are programmed by other people the user has to remember certain steps (for example, how to clear the screen and how to read the messages already stored). Such simple procedures are difficult for severely amnesic people to remember. Wilson and Moffat (1984) provide further discussion on the advantages and disadvantages of various electronic aids. All we need add here is the hope that recent developments in microcomputers and calculators will in time benefit the brain-damaged population.

If the memory deficit is one primarily involving verbal memory and little else, then visual imagery techniques should be seriously considered and investigated. As Moffat has described in the previous chapter, there are several visual imagery techniques and I will not refer to all of them here. The one I have used most often, and most successfully, involves drawing a picture of a name which is to be learned. 'Stephanie' may be drawn as a step and knees, and 'Dr Crossley' as a cross leaf. This has worked well for patients with left hemisphere damage (Wilson, 1981a; Wilson and Moffat, 1983) including patients with mild aphasia. Some patients with right hemisphere or bilateral damage may be able to use this technique although those with marked perceptual difficulties are unlikely to find it of much help. I have even known a few patients who perform worse with visual imagery than with no strategy at all. The face–name association procedure is a variation on the theme already described. Non-brain-damaged people do best when all the steps of this technique are included (McCarty, 1980). Both Glasgow *et al.* (1977) and Wilson and Moffat (1984) found that this was not true for certain brain-damaged people who were apparently unable to cope with all the face–name association stages. There are some who can benefit however so, along with other visual imagery procedures, it may be worth trying it out systematically with individual patients.

Some visual imagery techniques involve considerable verbal elements too. One such technique is the visual peg method, described in Chapter 4. There are patients who can easily learn the verbal pegs but who are unable to remember the images placed in or on the pegs. There are other patients who cannot remember the pegs but once these are provided they are able to recall the images with some degree of ease. Some patients with mild head injuries have learned to use the visual peg method in an experimental setting but everyday, practical applications may well be limited (although see Chapter 6).

Verbal strategies appear to work best for those with a reasonably intact language dominant hemisphere and whose memory problems are primarily of a non-verbal nature. Wilson (1982) described how a stroke patient was able to use a first letter mnemonic to solve a spatial memory task. A PQRST strategy was used with another patient in an attempt to prevent him asking the same question *ad nauseam*. (This strategy is described in Chapter 4: the letters stand for Preview, Question, Read, State and Test.) This particular man, who had suffered a right hemisphere sub-arachnoid haemorrhage following rupture of an anterior communicating artery aneurysm, constantly asked, 'Why have I got a memory problem?' After several weeks of answering this question several times a day it was decided to teach him the answer to his question using a verbal memory training technique. The patient wrote from dictation a summary of his illness, operation, resultant problems and prognosis. The PQRST technique was then followed with the patient selecting the key questions. The questions chosen were: (a) What has happened to me? (b) When? (c) What was the result? (d) What are my main problems now? (e) How long will I be here at the rehabilitation centre? (f) What is the long-term prognosis? Each weekday for the next three weeks the patient was asked the selected questions at the beginning of each session. The correct answer was supplied if he failed to answer or answered incorrectly. This was followed by giving him the summary sheet and going through the whole PQRST strategy again. At the end of three weeks he 'knew' the correct answers to all the selected questions. The procedure was experimentally but not clinically successful for in spite of 100 per cent correct responses when the therapist asked the questions, the man still repeated his original question several times a day. It would appear that although he 'knew' the answer he could not or would not search his memory for the information. This situation is very like that described by Walsh (1978) when he wrote 'at other times frontal patients act as though they have lost the "strategies of recall" which enable them to utilise the information which they have already stored' (p. 319).

For some non-verbal memory problems, such as difficulty in remembering the way from one place to another, it may be possible to teach patients to make the task a more verbal one by verbalising the steps required. Thus, for example, instead of using spatial memory to find the way to the newsagent it might be possible to learn the following instructions: 'Go down the road towards the big white building. Look for the telephone box and turn down the road next to it. Look for the house with the yellow door, and the newsagents is two doors further on.'

As well as problems with specific material (that is, verbal or non-verbal), some people encounter difficulty in certain modalities or when the material is presented in a certain way. Sometimes, then, the memory problems may be restricted to the visual modality. In the former, patients are unable to remember much of what they see and in the latter they remember little of what they hear. If the memory deficit is modality rather than material specific other treatment techniques may be called for. Those who demonstrate problems in the visual but not the auditory modality may have a unilateral spatial neglect or visual scanning problem, and may need treatment to improve their scanning. Diller and Weinberg (1977) describe some methods successfully used to reduce hemi-inattention. Alternatively, it may be possible to change the task from a visual to an auditory one either by describing the material to the patient or teaching the patient to verbalise the material.

When problems occur in the auditory but not the visual modality it is possible that speech therapy is required as this pattern may occur with language disorder. If a language disorder is not present it may be possible to teach the patient to change the task from an auditory one to a visual one by visualising or drawing information as much as possible.

The final treatment approach to be discussed here is motor coding or using movement as a memory aid. It has been established that the motor memory of amnesic patients is less impaired than many other aspects of memory (e.g. Brooks and Baddeley, 1976). An interesting question for memory rehabilitation is whether or not we can capitalise on this intact ability in order to ameliorate deficits caused through impairment of other memory systems. There is no conclusive answer at present but partial success has been achieved with one severely amnesic young man treated at Rivermead. MC, whose case study has been described earlier in this chapter, has received many treatment strategies, on an individual basis and in a group situation. At present he remains disoriented in time and place and he is unable to identify any of the people who have treated him for the past two years. Several attempts have been made to teach him the names of people with whom he regularly comes into contact. Visual imagery has failed but he has learned to associate ten signs with names. He chose most of the signs himself, for example pretending to eat soup for 'Sue' and sniffing a rose for 'Ros'. If the sign is demonstrated to him he reliably recalls the name it is associated with. If one of the ten people concerned says 'What's my name?' and makes the appropriate sign he gives the correct answer. He cannot, however, reliably pair the sign with the correct person if several people or several photographs are placed in front of him and the sign is not given. His difficulty is confounded by a face-recognition problem. He has learned to pair signs with names and, perhaps, for a person with a severe amnesia without perceptual problems, movement as a memory aid may be effective.

Whatever strategy the memory therapist selects it is important to bear in mind the preferences of the person with the memory problem. Furthermore, one procedure may work for one particular problem but not for another. Visual imagery, for example, may be a good way of learning names but be an ineffective way for remembering a shopping list. Flexibility and ingenuity are likely to remain the therapist's best allies.

How to Teach the Strategies

Having decided what problems to tackle and what strategies to use to ameliorate these problems, the next step is to consider how best to teach the strategies. A behavioural approach to memory rehabilitation is recommended because (a) it is adaptable to a wide range of patients, problems and settings; (b) the goals are small and specific; (c) assessment and treatment are inseparable; (d) treatment can be continuously and easily evaluated and (e) there is evidence that this approach can be effective (e.g. Wilson, 1981a, 1982).

A behavioural programme for the treatment of a memory impaired person should be organised in the following stages:

1. Specify the behaviour to be changed. 'Inability to learn people's names' or 'Difficulty in remembering short routes' would be appropriate ways of describing the problems. Vague and general descriptions such as 'Impaired concentration' would be unhelpful.

2. State the goals or aims of treatment. Again, these should be as specific and precise as possible. Appropriately expressed goals would read like the following: 'To teach Mrs A the way from the ward to physiotherapy' and 'To teach Mr B to check his notebook every half hour'.

3. Measure the deficit in order to obtain a satisfactory baseline. This may be achieved in several ways. For example, by recording 'how often Mr C repeats the same question in a week' or 'how many times Mrs D forgets to put her wheelchair brakes on before transferring'.

All the recording methods used in behavioural assessment and treatment are of potential use. It may also be necessary to carry out a more detailed analysis of factors affecting the memory failures. For example, does stress make the problem worse? Is relaxation training indicated? Does it help to pace information, that is, present it at a slower rate? Does extra rehearsal improve matters? What happens if the material is written down? What happens if another person presents the information?

4. Decide on the most suitable treatment strategy for the particular individual. (The suggestions in the previous section may help here.)

5. Plan the treatment. The following questions will provide guidance for the therapist through this stage (although it may not be necessary to go through *all* of these questions in each particular case):
   (i)   What particular strategy should be used?
   (ii) Who is to do the training?
   (iii) When is the training to be carried out and where?

    (iv)   How is it to be conducted and how often?

    (v)   What happens if the patient succeeds in remembering the task?

    (vi)   Will such success be sufficient reward in itself?

    (vii) May some further reinforcement be required?

    (viii) How do you measure success?

    (ix)   What happens if the patient fails at the task?

    (x)   In the event of such failure is the patient to be reminded?

    (xi)   Who will be responsible for keeping records? Will it be the therapist, the patient, the family or an independent observer?

6. Begin the treatment.
7. Monitor and evaluate progress according to the plan outlined in Stage 5.
8. Change the procedure if necessary.

Although these guidelines will be familiar to people involved in designing behaviour modification programmes there are, perhaps, fewer people aware of their usefulness in the field of memory rehabilitation. Table 5.3 is an example of one successful programme for a man who was unable to remember people's names.

Throughout this chapter, there has been some emphasis on the teaching of names. As well as highlighting techniques which can be applied to other problem areas, names are important in themselves. Inability to remember names is one of the most frequent complaints found among the memory impaired so patients *want* to learn them. In addition, it is usually possible for therapists to find a way of teaching at least a few names. Finally, because patients achieve some degree of success in this area they may be encouraged to apply strategies to other problem areas.

Other principles from behavioural psychology which have a part in memory rehabilitation include shaping, changing, prompting and modelling. Shaping, or gradually working towards the final goal, is a long-established procedure which has some limited value in memory training. The following description illustrates one way in which it has been used at Rivermead:

Patient MC (see above) with severe memory and perceptual problems was unable to remember any of the names of his therapists. It was decided to teach him one name — that of the clinical psychologist. Baselines were taken by telling him her name and asking him to

Table 5.3: Programme to Teach Mr AK to Remember Names

1.	Specify behaviour	Inability to recall people's names.
2.	State aims	To teach Mr AK to remember ten names of people in the rehabilitation centre.
3.	Measure deficit	Mr AK failed to recall any name (i.e. failed to give the correct answer within 30 seconds) on two consecutive occasions.
4.	Decide on treatment strategy	Visual imagery (therapist to draw each name).
5.	Plan treatment	One image to be introduced at a time. Verbal rehearsal for all other names. Two sessions per week.
6.	Begin treatment	Treatment started.
7.	Monitor and evaluate progress	Visual imagery successful. Rehearsal alone not successful.
8.	Change procedure if necessary	Not necessary. Mr AK learned ten names in 22 sessions.

recall it after intervals ranging from five seconds to three minutes. The intervals were filled with general conversation. It was established that he reliably recalled her name whenever the interval was 30 seconds or less. After 30 seconds he made mistakes. A timer was used in an attempt to shape his behaviour. The timer was initially programmed to sound every 30 seconds during the daily memory group, which lasted an hour. Each time the alarm sounded he was required to say the psychologist's name. After four consecutive correct responses, the interval was increased by five seconds. Over a period of three weeks the interval was extended in this manner until the time lapse reached 10.5 minutes. At this point the timer was removed in order to see whether success was due to a general improvement or to the specific effects of the treatment. We continued asking him the psychologist's name at random intervals during the memory group sessions and it was noted that over the next two weeks his recall deteriorated until he was making errors after 1.5 minutes. The timer was then reintroduced and within a week the young man was able to retain the name for eight minutes without making errors. The final goal of teaching him the name permanently was never reached but the shaping procedure increased retention span considerably. Other therapists may think of different ways this strategy could be implemented.

Chaining is a useful and adaptable technique for teaching new skills and would appear to have much to offer memory rehabilitation. It involves breaking down any piece of behaviour into a series of steps or links in a chain. Only one step is taught at a time. Once the first step has been learned, the second is added, then the third and fourth and so on. (See Yule and Carr, 1980 for a more detailed description of this procedure.) Chaining has been used at Rivermead to teach patients to remember how to transfer from wheelchairs to ordinary chairs. Usually the physiotherapist works out the necessary steps. For example:

1. Position wheelchair correctly.
2. Check brakes are on.
3. Remove feet from foot rests.
4. Move bottom forwards.
5. Position feet correctly.
6. Position arms correctly.
7. Lean forward.
8. Lift bottom.
9. Swing bottom towards seat of the chair.
10. Sit down.
11. Move feet and straighten up.

If forward chaining is the method of choice then the patient is expected to complete the first step unaccompanied. Once this is achieved the therapist reminds or guides the patient through each successive step. In *backward* chaining the reminding or guiding is carried out up to the last step, which the patient is expected to complete unaided. When the patient is able to do this the preceding step is attempted and so on until the first step is tackled. Although backward chaining is probably more often used in mental handicap, there is no evidence to suggest which of the two is more effective as a teaching technique. Indeed, choice may depend ultimately on the nature of the particular task being learned.

Prompting is another useful behavioural procedure for the memory therapist. Physical, verbal and gestural prompts may be used, either alone or in combination. The prompts are gradually faded out as the person became more able to manage alone. Physical prompting may prove useful in teaching a memory impaired person new skills. For instance, working a machine will require guidance through the task at the start with the therapist providing less and less physical prompting as the trainee becomes more adept.

Jaffe and Katz (1975) used verbal prompting and fading to teach a Korsakoff patient two names. This man had not learned anyone's name in five years of hospitalisation. The patient was told: 'This person's name is Paul Doty, try to remember the initials P and D.' The next time PD was introduced as Paul D and the patient asked to supply the full name. The verbal cues were gradually reduced and two names were learned in this way over a period of two weeks. A somewhat similar procedure was used at Rivermead to teach a young head-injured woman the correct month, to help her overcome her disorientation in time. Songs were used as verbal prompts. In June the song chosen was 'June is Busting Out All Over'. The next time the young woman was asked the month and gave an incorrect answer she was asked 'What song did we have?', and she was able to supply the correct answer. Over the next two days the cue was reduced to 'What song?' then 'Song?' after which she reliably said 'June'.

Modelling, or learning from imitating others, has been used with phobic patients and obsessive compulsives. It may also have an important part to play in memory training. A modelling technique was employed to teach a severely aphasic man some limited communication skills (Wilson, 1981a). It may also be of value in persuading some memory impaired people to use notebooks and other external aids. If they see other people with similar problems making use of such aids they may be more willing to employ them. From research on modelling we know that people are more likely to imitate peers than someone less like themselves. Also they are more likely to imitate people with high prestige than with low prestige. Sex, age, social class, ethnic status and the competence of the model are other influencing factors (Carr, 1980). Active participation leads to better results than passive observation of others, and live models are better than filmed ones. All these findings can be incorporated into memory training programmes, and may be particularly pertinent for the organisers of memory groups.

This is not a fully exhaustive list of teaching methods. Other techniques such as self-instruction may prove equally useful in some cases. Moffat (Chapter 4) describes these in detail. The role of computers, drugs, external aids and group training are all discussed elsewhere in this book. Finally, the motivated and interested therapist may be able to find new methods from other fields and other disciplines which can be adapted for the benefit of memory impaired people.

6 COMPUTER ASSISTANCE IN THE MANAGEMENT OF MEMORY AND COGNITIVE IMPAIRMENT

Clive Skilbeck

Introduction

Advantages of Microcomputers

Microcomputers have been widely available for only a few years. During this period, their relative cost has fallen dramatically, to the point where they are now very cheap. At the same time manufacturers have extended their storage capacities and their flexibility. Two of the most popular machines for clinical settings in the UK and USA are the 'PET' and 'APPLE', both of which have extensive software support (programmes) available.

Although they have often adopted innovative roles within the National Health Service, clinical psychologists have perhaps been slow to exploit the potential of microcomputers. Such machines are not yet commonplace in departments of Clinical Psychology, and where they do appear their use often seems restricted to the data storage and statistical analysis functions of the computer. Given that the cost of a complete PET system, including Disc Drives and Printer, can be less than £2,500 Clinical Psychology departments should be able to justify the purchase cost to their District Health Authorities.

Other contributors to this book have pointed to the developing role of psychologists in memory rehabilitation. If we recognise that research into memory rehabilitation in general is at an early stage, and presume that psychologists' involvement in the remediation of memory deficits can only increase, then we should acknowledge a manpower problem. Psychologists will have to be involved not only in the delivery of a memory retraining service, but also in its evaluation.

The aim of this chapter is to present the general case for employing microcomputers in the management of memory disorders, to review historical developments, and to provide some illustrative clinical examples.

The general case for using microcomputers in clinical settings is very strong and rests on a number of points:

112

(a) Cost/Time-saving Considerations. Clinical Neuropsychologists are a scarce resource. Given that microcomputers are not inexpensive, it only requires delegation to the computer of a small proportion of a psychologist's patient contact time, either in terms of memory assessment or retraining, to make its purchase cost-effective. This can gain extra time for the psychologist to accept more referrals, which is particularly useful in a specialty such as Neuropsychology where there is a high degree of face-to-face contact. One possible risk in such a strategy is that the psychologist comes to spend undue time in computer programming. Programming can be addictive!

Compared with the cost of employing an additional psychologist, the price of a microcomputer appears very cheap. Microcomputers are now highly reliable, and virtually maintenance-free: repair/service costs should be negligible.

(b) Provision of Standard/Controlled Conditions. An important problem in Neuropsychology is the assessment of progress or outcome following retraining or other treatment. There is a need to interpret 'recovery' data — has any noted improvement resulted from spontaneous recovery, the specific retraining procedure used, or because of other (uncontrolled) factors? The employment of a microcomputer provides an obvious advantage over face-to-face interaction in maintaining controlled testing or retraining conditions. The field of memory and cognitive rehabilitation is new in terms of the number of available research papers. Microcomputers can be of particular assistance in its evaluation by allowing the standardised, controlled, presentation of test items and recording of patient responses.

(c) Flexibility. Microcomputers can change the execution of a programme whilst that programme is running. This can be extremely useful in the area of memory retraining. For example, if a patient who is receiving orientation training via computer (see below) correctly answers a test item on three consecutive trials, the computer can be pre-programmed to omit that item on succeeding trials. Similarly, if an item proves too difficult, the computer can re-present it in an easier form. Such adjustments might be very difficult when face-to-face, given the necessity of preparing materials beforehand.

(d) Production of Timed Responses. It can be argued that the accurate timing of a patient's response latencies is very useful in assessing the success of cognitive rehabilitation. Timed measures may be more

Plate 6.1: PET Microcomputer System

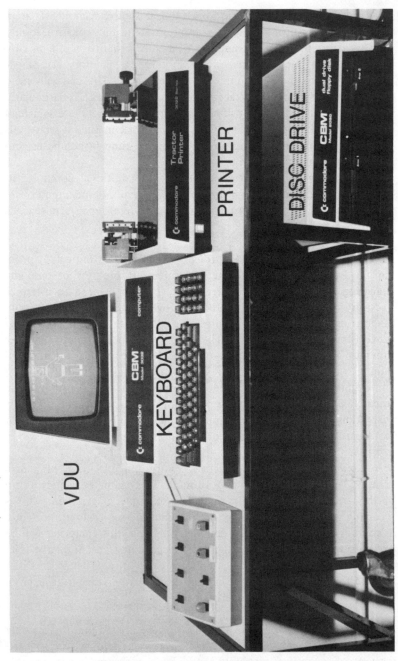

sensitive than accuracy alone to the process of cognitive recovery. Improvement in the attentional deficit noted frequently in patients who have suffered a severe head injury may be first observed in a faster visual reaction time performance.

(e) Patient Acceptability. Although the research to date is very limited, there is no evidence to suggest that a patient will respond less favourably via a computer than in a personal interaction. Indeed, patients may prefer its non-judgemental approach. A lack of interference from interpersonal and social factors may make a computer-administration a very attractive technique for patients relearning a skill.

(f) Ease of Data Analysis. This advantage really speaks for itself. Once a patient has answered the computer's questions, an immediate print-out of the responses and descriptive statistics (for example, mean, standard deviation, appropriate norms) can be obtained. The patient's results can also be immediately 'written' on to computer disc for permanent storage and future analysis.

All of the above points are relevant to the use of a microcomputer in the management of cognitive impairment. Besides being inexpensive, these types of computer system are compact. Plate 6.1 shows a complete 'PET' system, including a patient response board in position.

Disadvantages of Microcomputers

Whilst it is relatively easy to document the advantages of employing microcomputers, a corresponding list of the possible drawbacks to their use is more difficult to produce. Perhaps the obvious risk is that the computer will 'take over' and dictate the psychologist's thinking as to which are the most appropriate tests and retraining procedures to employ; that is, if the procedure is not machine-compatible, then don't bother to develop it.

Although this risk can be guarded against, a more insidious problem is that of programming addiction. The addict is forever thinking of new programmes to write that 'might be useful at some time', or seems unable to leave a completed programme alone — he/she continues to add on further options or refinements (termed 'hacking'). Without realising it, the addict spends more and more time in programming rather than in clinical work.

Another possible disadvantage of using microcomputers is that the psychologist may come to employ tests and procedures merely because their use has been made possible by the introduction of the microcomputer, without fully considering the implications from psychological theory. This disadvantage is not specifically directed against microcomputers, but rather arises every time advances in technology offer psychologists new tools. A related argument is that employing a microcomputer distances the psychologist from patients. This point is valid only if the psychologist moves towards the exclusive use of a computer for patient assessment. Clinicians should recognise that some valuable information can only be obtained from face-to-face contact with their patients.

Historical Review

Because microcomputers have only recently been adopted in clinical settings, there is a dearth of relevant studies on their use. The basis of the available literature is automated testing developed in psychology laboratories for the purposes of human and animal experimentation. For some time isolated automated devices have been employed to present particular psychometric tests, though the facility to administer a range of different tasks dates from the work of Gedye and Miller (1970). At about the same time, Elithorn and Telford (1969) described a computer-based system to assess intellectual skills. Workers naïve in the area might find Gedye and Miller's paper somewhat intimidating (see, for example, pp. 747–51). These authors described automated assessment of geriatric patients' learning ability using the Pictorial Paired Associate Learning Test. More recently, Volans and Levy (1982) have pursued this type of system using a Picture Matching Test.

The general case for automating standard intelligence tests was argued strongly in the late 1970s by Waterfall (1979). His research, like that of Gedye and Miller, had the aim of developing a slide projector unit to administer multiple-choice tests automatically to patients. Waterfall chose the Raven's Standard Progressive Matrices (Raven, 1960) as an example test, and incorporated an optional time-limit into the procedure (one minute being allowed for each of the 60 items). If no response occurs within the time limit the next slide item is presented and the failure to respond is recorded. Waterfall found that his procedure was reliable when used with a large number of patients, nurses and students, and required minimal instructions to subjects. Waterfall, like other researchers (e.g. Evans, 1975) reported that subjects enjoyed the automated testing procedure.

Waterfall (1979) discussed the possibility of the general introduction of *mini*computers into assessment, because of their flexibility in allowing a range of tests to be presented via the same equipment. However, he argued against the introduction of the then-existing microcomputers on the grounds of cost (at that time more than £20,000), portability (minicomputers are at least cabinet-sized) and the fact that 'few potential users, e.g. psychologists . . .' would be capable of learning to operate a computer! This quote from 1979 illustrates how quickly the field of microcomputers has been introduced and developed, and how predictions in this area are likely to become rapidly obsolete.

Although some researchers have continued to pursue the slide projector and 'controlled logic', or isolated microprocessor, approach the development of microcomputers has altered the direction of research in a very short period of time. Personal/microcomputers first began to appear in the mid-1970s the most popular versions produced by Commodore (PET) and APPLE being introduced in 1978. In the first six years sales of microcomputers have increased one hundredfold. An historical review of the development of microcomputers has recently been provided by Toong and Gupta (1982).

The 'clinical' roles for micros have developed rapidly. An early study by Lucas (1977) on patients' attitudes to interview via computer demonstrated that 82 per cent were favourably disposed towards computer interrogation, almost half preferring it to that conducted by the doctor. A study by Carr *et al.* (1983) on obtaining psychiatric histories from patients via microcomputer interview showed a 90–93 per cent accuracy compared with the information gathered by the psychiatric team. In addition, 88 per cent of the patients found computer interrogation to be as easy as clinical interview, and for most of the patients the computer interview uncovered relevant items of information that were not known to the psychiatric team.

Besides the interviewing role, microcomputers have been shown to be useful in the diagnostic process. For example, when fed with relevant information on a patient's symptoms they can be used to produce probability statements as to the cause of disease (De Dombal and Gremy, 1981). Other programmes available include one to yield neurological diagnoses from neuropsychological data.

In the future, microcomputers should hold a key position in clinical and educational assessment. For clinicians one of the most important developments in the administration of cognitive tasks using a microcomputer arises from the work of Acker (1980). His test battery is now commercially available for the PET microcomputer through NFER-Nelson Publishers Ltd. The battery includes visual memory, visuomotor speed, visuospatial, and right-left orientation tasks, among others. Practice items are generally included.

The visual memory task employs items that are impossible to code verbally, unlike some other clinical tests of memory such as the Benton Visual Retention Test (Benton, 1974). The task, described below in the section on the assessment of memory, employs a multiple choice procedure.

A similar multiple-choice response format is provided for the visuospatial analysis task: patients are presented with three designs, two of which are identical. The task is to indicate, by pressing one of three buttons, which is the 'odd man out' (Figure 6.1).

Figure 6.1: Visuospatial Analysis Problem

The 'different' design may differ in only two blocks (hard condition) or in four (easy). The computer print-out provides accuracy and response latency data (Table 6.1).

Table 6.1: Visuospatial Analysis Print-out

2 Different ('hard')						
Correct :	5	RT :	7.14,	SD :	6.10
Wrong :	7	RT :	4.38,	SD :	2.47
4 Different ('easy')						
Correct :	8	RT :	4.34,	SD :	1.55
Wrong :	4	RT :	3.56,	SD :	0.74

The visuomotor speed task (termed symbol digit) is very similar to the digit symbol sub-test of the Wechsler Adult Intelligence Scale (Wechsler, 1955). The major differences are that in the former, number responses correspond to symbols (rather than vice versa), and the patient's answers take the form of pressing the appropriate button for each presented symbol rather than drawing the symbol (Figure 6.2).

Accuracy and speed print-outs are provided for the first 20, middle 20, and final 20 trials separately (Table 6.2). This provides a check on any fatigue or 'warm-up' factors that may be operating.

Figure 6.2: Symbol Digit Task

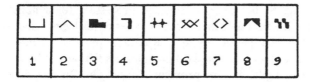

Table 6.2: Symbol Digit Print-out

1st 20 Trials =	7.02	SD	= 5.31
		Mistakes	= 0
2nd 20 Trials =	10.18	SD	= 10.85
		Mistakes	= 2
3rd 20 Trials =	5.85	SD	= 4.12
		Mistakes	= 8
All Trials =	7.58	SD	= 7.47
		Mistakes	= 10

The full battery has been described elsewhere (Acker, 1980).

In the field of special education and rehabilitation evidence is also accruing on the usefulness of microcomputers. A recent article by Saunders (1980) argues for their use in teaching the mentally handicapped; he suggests the teaching of basic alphabet and mental arithmetic skills as typical examples, though clear thinking is required in the preparation of problems for the user (patient). Lally (1981) has also recommended microcomputer assistance in teaching word recognition to mentally handicapped children (mean IQ: 60) in a study employing voice synthesis. The experiment involved comparing the usual teaching procedure with 'usual procedure plus computer instruction'. Lally's results were highly significant ($p < .001$), the computer-assisted group showing average rises over five assessment sessions from an initial level of 38.5 to 70.9 words correctly recognised. The comparable rise for the group without the computer aid was from 37.5 to 47.2 words.

Whilst acknowledging that the use of microcomputers in rehabilitation is in its infancy, an editorial by Vanderheiden (1982) reviews some of the possible future developments in this field. Vanderheiden points out that the use of micros can reduce the cost of providing aids to the disabled due to mass production. An available micro can reduce the amount of paperwork or physical output required of a disabled person, and a very flexible system can be constructed to meet specific requirements of the patient, via modified (or 'customised') hardware. The possibilities of providing intelligent prostheses to help overcome the patient's disability are also referred to by Vanderheiden; in particular micros are beginning to be used as language processors for aphasic patients. Vanderheiden feels that there are a number of problems which require research. For example, it would be useful for physically handicapped people to have access to standard programmes that are available to non-handicapped people, and the problem of rapid obsolescence due to rapid technological development needs to be tackled. At present the BBC microcomputer appears the best available machine in terms of adapting for future development.

A good illustration of what can be achieved for non-verbal patients who have a motor handicap has been provided by Pollak (1982). He describes a system based upon an inexpensive microcomputer (PET), with special response devices and keyboards, including 'suck' and 'blow' controls. The patient is easily able to select individual words or phrases/sentences for communication from an expandable vocabulary store, and required messages are built up on the micro's VDU. The VDU is also used to display user guidance notes. Inclusion of a 'self-scanning' keyboard, by which the micro automatically highlights possible items, one by one, only requires the patient to stop the scanning sequence at a desired item. This keeps the necessary motor activity to a minimum for patients with severe motor handicaps.

Another useful computer-based communication aid is BLISSAPPLE, which promotes communication based on the international symbol language. The partially-sighted and blind may be helped via microcomputer, the range of appropriate applications being from the simple display of very large letters on the VDU to extremely sophisticated developments such as the Telesensory 'optacon' system which allows blind people to 'read' printed text.

Microcomputer Applications in the Management of Memory Impairment

Microcomputers can assist in the management of memory disorders by helping to:

(1) assess the memory deficit;
(2) measure the effectiveness of any intervention (for example, involving drug treatment);
(3) in the retraining procedures themselves.

Assessment of Memory Deficit

It is obvious that microcomputers are excellent for presenting items in visual memory tasks. Using the machine's capacity for display graphics, it is easy to produce abstract visual designs for memory testing. These designs do not suffer from one of the difficulties, namely confounding verbal coding, inherent in some psychometric visual memory tests such as the Benton VRT.

An example of a computer-administered visual memory test is that devised by Acker (1980) as part of his Bexley–Maudsley Automated Psychological Screening. In the test the patient receives 36 memory trials. On each trial he is first invited to press a button to see the to-be-remembered visual stimulus. This memory item (Figure 6.3) appears for a few seconds, followed by a delay period of 1, 5 or 10 seconds.

Figure 6.3: Visual Memory Stimulus

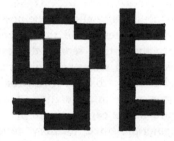

After the delay the patient is presented with three designs (Figure 6.4), one of which is identical to the original memory item. The patient indicates which design he believes was the memory item via buttons on a response panel.

Figure 6.4: Visual Memory Multiple Choice Response

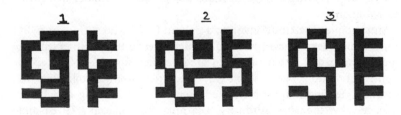

Table 6.3: Visual Memory Print-out

		1 sec. delay					
Correct	=	11 Mean RT	=	1.96,	SD	=	0.59
Wrong	=	1 Mean RT	=	8.33,	SD	=	1.15
		5 sec. delay					
Correct	=	9 Mean RT	=	4.10,	SD	=	3.36
Wrong	=	3 Mean RT	=	10.16,	SD	=	3.96
		10 sec. delay					
Correct	=	7 Mean RT	=	3.33,	SD	=	0.76
Wrong	=	5 Mean RT	=	5.63,	SD	=	2.80

At the end of the test the microcomputer can print out accuracy results, according to the three delay periods, and also provides mean and standard deviation data for both correct and error responses (Table 6.3).

Such response latency data would not be possible with traditional 'pencil and paper' memory tests, and the microcomputer saves the psychologist having to spend time scoring the test. Further, the computer's multiple-choice format seems particularly appropriate for those patients (for example, with stroke or Parkinson's disease) in whom motor impairments may make interpretation of traditional test results difficult. In the future we are certain to see the introduction of standardised microcomputer-presented memory tests, accompanied by appropriate normative data.

Measuring the Effects of a Therapeutic Intervention

As mentioned earlier, the timing of response latencies is a particular feature of microcomputers. The timing can be made very accurate, as it is easy to convert the machine to act as a millisecond timer by means of a short programme. I have been using a PET in this way as part of Reaction Time investigations of memory scanning in neurological patients.

An example case study involves a patient (KW) who suffered a right frontal lobe haemorrhage, with subsequent neurosurgical intervention to clip the causal aneurysm. Repeated testing suggested that KW's cognitive functions were stable in the three months following his operation, leaving him with marked memory and learning deficits as evidenced by the Rey Auditory Learning Test (Lezak, 1976) and Wechsler Memory Scale Factor scores (Skilbeck and Woods, 1980). In conjunction with a neurosurgeon, it was decided to use Desmopressin

(DDAVP) on an experimental basis with KW, there being some research to suggest its potential usefulness following brain injury.

After baseline testing, KW was assessed approximately every two weeks for three months, alternately 'on' and 'off' the drug. Testing included visual reaction time (RT) meaures of memory scanning, using a paradigm well-known in experimental psychology (Sternberg, 1975). The design involved providing KW with a number of digits (the 'positive' set), and then presenting single digits to him visually through the computer. On each trial KW was required to press one response key if the presented digit belonged to the positive set, and another response key if it did not (that is, a 'negative' set digit). At each assessment KW was tested under four conditions of positive set size (1, 2, 3 or 4 digits). Figure 6.5 depicts the mean RT results for the four positive set size conditions, at each testing session. It can be seen that the plots for set sizes 1, 2 and 3 all show beneficial effects from the 'standard' dose of the drug, in terms of faster memory scanning. In contrast, plot 4 failed to show consistent changes according to drug condition. Also, when the drug dose was doubled plots 1 and 2 deteriorated (point 6).

Although the results obtained were not totally consistent, they do suggest that medication may have some role in the amelioration of deficits in at least one area of memory structures. The deleterious

Figure 6.5: Patient KW: Mean RT and Drug Administration

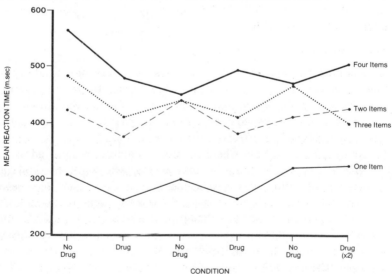

Figure 6.6: Patient TA: Median RT and Medication Level

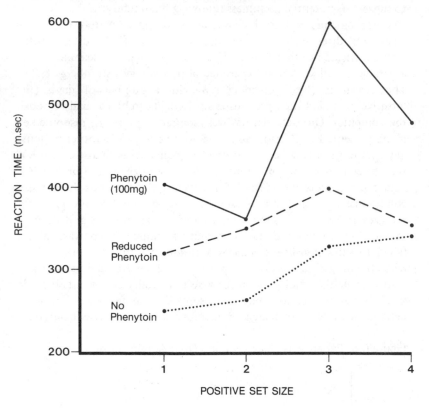

effects noted from doubling the drug dose highlight the careful experimental work that is required in the field of drug effects and cognitive performance. Although in this case the microcomputer was not directly involved in the process of remediation, it did prove a useful tool in assessing the beneficial effects of the 'memory drug'.

Another case example where the microcomputer has proved useful in assessing cognitive change is that of TA, who was a head-injured patient almost four years post-accident when first seen. Because of benign neglect, or medical oversight, TA was still taking a 100 mg daily dose of Pheytoin, on which he had been placed prophylactically immediately after his injury. Rather than just stop the anti-convulsant medication immediately, a baseline measure of his memory scanning performance with the existing level of medication was obtained. The drug dose was then halved and two weeks later he was reassessed.

Finally, he was seen a further two weeks later, after he had been off medication for two weeks. Figure 6.6 shows TA's median RT performances under increasing memory load (that is, with positive set sizes 1-4, according to Sternberg's paradigm).

On his original dose, TA's performances were both slow and somewhat erratic. When the medication dose was halved his performances generally were faster and the shape of the RT graph became nearer to that expected of a normal individual. After he had been off Phenytoin for two weeks, his performances were both fast and displayed a normal shape.

Involvement in the Retraining Procedures Themselves

As is described elsewhere in this book (for example, Chapter 4), recent research has suggested that it is possible to assist a patient's impaired memory using a number of internal or external aids. One such example of an internal aid is the 'Peg' system. The patient is first taught the 'Peg', which has ten points, each built around a rhyme: 'one is a bun, two is a shoe, three is a tree' . . . 'ten is a hen'. After acquiring the steps in the peg the patient can use the system to help him remember lists of items. Each item to be recalled is linked to the peg using a visual image: for example, if trying to remember the word 'blouse', a scene might be imagined in which a hen is wearing a blouse. It is claimed that the more bizarre and elaborated is the image, the greater is the probability of recalling the item (Lorayne, 1979).

A relevant case example, with whom I used a microcomputer, is that of an eleven-year-old girl (SO) who suffered a severe head injury and associated haemorrhage of the left frontal lobe. Her most prominent cognitive deficit was impaired memory, particularly in the area of spontaneous recall. However, her visual memory ability seemed well-preserved. One of the things that SO most missed following her head injury was being able to go shopping for her mother without having to write down all of the items required. For this reason, the peg retraining focused upon items of food shopping. Comparison was made of SO's recall of items linked to the peg system, with the level she achieved by mere repetition (three presentations); incidently, although SO had severe recall difficulties she needed only four presentations of each peg point ('one is a bun', etc.) to acquire the peg permanently. Both 'peg' and 'repetition' shopping items were presented through the microcomputer, and SO's learning and recall were tested approximately weekly. Figure 6.7 depicts the 'Peg' and 'Repetition' results, and indicates that SO was able to improve her recall, over and above the

Figure 6.7: Patient SO: Recall of Shopping List, Peg v. Repetition

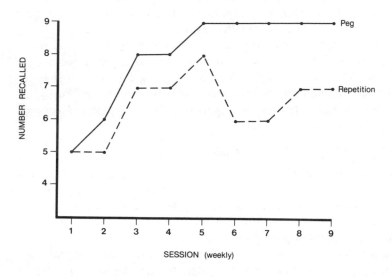

effects of repetition, using the peg system.

This patient has been tested on a number of occasions over the last three years. Generally, the peg system has allowed her to recall 100 per cent (or close to it) of a limited amount of information without many practice sessions. In contrast, regular repetition of the same amount of similar material has usually resulted in only about 60–70 per cent recall.

The results with this patient using microcomputer presentation of the peg system have, therefore, been encouraging. It is interesting that SO has been able to follow instructions from the computer to adopt the visual image described by the computer. In fact, only a verbal description, through the computer, of the desired image has been used. For example, when trying to remember the shopping item 'TEA', the instruction printed on the computer screen was – 'one is a bun, – TEA. Imagine a bun floating on a cup of tea'. The computer was not programmed to depict figurally the scene she was to use. The results obtained demonstrate that SO is able to follow such verbal instruction, but it may be that the beneficial effects of the peg could have been enhanced for her using the computer graphics facility. Similarly, many patients with memory deficits will not have the well-preserved visual imagery ability that SO displays. This may not present a great barrier to computer administration of memory retraining using visual imagery as there are a number of microcomputers that can offer excellent graphics (for example, the APPLE and Commodore 64). The standard is now so high that psychologists using visual imagery in the retraining of their patients will not even have to make do with 'static' pictures on their microcomputer — often they will be able to programme moving or 'cartoon' graphics to increase the vividness of the image for the patient's use.

A second area where microcomputers have been involved in memory retraining is that of orientation. Such an application may be appropriate for patients who have sustained severe damage as a result of head injury or stroke. The application originated in the field of psychogeriatrics, where a common problem is the 'confused' patient. This type of elderly patient may become so disorientated in time, place and person as to be unable to remember the name of the hospital, what day of the week it is, or even his wife's name. In the last few years psychologists working with the elderly have carried out research into techniques that may help to ameliorate these severe memory impairments. The most important development so far seems to be the introduction of Reality Orientation Therapy (ROT). As its name suggests, ROT focuses upon improving a patient's level of orientation (Holden and Woods, 1982), generally by frequent, daily reminders to the patient of items of information that should be familiar to him.

Many neurological patients, for example those who have suffered a severe head injury or stroke, manifest similar difficulties in orientation to those seen in the field of psychogeriatrics. From the therapy point of view, a major problem in trying to reorientate patients is that techniques such as ROT are time-consuming. It is rarely that a psychologist, or one of the physical therapists working with the patient, has the time available to improve a patient's level of orientation. It can be argued, however, that this long and monotonous aspect of memory retraining can largely be delegated to a microcomputer.

It is relatively easy to write a programme that involves the computer asking a patient orientation questions of personal relevance. Each question can be presented on the computer's screen, along with a number of possible answers; an example is shown in Table 6.4. The possible answers are numbered, so that all a patient has to do is to press the button number corresponding to the answer that he believes to be true. For this purpose the patient is provided with a response board containing the numbered buttons which fits over the computer's usual keyboard to prevent the patient inadvertently 'crashing' the programme (that is stopping it running).

With this arrangement, it has been our experience that the large

Table 6.4: Patient Re-orientation Programme

What day is it today?
1.   Monday
2.   Wednesday
3.   Thursday
4.   Friday

majority of neurological patients can comprehend the task instructions and follow the system.

The 'reorientate' computer programme is written so that each time it runs it first requires the insertion of the orientation questions and possible responses. This allows flexibility in the retraining system (so that different orientation questions can be used, as appropriate), and also allows the psychologist to vary the number of items to be included on any particular run. Patient boredom is unlikely to occur. The method does not require that the same question has to be re-entered every time it is used at a particular session: the programme is written so that it loops round and round to present the item a number of times, the number of 'loops' being determined by the psychologist on each occasion that the programme is run.

There are a number of features of computer-administered retraining programmes that are worth mentioning.

The first is that maintenance of the patient's attention can be aided in a number of ways: for example, attention to the question presented can be maintained by adding an underlining to the question shortly after it has been displayed. Attention could be further enhanced by flashing the underlining off and on, or varying the colour in which the question is presented. Retraining of orientation via computer can be made far more interesting for the patient than the corresponding face-to-face interaction with the psychologist or therapist! Overloading the patient with the sudden appearance of a screenful of alternative responses to a question can be avoided by temporarily sequencing their appearance on the screen. The patient should then be able to 'take in' the information more easily. Another potential problem that can easily be avoided is that of 'positional effects' operating on response selection. By the simple insertion of two lines of programming the order in which the alternative responses are presented to the patient can be randomised. As is the case with interpersonal retraining of orientation, it is important to provide the patient with feedback to reinforce selection of the right response or correction of a wrong response. A number of feedback statements, therefore, need to be included in the programme. Those confirming a correct response might include 'you are right —', 'that is correct —', or 'yes! —', followed by a restatement of the correct response, and those when the wrong answer has been chosen might be 'don't forget —', and 'try to remember —', followed by the correct answer. Obviously a time-limit has to be set so that if the patient fails to respond within, say, ten seconds the computer automatically provides the correct answer. It is relatively straightforward to write the programme so that questions which the patient finds very easy (that is, always answers them correctly and speedily) can be omitted on later 'loops' of the programme. Similarly, items that a patient finds too difficult can be omitted or represented in an easier form.

In addition to reducing the tedium for the psychologist, or therapist, who has frequently to repeat these orientation items, using a micro-computer has the further advantage of providing accurate measurement of response latency. The ease with which a patient retrieves an item from memory can thus be gauged, as can the beneficial effects of presenting a particular item a number of times. Finally, the computer can provide a 'hard copy', or permanent record of a patient's reorientation session without detailed notes being necessary. Table 6.5 provides an example record showing the presented questions, the patient's responses, whether the answers were correct, and the times taken for the patient to respond.

This particular type of programme has been used with a number of patients in our unit who have memory and orientation difficulties. The data produced from our studies of these patients clearly indicates shorter response latencies and greater accuracy, both between sessions and between trials within one session. For the example case below, I am indebted to my colleague John Welch, Principal Psychologist in the Regional Neurological Centre, Newcastle.

RM was a longstanding severe head-injured patient when first seen for retraining. He had major memory and orientation difficulties. Using the programme 'reorientate' he was given 21 orientation questions (on four repetition loops each session), over a number of weeks. The questions were divided into seven questions which were repeated at each session (for example, 'Which famous film star died in 1982?'), seven questions which related to current news items, and seven questions which related to recent personal information. RM ran through the orientation programme weekly, the results obtained demonstrating that his mean response latency for repeated items decreased over the weeks (Table 6.6). In addition, mean response time decreased over the four

Table 6.5: Re-orientation Programme Print-out

RESULTS FOR	:	PATIENT ID
DATE	:	
RUN NAME	:	
Q : WHAT MONTH IS IT?		
CORRECT ANSWER	:	DECEMBER
PATIENT ANSWER	:	DECEMBER
RIGHT, TIME	:	3.35 sec.
Q : HOW OLD ARE YOU?		
CORRECT ANSWER	:	34
PATIENT ANSWER	:	33
WRONG, TIME	:	6.4
Q : WHO IS PRESIDENT OF USA?		
CORRECT ANSWER	:	REAGAN
PATIENT ANSWER	:	CARTER
WRONG, TIME	:	5.7

Table 6.6: Patient RM: Mean Response Latency (sec.) Across Sessions

		Session (Week)				
		1	2	3	4	5
Repeated Questions	:	4.1	2.8	2.8	2.0	0.8
New Questions	:	2.4	3.2	2.8	2.5	2.5

Table 6.7: Patient RM: Mean Response Latency (sec.) Within Sessions

		Trial			
		1	2	3	4
Session (week)	1	6.3	2.8	2.1	1.7
	2	5.4	2.2	1.9	2.5
	3	4.3	2.1	2.2	1.9
	4	4.1	2.7	1.3	1.2
	5	2.3	2.3	1.3	1.4

loops within a session (Table 6.7).

RM's performance using computer-administered questions was compared with his results in a more traditional face-to-face orientation retraining. Very similar results obtained in the two conditions for repeated items (Table 6.8), and for items which changed week to week (Table 6.9) although performance on computer items at week five broke the pattern.

Our results with RM show that learning does take place across trials in any particular session, and across sessions. Although there is little available data, our findings do not suggest that major differences should be expected between computer-administered and face-to-face orientation retraining. The computerised condition offers the benefits of a non-judgemental approach and economy in terms of time spent in face-to-face retraining.

Table 6.8: Patient RM: Orientation Errors for Repeated Questions

		Computer Trials				Non-computer Trials			
		1	2	3	4	1	2	3	4
Session	1 :	7	3	1	0	7	2	1	0
	2 :	4	2	1	0	4	1	1	0
	3 :	6	0	0	0	0	0	0	0
	4 :	0	0	0	0	0	0	0	0
	5 :	0	0	0	0	0	0	0	0

Table 6.9: Patient RM: Orientation Errors for New Questions

		Computer Trials				Non-computer Trials			
		1	2	3	4	1	2	3	4
Session	1 :	6	3	0	0	10	4	2	0
	2 :	4	3	0	0	7	4	0	0
	3 :	7	2	2	0	9	4	1	0
	4 :	6	1	0	0	6	1	0	0
	5 :	9	7	2	3	7	3	1	0

Future Developments

Almost certainly developments in the field of microcomputers will reflect continuing technological progress which will take place surprisingly rapidly.

It is to be expected that in the near future a range of standard micro-computer-administered tests will become available for routine clinical use. The tasks which will first appear are likely to be those assessing visual memory and visual perceptual/spatial functions. Auditory tests presented via a micro are now a real possibility, given progress in developing voice synthesis systems for use with computers. Further ahead, and much more difficult to predict accurately, lies the introduction of voice recognition systems. Such systems still require perfecting, but when they do appear they will allow computer presentation of tests, and response recording, in both auditory and visual modalities.

The development of the above features will also help to expand the microcomputer's role in the rehabilitation process. Some of the most innovative recent research has been carried out in the field of communication disorders (see p. 120 above).

7 DRUG TREATMENTS, NEUROCHEMICAL CHANGE AND HUMAN MEMORY IMPAIRMENT

Steven J. Cooper

Introduction

Some memories are short-lived. Others, however, are persistent, and we may retain certain memories for the greater part of our lives. In old age, when there may be increasing difficulty in holding on to our memories, it often proves possible to recall distant events, stretching back over a lifetime. It is generally accepted that certain changes must take place within the brain which are essential to the formation and retention of memories. Damage to the brain, arising for example from blows to the head in accidents, can result in both temporary and permanent losses of memory (amnesia). When the brain begins to show signs of degeneration, for example in some elderly patients, the capacity to form new memories may become seriously impaired.

What events occur within the brain which correspond, in at least some way, to the formation of memories? One answer might be that certain nerve cells (neurones) within the brain, perhaps specialised to perform memory functions, become more efficient in communicating among themselves. Neurones signal to each other across narrow, dividing synaptic junctions. The synapse separates the enclosing membrane of one nerve cell from that of a neighbour. A neurone can produce an effect on an adjacent neurone by releasing a very small amount of a chemical substance (a neurotransmitter) which diffuses across the narrow synaptic gap and initiates changes in the adjacent neurone. For a brief time, the neurotransmitter molecules couple with specialised receptors or recognition sites, which are situated in the cell membrane of the neighbouring neurone, and then depart. It is the amalgamation of the neurotransmitter molecules with specific recognition sites which determines the nature of the signal passing from one nerve cell to the next. One important hypothesis of memory is that as a result of learning or training, certain synapses in the brain become more efficient in the transfer of information between neurones, and that this enhanced efficiency is a prerequisite of memory storage. It follows that anything we can do to modify chemical neurotransmission at synapses within the brain may carry implications for the functions of remembering and forgetting.

We are aware that neurones within the brain make use of a fairly large number of neutrotransmitters, in their business of passing information among themselves. It is quite unknown how many of these neurotransmitters participate in memory processes, and the 'memory' neurones have never been isolated. Nevertheless, some tentative steps have been made in identifying some, at least, of the neurotransmitters which may contribute to the formation and retention of memories, as well as their retrieval. In particular, a good deal of experimental and clinical investigation has concentrated upon a neurotransmitter called *acetylcholine*. The name is usually abbreviated to ACh. Nerve cells which release ACh at synapses in order to signal to other cells are called *cholinergic* neurones. This signalling process is often referred to as *cholinergic neurotransmission*. Professor J.A. Deutsch, and others, have put forward the idea that the formation of memories, their retention and their forgetting depend to some degree upon the level of efficiency or sensitivity of transmission at cholinergic synapses. An important point to note is that certain drugs are available which can be used either to assist or to impair cholinergic neurotransmission. They must, therefore, if the theory is correct, either help to promote and preserve memories, or to hinder memory processes and so produce forgetting and amnesia.

It will be helpful to know a little more about the origin and fate of acetylcholine in order to appreciate how the drugs we shall be discussing produce their effects on cholinergic neurotransmission.

Lecithin is a dietary constituent, and is a primary source of choline. Once inside the cholinergic neurones of the brain, the choline is converted into ACh, through the agency of the enzyme, choline acetyltransferase (CAT). After release, ACh acts at cholinergic receptors, and then detaches from the receptor. It is converted back to choline by the enzyme, acetylcholinesterase (AChE). By taking more choline, or by adopting a diet which is rich in lecithin, the levels of ACh in the brain can be significantly elevated (Wurtman and Growdon, 1979). ACh levels can also be increased by inhibiting the activity of the enzyme which is responsible for destroying ACh, acetylcholinesterase (Figure 7.1). Cholinergic neurotransmission can be interfered with, on the other hand, either by damage which destroys cholinergic neurones, or by giving a drug which impedes the access of ACh to cholinergic receptors.

The main purpose of this chapter is to consider the evidence that

Figure 7.1: Acetylcholine Synthesis and Metabolism

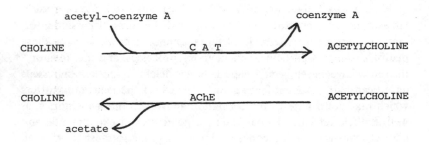

cholinergic neurotransmission is closely involved in memory processes. The evidence derives from both human and animal experimental studies. Furthermore, if degeneration takes place to reduce the numbers of cholinergic neurones in the brain, we may have an explanation, at least in part, for the deteriorating memory encountered in elderly patients who show signs of dementia. Particular attention will be paid to the condition known as Alzheimer's disease, in which there is progressive deterioration of brain function, accompanied by memory failures, personality changes, lessening of intelligence and other psychological impairments. Alzheimer's disease involves a selective loss of cholinergic neurones. To what extent are the mentally-crippling features of the disease reversible? An approach to the question, using drug therapies, may not only open avenues to possible treatments of this and other, related diseases, but also throw more light on the part that cholinergic cells play in memorising, remembering and forgetting.

Acetylcholine and Memory in Animals

The results of memory experiments using animal subjects suggest that after training or learning, the strength of memories for the events of training experience first increases with the elapse of time, and then begins to diminish with further elapse of time (Deutsch and Rogers, 1979; Squire and Davis, 1981). In other words, following learning, memories first consolidate, and later extinguish or fade, leading to forgetting. The time over which the changes take place can be minutes, days, months and years. Extensive training will help to promote the retention of memories, whilst poor initial learning will result in difficulties in retention. Deutsch has proposed that memory strength depends upon the level of information transmission at cholinergic neurones, which should therefore, in turn, depend upon the success of the initial training experience and upon the time that has elapsed between training and later recall. He has reviewed the series of experiments undertaken by his colleagues and himself which support his hypothesis (Deutsch, 1971; Deutsch and Rogers, 1979). In their experiments, *anticholinesterases* and *anticholinergic* drugs were used. The former increase ACh levels in the brain by inhibiting the activity of the degradative enzyme, AChE (Figure 7.1). The latter reduce ACh activity by blocking the effects of ACh at cholinergic receptor sites.

Deutsch and his colleagues trained rats to run to an illuminated arm within a Y-shaped maze. Eventually the rats satisfied a criterion of learning by running correctly to the lit arm on each of ten successive trials. If the animals were retested 14 days after completion of the training, they showed evidence of excellent retention of the learning experience. They remembered to run to the lit arm of the Y-maze. However, if the retesting was left until 28 days after the completion of training, the animals' recall was poor, indicating that the original learning had been forgotten. Deutsch showed that an injection of an anticholinesterase immediately before the recall test, when a 28-day period had elapsed from the completion of training, resulted in a strong improvement in memory. Increasing cholinergic activity, therefore, overcame the process of forgetting. Hence, forgetting may occur as a consequence of diminishing activity at cholinergic 'memory' neurones.

In other experiments, Deutsch and his colleagues showed that an anticholinergic drug, scopolamine, given just before a recall test which was carried out only one or three days after training, produced an appreciable impairment in memory. Relatively 'fresh' memories, therefore, appear to depend on active, ongoing cholinergic transmission. When the cholinergic activity was blocked by the action of scopolamine, loss of memory or amnesia occurred.

Memory strength can depend upon the effectiveness of the original learning. Deutsch examined the effects of anticholinesterase injection on the retention of either well-learned or poorly-learned habits. His results showed that the drug treatment produced an improvement in the performance of the poorly-learned habit, but not in that of the well-learned habit, in a subsequent test of retention. His interpretation of these results is that since cholinergic neurotransmission improves with learning, it must remain at a comparatively low level in poorly-learned habits. The anticholinesterase treatment increased cholinergic activity and so facilitated recall in the test of retention of the poorly-learned habit. The well-learned habit, on the other hand, would retain a high level of cholinergic activity, which would not be improved by the anticholinesterase treatment.

These results, and others, are described in review articles (Deutsch, 1971; Deutsch and Rogers, 1979). Taken together, the experiments suggest strongly that cholinergic neurotransmission is involved in some way, in learning and memory processes in animals. They also imply that amnesia may result as a consequence of a loss of cholinergic activity within the brain.

Acetylcholine and Human Memory

Animal studies indicate that synaptic transmission between neurones in the brain which utilise ACh may be especially important in memory processes. There is evidence which also implicates cholinergic neuro-transmission in human memory. Experiments have been performed which tend to show that enhancement of cholinergic activity leads to improvements in performance with memory tasks, whilst antagonism of cholinergic activity results in significant impairments.

For the brain to manufacture ACh it requires a supply of choline in the blood plasma which supplies the brain (Figure 7.1). Choline is converted into ACh by the enzyme choline acetyltransferase (CAT) within the brain's cholinergic neurones. Choline is a constituent of human diet, and its principal source of lecithin. It has been found that administering additional choline or lecithin to people results in an elevation of brain ACh levels (Wurtman and Growdon, 1979). The brain responds to the additional supply of choline by manufacturing more ACh. This may, therefore, provide a method for improving performance in memory tasks.

In one study which examined this idea, ten volunteer subjects were tested on two learning tasks. The first, a serial learning task, consisted of learning a fixed sequence of ten unrelated words. The second, a selective reminding task, examined the recall of common words which were either highly imageable (for example, a word like *table*) or had low imagery value (for example, *truth*). The subjects consumed either 10 g of choline chloride elixir or an inactive elixir which was matched for colour and taste (the placebo condition). In this experiment,

Sitaram and colleagues found that choline treatment produced a small but significant improvement in the recall of unrelated words, but discovered that overall performance on the selective reminding task showed no difference between choline and placebo conditions (Sitaram, Weingartner, Caine and Gillin, 1978).

They did observe, however, that under the placebo condition, high imagery words were recalled better than low imagery words. This difference disappeared in the choline condition. Thus, a very interesting effect of the choline treatment was to improve the recall of the low imagery words, without affecting the recall of the high imagery words. Choline treatment appeared, therefore, to improve poor memory performance, but did not produce an additional improvement in good memory performance.

Cholinergic activity in the brain can also be increased by administering a substance which mimics the effects of ACh at cholinergic receptors in the brain. If cholinergic activity at the receptors is important in memory, then it may prove possible to detect improvements in memory as a result of such mimicry. In another study, Sitaram and colleagues, administered *arecholine*, a drug which acts like ACh at cholinergic receptors, to volunteer subjects (Sitaram, Weingartner and Gillin, 1978). The subjects were required to learn a fixed sequence of ten words belonging to a familiar category (for example, vegetables, cities, fruits), and their performance was compared after arecholine (2 mg or 4 mg) or placebo treatments. The results of the study showed that the arecholine at the higher dose (4 mg) did accelerate the learning of the words in serial order. Mimicking cholinergic activity, therefore, may lead to improvements in human memory which would be reflected in better performance in the serial learning task.

A further method for enhancing cholinergic activity is to administer a drug which inhibits the effects of the enzyme, acetylcholinesterase, which acts to remove ACh from cholinergic synapses. Davis and colleagues planned at study which required a comparison between intravenous infusion of either 1.0 mg physostigmine (an acetylcholinesterase inhibitor) or placebo (Davis, Mohs, Tinklenberg, Pfefferbaum, Hollister and Kopell, 1978). The volunteer subjects were tested in tasks which were designed to test short-term (STM) and long-term (LTM) memory functions. Two tests of STM function were employed: the digit span and a memory scanning task. Physostigmine was found to have no effect, compared to the placebo condition, in either task. LTM functioning was assessed by two verbal learning tasks, and it was found that, in this case, physostigmine significantly improved the recall of learned items during subsequent recall trials. Davis and his colleagues concluded that the enhancement of cholinergic function might improve LTM in, at least, certain situations.

These three studies are consistent in suggesting that stimulating cholinergic activity in the brain, by (i) increasing ACh synthesis or manufacture by providing additional amounts of dietary choline; (ii) stimulating cholinergic receptors by arecholine, a drug which mimics actions of ACh; (iii) inhibiting the breakdown of ACh by the cholinesterase inhibitor, physostigmine; can lead to detectable improvements in human performance which may reflect improvement in memory processes. It is difficult to draw further conclusions on the basis of so few experiments; but the data are suggestive that enhancing cholinergic actvity in normal volunteers may confer some benefit in tasks which require LTM involvement, and in circumstances where performance may be relatively poor under no-drug (placebo) conditions.

There are complementary studies in the literature which demonstrate that significant impairments in human memory can be produced by drug treatments which tend to act against cholinergic transmission at synapses in the brain. These studies have relied on the drug *scopolamine* (*hyoscine*), which antagonises the effects of ACh at cholinergic synapses. The results of representative studies are briefly indicated in Table 7.1. The subjects in these studies were young normal volunteer subjects, university or medical school subjects of either sex.

As a general rule, impairments in performance can be difficult to interpret, since there are many ways to produce them. Impaired performance in a memory task, for example, may not reflect an inferior memory but may arise from some generalised disruptive or interfering effect on behaviour. It is known that scopolamine can produce sedation in subjects, and there are cases where scopolamine has induced hallucinations. Inspection of Table 7.1, however, indicates that *not* all performance in a variety of learning and memory tasks was impaired by relatively small doses of scopolamine. This tends to indicate that the cases in which significant impairment of performance was detected after scopolamine treatment, did not occur simply as a consequence of sedation or other side effects.

Performance on tasks which impose no delay between exposure to test items and recall of those items (digit span; immediate free recall of verbal material) show relatively little or no effect due to scopolamine treatment. In contrast, whenever a delay is introduced, or when learning proceeds over several trials, scopolamine does appear to impair

Table 7.1: Representative Studies which Report Performance Impairments in Learning/Memory Tasks Following the Administration of Scopolamine (Hyoscine) to Young Normal Volunteer Subjects (male and female)

Authors (date)	Scopolamine dose; route of administration[a]	Learning/memory task	Drug-related effects
Crow and Grove-White, (1973)	0.4 mg, i.v.	(i) immediate free recall	some impairment
		(ii) delayed free recall	marked impairment
		(iii) number-colour associations	some impairment
Crow et al. (1976)	0.4 mg, i.v.	(i) immediate free recall	no impairment
		(ii) delayed free recall	significant impairment
Drachman and Leavitt, (1974)	1.0 mg, s.c.	(i) digit span	no impairment
		(ii) digit sequence learning	impaired performance
		(iii) multitrial immediate free recall	marked impairment
		(iv) retrieval by category	some impairment
Ghoneim and Mewaldt, (1975)	0.6 mg/70 kg body weight, i.m.	(i) immediate free recall	impaired performance
		(ii) delayed free recall	impaired performance
		(iii) delayed recognition	non-significant impairment
		(iv) immediate recall of digit sequences	no effect
		(v) visual recognition	no effect
Sitaram et al., (1978)	0.5 mg, i.m.	(i) categorised serial learning	learning impairment
Jones et al., (1979)	0.3 mg, oral	(i) digit span	some impairment on early serial positions
		(ii) category clustering	no effect

Note: a. Abbreviations: i.v. = intravenous; s.c. = subcutaneous; i.m. = intramuscular.

performance quite reliably (Table 7.1). This distinction may be taken to indicate that scopolamine may have relatively little effect on STM processes (at least at the dose levels employed in the cited studies), but can impair performance in tasks which incorporate LTM functioning. If so, LTM processes may be particularly susceptible to impairment as a consequence of the antagonism of cholinergic neurotransmission in the brain. It would be particularly interesting if it could be shown that the impairments in learning and memory due to scopolamine treatment could be reversed. Indeed, there are data which show that physostigmine, which increases cholinergic activity in the brain, will overcome scopolamine-induced impairments in learning and memory (Ghoneim and Mewaldt, 1977; Mewaldt and Ghoneim, 1979).

Thus, experimental evidence exists which suggests that enhancing cholinergic neurotransmission can aid human memory in some circumstances, whilst antagonising cholinergic neurotransmission can impair it. Drachman and Leavitt (1974) noted that the pattern of memory impairment seen in young volunteer subjects following scopolamine administration bore a marked similarity to the impairments in memory observed in elderly patients. They proposed that the cognitive and memory disturbances which occur with ageing may reflect a relatively specific impairment of cholinergic neurotransmission. This is an important hypothesis, which will be considered in detail in the next two sections. The focus of the following sections will be Alzheimer's disease and senile dementia, conditions in which memory impairment is very common and often pronounced, and in which degeneration of cholinergic neurones in the brain is known to occur.

Alzheimer's Disease: A Cholinergic Involvement

Dementia refers to a progressive loss of cognitive and other intellectual functions as a result of organic brain disease. The term *senile dementia* has been used for those cases of dementia where the age of onset is 65 years or over. The description *Alzheimer's disease*, however, is applied to those cases in which the patients are younger than 65 when the disease is first diagnosed. Although there has been some debate concerning the relationship between the two categories of dementia, many authorities now consider that Alzheimer's disease is essentially the same as the most common form of senile dementia. This latter category can be referred to as senile dementia of the Alzheimer type, or SDAT as an abbreviation (Terry and Davies, 1980).

Contrary to some views, dementia is not a necessary feature of living into old age. In the United States, for example, it has been estimated that about 15 per cent of those over 64 years show some signs of dementia. About 5 per cent of the same population are afflicted with severe dementia. It is thought that about half the patients with some form of senile dementia have the Alzheimer type. This disease is progressive and irreversible; patients do not recover and may show so much deterioration as to require total nursing care. Death is usually due to an infection. In younger patients, the course of Alzheimer's disease lasts on average about ten years, whereas in senile patients it is only three years (Nielsen, Homma and Biorn-Henriksen, 1977).

The clinical features of Alzheimer's disease have been clearly portrayed by Strub and Black (1981), in a recent text dealing with organic brain syndromes (pp. 119-64). The initial symptoms and signs of Alzheimer's disease can be described in terms of several categories. Emotional changes can be among the first to occur, and may include loss of interest in work and family, increased irritability, and hypochondriasis. Restlessness, fatigue and loss of initiative, coupled with anxiety and depression, may also be present. Early in the disease, cognitive changes also occur, and the most common feature is a disturbance of memory. Forgetfulness and difficulties in learning or retaining recent memories are characteristics. The more remote, well-established, memories remain intact, however.

The disease progresses through several stages, marked by a progressive deterioration in intellectual abilities, communication with others, in the ability to attend and in the execution of learned skilled movements. In the final stages of the disease, patients become completely dependent on others for care. They become incapable of communicating, may show involuntary emotional expression, and eventually become totally apathetic and withdrawn.

Alois Alzheimer, a clinician and neuropathologist, published a report in 1907, in which he described the case of a 51-year-old woman whose symptoms began with loss of memory and disorientation (Alzheimer, 1907). The woman eventually became profoundly demented and died within five years. Alzheimer also described some unusual pathological features in the woman's brain, which he had examined microscopically at autopsy. In addition to the observation that the cortex had atrophied, he noticed the presence in the neural tissue of what are described as *neuritic* or *senile plaques*, and detected many cortical neurones which contained *neurofibrillary tangles*. Simchowicz later added the observation of *granulovacuolar degeneration* of the pyramidal cells of the hippocampus (McMenemey, 1970). Descriptions and interpretations of these neuropathological changes associated with Alzheimer's disease are provided by Terry and Wisniewski (1970) and Terry and Davies (1980).

It seems very likely that the neuropathological finaings indicate stages in the degeneration and loss of certain neurones within the cortex. The cause of the neuronal degeneration remains unknown, although a transmissable, infectious agent is suspected (Terry and Davies, 1980). An important recent advance in the understanding of Alzheimer's disease is the discovery that the neurones which are most involved in the degenerative process are cholinergic in nature.

Recently, several groups of investigators have reported 60-90 per cent reductions in the activities of *choline acetyltransferase* (CAT) and *acetylcholinesterase* (AChE) in the brains of patients with Alzheimer's disease and SDAT (Bowen *et al.*, 1976; Davies and Maloney, 1976; Davies, 1979; Perry *et al.*, 1977, 1978; White *et al.*, 1977). These enzymes are 'markers' for cholinergic neurones, since both are contained within them. CAT is an enzyme that manufactures or synthesises ACh, while AChE is an enzyme that inactivates ACh (Figure 7.1). Neurones which contain neurotransmitters other than ACh do not appear to be as markedly affected in the disease. The most consistent and severe neurochemical loss in Alzheimer's disease is a reduction in cholinergic activity in the cortex, and this finding indicates a specific degeneration and loss of ACh-containing neurones.

Interestingly, the neurones which contain ACh do not originate in the cortex. Instead they reside as large cells in various regions of the basal forebrain, and project fibres to the cortex, where they form synaptic connections with cortical neurones (Price *et al.*, 1982). It has been proposed that the degeneration of these ascending cholinergic fibres gives rise to the neuritic plaques in the cortex, described by Alzheimer, and that the impairment of memory, learning and other cognitive functions may result from the loss of cholinergic transmission (Price *et al.*, 1982). These findings raise the challenging question of whether there are ways to prevent, or to repair, degeneration of the cholinergic neurones which innervate the cortex. If ways are found, they may contribute to the amelioration of Alzheimer's disease.

Cholinergic Treatments in Alzheimer's Disease

The two preceding sections show, firstly, that memory processes may be affected by drug-induced manipulations of cholinergic activity in young normal volunteer subjects, and secondly, that in Alzheimer's disease and in senile dementia of the Alzheimer type there appears to be a drastic and selective degeneration of cholinergic neurones in the brain. If the subsequent impairments in cholinergic activity are responsible for the cognitive and memory impairments associated with Alzheimer's disease, it may prove possible to alleviate the impairments in some degree by attempting to raise cholinergic activity in the brain. A number of studies have been performed with this aim in mind, to enhance cholinergic activity in elderly patients with Alzheimer's disease in the expectation of some improvement in cognitive and memory functioning. Representative studies are listed in Table 7.2.

In the majority of studies, choline (either alone or as a constituent of lecithin) has been administered over extended periods (Table 7.2). The rationale for the treatment is that the choline treatment might lead to elevations in brain ACh levels. However, as can be seen, there has been very little indication that choline treatment secured any specific cognitive improvement, although general improvements in behaviour may have occurred. In one study, Signoret *et al.* (1978), there was some evidence of slight improvement with choline treatment. Perhaps significantly, the improvement was detected in younger patients with a short disease duration. Most of the patients examined in these studies were of an advanced age, and because of the progressive nature of the disease, would be expected to display signs of severe dementia. Under those circumstances, it may prove impossible to enhance remaining cholinergic activity sufficiently to produce any discernible effect on behaviour. Choline can only be converted to ACh if cholinergic neurones remain intact. If the cholinergic system of the brain has undergone severe degeneration, choline treatment may be of little avail in stimulating cholinergic activity.

With this important consideration in mind, the report of Smith and Swash (1979), which is concerned with a relatively young patient at an early stage in Alzheimer's disease, is particularly relevant. In several memory tests, they found that physostigmine, which inhibits the breakdown of ACh, did not affect the number of correct responses, but did reduce significantly the number of intrusion errors. In this patient, the level of choline acetyltransferase (CAT), a marker for the presence of cholinergic neurones, was only 23 per cent of the value for control brain levels. Facilitating cholinergic activity by drug treatments, early in the course of Alzheimer's disease, may confer some benefit. Smith and Swash's study showed that the number of inappropriate

Table 7.2: Outcomes of Treatments Designed to Enhance Cholinergic Activity in Elderly, Demented Patients

Authors (date)	Patients	Treatment	Dose	Duration	Outcome
Boyd et al. (1977)	7 patients with Alzheimer-type senile dementia. One 70 yr, one 78 yr, five 80+ yrs.	choline	5 g/day	4 weeks	Little change, but some improvement in behaviour.
Etienne et al. (1978)	3 patients, ages 76, 81, 88 yrs. Advanced Alzheimer's disease.	choline	up to 8 g/day	1 month	No definite clinical or laboratory signs of improvement.
Smith et al. (1978)	10 patients with Alzheimer's disease (mean age 77).	choline	9 g/day	2 weeks	No improvements.
Signoret et al. (1978)	8 patients with Alzheimer's disease (ages 59–78 yrs).	choline	9 g/day	21 days	Memory improvement in younger patients with short disease duration.
Christie et al. (1979)	11 patients with Alzheimer's disease (ages 53–67 yrs).	choline lecithin	2.5 g/day 40–100 g/day	9 days periods up to 3 mths.	No effect. No effect.
Corser et al. (1979)	4 patients with Alzheimer-type senile dementia (65–76 yrs).	lecithin	20 g/day	6 weeks	Modest general improvements.
Etienne et al. (1979)	7 patients with Alzheimer's disease (ages 42–81 yrs).	lecithin	25–100 g/day	4 weeks	Some improvements in 3 patients.
Smith and Swash (1979)	1 patient (42 yr) with Alzheimer's disease.	physostigmine	1 mg		Reduction in number of inappropriate responses in memory tests.

responses in memory tasks can be reduced. Clearly, more studies are required in patients who are at an early stage of the disease. However, the disease is difficult to diagnose in its early stages. If drug treatments are to be tried, it may prove worthwhile to investigate the effects of drugs which act directly at receptors to mimic the effects of ACh (for example, a drug like arecholine), since it is known that ACh receptors remain intact in Alzheimer's disease.

It is too early to decide whether or not drug treatments which modify cholinergic neurotransmission in the brain can have any lasting benefit in Alzheimer's disease or in cases of senile dementia. Directly-acting drugs which mimic the effects of ACh need to be investigated, since such drugs may prove of more benefit than pharmacological manipulations which depend upon residual intact cholinergic neurones. Animal and human studies indicate that cholinergic neurones are involved in memory processes. We need to know much more about the course of the degeneration of cholinergic neurones in Alzheimer patients, and to discover how this process relates to the course of deteriorating memory and other intellectual functions. Only then, perhaps, will it be possible to design drug therapies which either act to arrest the processes of degeneration within neurones or act to restore diminished cholinergic activity.

In the final section of this chapter, there will be a brief consideration of the effects of other varieties of drugs which have been used in efforts to treat the cognitive deficits of the elderly.

Miscellaneous Drug Treatments in Senile Dementia

A wide variety of drug treatments have been tried in the treatment of cognitive and behavioural disorders which are associated with the progressive brain degeneration in senile dementia. The treatments have been reviewed recently (Funkenstein, Hicks, Dysken and Davis, 1981; McDonald, 1982; Reisberg, Ferris and Gershon, 1981), and therefore only brief mention of some compounds will be made here.

Dehydroergotoxin (*Hydergine*) is a mixture of ergot alkaloids (dihydroergocristine mesylate, dihydroergokriptine mesylate, and dihydroergocornine mesylate). It is thought to be the most frequently prescribed drug for the treatment of senile dementia. Improvements have been observed with hydergine treatment in cases of senile dementia, but the mechanism of action remains unresolved. It is not clear whether improvements are primarily cognitive, or whether the hydergine treatment produces improvements in mood as a consequence of reducing anxiety and/or depression, which affect elderly demented patients.

Gerovital H3 is a solution which was developed by Dr Anna Aslan in Rumania. Its primary active ingredient is procaine hydrochloride. There is little evidence that the treatment confers any benefit on senile patients. What improvements there are may be due to improvements in mood, rather than in cognitive functioning.

Piracetam has been reported to have effects in both animal and human studies. Platel and Porsolt (1982) used the habituation of exploratory activity in mice as a screening test to detect memory-enhancing drugs. They advanced evidence that piracetam, among several other compounds used clinically to treat geriatric patients, may help enhance memory in the behavioural tests which they employed. Dimond and Brouwers (1976) reported that 14 days of treatment with piracetam in young normal volunteer subjects produced some improvement, compared with placebo treatment, in a verbal learning task. Piracetam has also been shown to have some beneficial effects in healthy ageing individuals (aged 50 years or more), in a variety of perceptual-motor tasks (Mindus, Cronholm, Levander and Schalling, 1976). However, no significant effects of piracetam treatment were found by Gustafson and colleagues, who administered the drug to a series of nine elderly patients, who displayed symptoms of mild to moderate dementia (Gustafson, Risberg, Johanson, Fransson and Maximilian, 1978).

A major problem in understanding the effects of piracetam on cognitive and other mental functions is that little is known about its physiological effects in the brain. A recent electrophysiological study has shown that piracetam increases the response of neurones within the hippocampus (Olpe and Lynch, 1982). Although this is an interesting finding, its relationship to any therapeutic effect of piracetam in geriatric patients is quite unclear.

Conclusions

Currently, there is little or no conclusive evidence which identifies particular neurotransmitters or particular neurones in relation to memory processes. There is consistent, suggestive evidence, however, from animal and human experimental studies that (i) facilitating cholinergic neurotransmission with drugs can lead to some improvement

in learning and memory, and (ii) impeding cholinergic neurotransmission with drugs can result in some amnesia. The level of activity
at cholinergic synapses may therefore be an important aspect of learning and memory processes. This statement has to be qualified, however,
since (i) we do not know if all or only a proportion of cholinergic
neurones are involved (ACh is distributed widely throughout the brain),
and (ii) there is no strong conclusion that can be drawn to relate
cholinergic activity to one or several of many stages or levels of processing which are believed to be involved in what we describe, in a global
fashion, as memory.

It is now recognised that in Alzheimer's disease and in related
conditions in the elderly, there is a selective loss of cholinergic neurones
in the brain. In the early stages of these progressive illnesses, impairments in memory are commonly detectable. It is hypothesised that
the loss of cholinergic neurones may be responsible in some measure
for the deteriorating memory functions. Direct evidence on this critical
point is required. If the degeneration of cholinergic neurones is prevent-
able, or may be arrested, and ideally, reversed, then the progressive
loss of memory, intellectual capacity and self-care in elderly patients
who suffer dementia may be held in check.

List of Drug Names

Chemical Name	*Proprietary (Trade) Name*
acetylcholine	Miochol
dihydroergotoxin	Hydergine
hyoscine ⎱ scopolamine ⎰	Pamine
physostigmine	Antilirium
piracetam	Nootropil

8 MANAGEMENT OF ATTENTION DISORDERS FOLLOWING BRAIN INJURY

Rodger Ll. Wood

Introduction

The emphasis on memory impairment following brain injury has possibly obscured the effect that such injuries have on attention and speed of information processing (Newcombe and Artiola i Fortuny, 1979). This is beginning to be remedied. Many clinical studies of closed head injury are extending their investigation of memory disorder to include the related problems of attentional control (Newcombe, 1982). This is an important area of study because patients with even mild and moderate injuries experience problems of concentration or speed of information processing which continue for months and sometimes years after injury (Russell and Smith, 1961; Miller, 1970; Van Zomeren and Deelman, 1978). Attentional deficits can exist when there is no measurable memory impairment, and evidence is beginning to implicate attentional variables in disorders of memory and learning following brain injury (Wood and Eames, 1981; Oakley, 1983).

Attention disorders following brain injury have been commented on since the beginning of this century. Meyer (1904) made reference to the difficulty that many traumatically brain-injured patients have in concentrating, even during simple and interesting activities. The problem was also mentioned by Conkey (1938) who described the poor performance of head-injured patients on tasks measuring concentration and focused attention. Goldstein (1939) also suggested that one of the most characteristic features of the 'brain damage syndrome' was a 'forced responsiveness' to stimuli. He thought that the patient's difficulty in concentrating on a task was due to involuntary attentiveness to other, non-essential, information available at the same time. Similar comments were made by Ruesch (1944) and Dencker and Lofving (1958) during observation of patients performing psychological tests. This, in effect, conforms to what McGhie (1969) describes as the most common form of attention deficit to be associated with brain damage, 'the failure of the normal inhibitory process resulting in distractibility'. This results in patients being unable to focus their attention on a particular stimulus because they are distracted by a 'forced responsiveness' to external noises or any other event which would usually be ignored. More recently this problem has been recognised by Ben-Yishay, Rattok and Diller (1979), who refer to disturbances of concentration which they describe as 'impersistence', the inability to sustain focused attention long enough to complete even simple perceptual or motor tasks.

Given the apparent inportance and pervasiveness of this problem, there is little in the clinical psychology literature that offers help for those therapists faced with the rehabilitation of a patient with this kind of disturbance. This may be because of the confusion regarding the concept or mechanism of attention. Until recently there was not even an acceptable model of attention, and even when one did emerge it aroused much controversy and theoretical debate. Moray (1969) stated that the terminology relating to attention was 'at best confusing, and at worst a mess'. There is, however, some consensus about three components of attention: alertness, selectivity and effort (Posner, 1975; McGuinness and Pribram, 1980).

Alertness

In one sense, attention refers to a state of alertness or arousal which allows us to recognise that information is present and direct our attention towards it. Sokolov (1963) described this as an orienting response. Alertness refers to a fluctuating condition of the central nervous system which may vary from a low level during sleep to a high level during wakefulness. Changes in alertness affect our performance on a variety of tasks. It can be measured by changes in the electrophysiological state of the brain and thus has become an area of study dominated by the psycho-physiologists (Elliot, 1969; Lacey and Lacey, 1970) and as such is clearly outside the scope of this chapter. It is important to recognise, however, that this aspect of attention is probably related to an important characteristic of motivated behaviour described as *drive*. The mechanism of this is not clearly understood, but it would appear to be related to the effort component of attention, which will be referred to later. (For a more detailed discussion, refer to Eames and Wood, 1983.)

Selectivity

Selective attention refers to the process of choosing some item of information from the environment in preference to others. Selected items are more likely to affect our awareness, memory or behaviour than non-selected items which may be present at the same time. This aspect of attention was originally described by William James (1890) who made the by now almost immortal comment 'Everyone knows what attention is.' He described it as 'taking possession by the mind, in a clear and simple form, one out of what seems to be several simultaneously possible objects or trains of thought'. In saying this, James opened the door for studies on selective attention which have preoccupied academic research on human attention ever since (McGuinness and Pribram, 1980; Stevens, 1981). Although James explained a number of attention characteristics, including the behavioural manifestations of attention, he never quite solved the problem concerning the mechanics of attention, especially its controlling process. This probably led to the study of attention being rejected by behavioural psychology in the late 1930s, which regarded it as too mentalistic a concept to be worthy of scientific research.

Research into psychological aspects of selective attention was ironically revived by the behaviourists themselves, when experimenters were forced to admit the importance of attention when animals were found to notice some stimuli but ignore others, in studies, for example, of cue sampling and discrimination learning (Trabasso and Bower, 1968; Honig, 1969). Data suggesting the presence of attentional variables were explained in terms of cue salience, assuming that particular stimulus parameters were more noticeable or meaningful to the animal than others. This led to other studies on attention and learning, one of the most notable in this context being that dealing with attention and learning in the mentally handicapped (Zeaman and House, 1963).

Effort

The final aspect of attention involves the conscious effort that one gives to monitoring a stimulus. This implies a control process (Stevens, 1981; McGuinness and Pribram, 1980) that co-ordinates alertness, arousal and selectivity to direct attention towards significant features of the environment. Van Zomeren and Deelman (1978) describe this aspect of attention as 'tonic alertness', a continuing receptivity to stimulation extending over minutes or hours. The lay person would describe this aspect of attention as 'concentration' and as such it is clearly a very important component of attention and vital to the learning process. It is this aspect of attention that appears particularly vulnerable to the effects of brain injury, because patients characteristically describe difficulties of concentration. In addition, many demonstrate distractability by frequently diverting their attention from a training task towards some other stimulus within their environment.

Attention and Memory

The memory system can be divided into three storage structures, each of which deals with a different stage of information processing. The first stage has been described as the 'sensory register' because of the way information enters the system (by one or more of the five senses). Information is held in this structure in sensory form (for example, visual information is stored according to sensory characteristics such as lightness or hue) but only for very short periods of time. While it is there, a process of pattern recognition takes place whereby the sensory characteristics of the information are compared to previously acquired knowledge and some meaning is given to the stimulus.

Pattern recognition is a way of encoding sensory information so that it can be passed to the second of the storage structures – short-term memory. Information stored here has some meaning to the system and can be prevented from fading by a process of rehearsal. This allows information to be held in temporary storage while its value is being assessed to determine whether further processing is necessary. Only a limited amount of information can be held in this system at any given time before overloading occurs, and items become lost (forgotten). It is likely that as a result of brain injury the capacity of this system is reduced.

The third storage structure is long-term memory. This has been described as a depository for vast amounts of information, stored permanently as part of our knowledge about the world. It appears that long-term memory is more than just a passive information store, because its existence is crucial to earlier processing of information (for example, it is necessary to be able to recognise a stimulus as familiar or important in the first place), as well as forming part of later processing when meaning is given to sensory information. This memory process appears least affected by brain injury because even the most severe amnesics are capable of recognising information as being meaningful, even if they are unable to maintain a record of what it is they have processed.

Two features of this processing system are important if we are to understand the role of attention in memory. The first is that throughout the system information is being *controlled*, passing from one stage of processing to another in an organised way (Atkinson and Shiffrin, 1968). The other feature involves the *limitation* imposed on the system, either affecting the *time* information can be retained or the *amount* which can be stored. The limited capacity of the system demands that the flow of information is controlled, making both processes important characteristics of the attentional process.

When describing memory in this way, two concepts become apparent. One is the idea of memory *structures*, which have been described as storehouses of information. The other describes *processes* (for example, pattern recognition or rehearsal), which help to channel information between structures and which play an important role in the retrieval of such information. Attention exerts its effects on the *processes* of memory rather than the structures. This illustrates the importance of understanding the attentional aspects of memory because memory impairment – the failure to retrieve information – is assumed not to result from damage to the structures themselves (probably because they don't exist as such and are no more than hypothetical constructs of memory) but as a result of damage to the memory processing system.

Some support could be given to this theory by recognising that impairment of memory usually affects short-term capacity rather than the sensory register or long-term memory. This could result from the fact that more processing of information takes place at this stage (for example, giving meaning to the pattern recognition process, rehearsing information to prevent decay, and allowing further processing), all of which require considerable control and a degree of conscious effort. Possibly this is why Baddeley and Hitch (1974) referred to this stage as 'working memory', a term which reflects what we are immediately thinking about or working on. An impairment of attention would have an even greater effect if one accepted the Craik and Lockhart (1972) information processing approach to memory in which there are no structures as such, but instead there are different stages (called levels) of memory coding which rely on processes such as pattern recognition and rehearsal. It assumes that the more the information is processed the better the memory, mainly because semantic associations can be formed, which give the information greater meaning (depth of processing), thereby aiding retrieval. If the processing capacity of this system should become impaired, then information within it will not only be less well organised, but will also be more superficial (because of impaired processing capacity) and therefore more vulnerable to interference and forgetting.

Disorders of Attention, Memory and Behaviour

The effect of an attentional deficit can best be understood within the context of the two modes of information processing proposed by Shiffrin and Schneider (1977). They described an attention-dependent form of *controlled* processing, and a relatively attention-independent procedure called *automatic* processing. Controlled processing is required when a person has to cope with new information. It is a very conscious mode of processing which is limited in its capacity, mainly because of the attentional requirements of the situation. When learning a new task, an individual must focus full attention on the procedure involved to allow the most efficient information processing for learning to occur. This process will continue until the response is learnt, and with repetition of that response less attention is needed, until in the end even quite a complex response (for example, driving a motor car) can be made in an almost automatic way. Automatic processing therefore occurs without conscious control, and proceeds without stretching the capacity of the information processing system. Because little attention is given in the automatic mode, it allows an individual to expand his processing capacities. When, for example, one has learned to drive, it is possible to both drive and listen to the radio at the same time, whereas before driving proficiency has been attained, the radio would have been an unwelcome distraction in the learning process.

Observations of a patient's behaviour following severe brain injury suggest that many automatic skills have been impaired, forcing the patient to revert back to a more conscious, controlled form of information processing. This is illustrated when brain injury disrupts walking ability due to damage to the sensory motor cortex. When this happens, a previously over-learned and automatic skill becomes impaired, with the result that the patient must attend to many of the basic functions involved in walking (for example, joint position, limb placement and balance). Suddenly the fluent and effortless procedure becomes a process which is slow, hesitant, and requires focused attention to achieve control and co-ordination of movement.

In this shift from automatic to controlled processing, a brain-injured patient is ironically forced to use those aspects of cognitive ability which rely on attention and which are almost certainly damaged as a result of the injury. Consequently, thinking becomes slow and often concrete in nature, lacking the acuity and flexibility needed to rapidly adjust ideas and behaviour to changing environmental situations. Concentration is affected, and individuals find that they are unable to do many things which before their injury were carried out in an almost effortless manner.

Two basic forms of attentional disorder are revealed in this situation. One has been described as a 'focused attentional deficit' (FAD) which occurs when an automatic response is replaced by a controlled response (the above example of learning to walk illustrates an FAD). The other disorder of attention recognised by Shiffrin and Schneider (1977) is described as a 'divided attentional deficit' (DAD) which occurs when controlled processing is in use and where the limitations of the system fail to accommodate all the information necessary for optimal task performance. Deficits of this kind are common in everyday life. Van Zomeren (1981) gives an example of a DAD experienced when one has to cope with a variety of new information that might occur if one asked a stranger the way to an address in an unfamiliar part of town. The complicated list of instructions is more than most people can process within a specified time and, inevitably, in such situations one is left having to repeat the request for directions further down the road. This particular deficit probably explains why, for example, brain-injured patients are unable to cope with more than one or two items of information on a shopping list. Many patients who complain of a memory impairment affecting day-to-day behaviour describe the frustration of going to the corner shop for several items, but only being able to remember one or two because they do not have the memory (attention) span to be able to cope with more information. This can effectively be explained as a divided attentional deficit (see Eames and Wood, 1983).

In support of this divided attentional deficit Miller (1970) showed how the more alternatives a patient has to respond to, the slower and more unreliable his response will be. Miller felt that the effect of a head injury must be to slow down decision-making and therefore information processing, a conclusion later reached by Gronwall and Sampson (1974) and Van Zomeren and Deelman (1976). This latter study found that the amount by which the rate of information processing was slowed down was proportional to the length of coma after injury.

Reason (1979) also provides an explanation of the kind of errors we make in our day-to-day behaviour. This parallels many of the ideas proposed by Shriffin and Schneider (1977) and appears to explain well the difficulties presented by the head-injured patient. Reason describes the different levels of conscious control necessary for different behaviour. During the learning phase of an activity, the unskilled person relies heavily on the feedback available from a task and therefore consciously attends to the activity (controlled processing). Once the action is learned, the individual's performance is controlled by a series of 'pre-arranged instruction sequences' that act independently of feedback information (automatic processing), thus leaving the individual free to concentrate on other aspects of the same or different tasks. Reason suggests that 'critical decision points' occur, even in familiar and well-practised activities. If such a point occurs when actions or situations are common to two or more behaviours, then failure to attend correctly to the behavioural alternatives may result in a completely inappropriate behaviour occurring. The level of complexity of a particular behaviour and the predictability of the environment will influence the frequency with which these 'attentional switches' need to occur.

Attentional Retraining Procedures

The rest of this chapter contains various ideas and suggestions for developing attentional training programmes. The rationale for these programmes is based on experience with severely brain-injured patients, most of whom have attentional problems which interfere with their ability to learn skills, remember information or behave in a co-operative and attentive way during attempts at rehabilitative therapy. The reader must not expect to find details of a well establishing training procedure. Attentional training requires from the therapist/practitioner a degree of ingenuity, as well as a reasonable knowledge of the role that the information processing system plays in memory and behaviour at all cognitive levels.

The importance of attention training is threefold. First, it is important to realise that unless the patient has an efficient processing system, life events of any kind are not going to be reliably processed to the point where one can say they have become established in memory. This means that memory training methods may be rendered useless if patients whose recall ability one is trying to improve have an attentional problem which makes it difficult for them to register sufficient information to form a meaningful 'memory trace' in the first place.

Secondly, there are many behavioural characteristics of attention that are important to memory and learning, which may not be included in a memory retraining procedure. Short attention span and distractability are not uncommon sequelae following severe brain injury, and these produce behavioural changes which make such patients difficult to work with in *any* retraining context that requires concentration, co-operation and participation. It may be necessary, therefore, to deal with these aspects of attentionally-controlled behaviour first, before proceeding to other aspects of cognitive rehabilitation.

Finally, however imprecise, primitive or unorthodox these initial ideas and techniques may seem, they still serve to illustrate a significant problem in rehabilitation, and provide a platform from which better ideas can be developed. A lot of work still needs to be done to produce the carefully controlled studies that will show the clinical and social relevance of cognitive training generally and attentional training in particular. Such work needs to be linked to an acceptable rationale or underlying theory of attention, to provide a reasonably solid foundation for studies which aim to determine the clinical effectiveness of such procedures.

General Considerations

Recording Improvements

(i) Baseline Measures. Before beginning any retraining procedure it is necessary to establish a reliable baseline (Hersen and Barlow, 1976). This in effect will describe the level of performance that the patient *usually* achieves on a day-to-day basis. This not only provides an index for future improvement of specific abilities, but also allows the therapist to establish a level of task complexity with which the patient can be expected to cope, and thereby avoids the possibility of either ceiling or floor effects in a measure of their performance.

(ii) Behaviour Change. It is necessary to remember that our appreciation of a patient's attention difficulties is derived mainly from observations of behaviour within a situation that requires good attention. These behavioural observations may be substantiated by the patient's performance on tasks designed to measure aspects of attentional ability. This suggests that we should orientate our training procedures towards

the behavioural manifestations of attention and look for improvements within the behavioural repertoire of a patient.

(iii) Outcome Measures. It is of little value improving a patient's ability to perform well on measures of some attentional skill if such patients are not able to utilise that skill in the execution of some aspects of daily behaviour. This means that any training programme must contain outcome measures which are related to, but independent of, the actual training programme. These will include:

(a) A measure of improvement on the attentional retraining tasks themselves.
(b) Improvement in attentional performance on tasks similar to, but not included in, the training procedure.
(c) A record of observable behaviour change, especially those behaviours that are related to attention and concentration.

Feedback of Results

Attention training tasks may often be stereotyped or repetitive, and therefore essentially boring. This makes it important to maintain the patient's co-operation and motivation to participate, so reinforcement of some kind may be necessary. For those individuals with only subtle information processing problems, feedback of results, showing improvement in task performance, may be enough. The more severely injured patient who demonstrates behaviour as well as attention problems, may require more frequent feedback of performance which may need to be linked to some tangible reward (chocolate, drinks, cigarettes, etc.).

Time on Task Difficulties

Patients will vary according to the length of time they are able to co-operate with any retraining activity and in the level of complexity with which they are able to cope. Some patients are able to participate for 30 minutes or more, while others will be exhausted after 15 minutes. Reliable baseline recordings should give the therapist an indication of a patient's ability and stamina for this kind of activity, thereby allowing realistic levels of task difficulty to be established from the beginning of training. If the patient's performance improves, the therapist is then presented with two opportunities for increasing task difficulty. First, the *duration* of the task can be extended, requiring attention to be sustained for longer periods. Secondly, the task could be made more *complicated* by speeding up the required response time, or introducing more, less or different attention cues into the training procedure. This allows alterations to be made to the attention training programme, which accommodate any changes in the patient's performance as the training progresses, while avoiding the need to have a vast array of alternative training procedures.

Multi-systems Approach

The success of an attention training programme depends on how appropriate the training procedure is to the particular kind of attention deficit.

This requires the therapist to remember that attention is not a unitary concept. Attention strategies may vary according to the stage of information processing as well as the type of information being processed. It is not necessarily the case that someone who is being trained on an attention task in the visual modality will experience a generalised improvement that transfers to the auditory modality. This means that a training procedure must be modality-specific and also, to some extent, strategy-specific. For example, a task designed to improve sustained attention will not necessarily include many of the responses required for a selective attention training procedure.

To obtain the best results from attention training, therapists should first direct themselves to assessing, as accurately as possible, the nature of the attention deficit before selecting a training procedure. In broad (simple) terms, the various attention processes which offer themselves to a training approach can be described as follows:

(i) Sustained Attention/Vigilance. Training a patient to maintain an attentional set allows him to focus concentration for longer periods; helps reduce the effects of distractability and short attention span; improves concentration during therapy sessions; and provides the patient with better opportunity to learn new techniques. It is important to provide vigilance training in both the visual and auditory modalities. Initially, each modality should be trained separately, but when task performance has improved to some acceptable level, it may be useful to combine the auditory and visual tasks so that the patient has to respond to both task requirements at the same time. This has a logical basis, because social behaviour is (at least) 'bi-modal'. We are often required to respond to both visual and verbal cues, presented

simultaneously (for example, when a person emphasises a certain phrase both with verbal expression and with gesture).

Auditory vigilance training is an important aspect of verbal information processing and verbal memory functioning. Patients with attention difficulties often appear to be listening to verbal instructions, but if asked to repeat them either they appear to have forgotten what was said, or get the information mixed up, making it difficult to understand or communicate with another person. Visual aspects of attention, on the other hand, are also very important during a rehabilitation programme. The ability to discriminate between relevant and irrelevant items of a task, or the visual scanning which aids the perception of environmental cues, are vital factors in visual information processing and various kinds of occupational performance (for example, the ability to monitor the workings of a machine, read dials and gauges on an instrument panel, or even monitor changing road conditions).

(ii) Selective Attention. Once a patient is able to sustain an attentional set long enough to monitor information reliably, it becomes important to improve the efficiency by which one can discriminate between useful, important or unimportant stimuli. This is necessary not only in visual attention, when one is expected to select from an array of environmental cues those which are important to current behaviour, but also with regard to memory functioning, because during the processing of information we have to select and rehearse certain information which prevents information overload and improves recall capabilities.

As yet there is little hard evidence to implicate selective attentional deficits following head injury. However, the procedure involved in training this important attention characteristic has potential benefits for many aspects of cognitive ability. At the behavioural level at least, many patients seem unable to select efficiently from their environment those features which are important in the control or adaptation of behaviour. It also seems that within specific learning tasks, some patients have difficulty in recognising the salient aspects of a learning procedure, and take longer to learn as a consequence.

(iii) Sequential Attention. It is often necessary to remember information in some prescribed order. This may be regarded as a form of temporal memory: the ability to remember not only that a number of events has taken place, but to fix those events in time and in some kind of logical order. Similarly, when asked to remember a piece of

information, it is necessary to store the material in a meaningful way, which again requires some kind of sequential processing and ordering of data.

Psychological assessment of memory often reveals a disparity between that amount of information patients with brain injuries recall, and the sensible *organisation* of that information. The 'Anna Thompson Study' of the Wechsler Memory Scale provides an example of this. Many patients may recall an average number of information units, but these sometimes seem to have been plucked randomly from memory, and the order in which the information is retrieved bears little resemblance to the story as it was originally told. Similarly, the free recall of a word list may show that such patients are not conforming to the 'primacy-recency' effect which is usual in the free recall situation, whereby items are recalled mainly from the beginning and end of the word list. Rather, these patients will provide words from anywhere within the list, not necessarily the beginning or end. If the list is presented on repeated occasions, this random selection from memory appears to continue, and patients fail to establish a platform of words remembered at the beginning or end of the list, using that to cue the recall of other words which have semantic similarity, or which are next to them within the list. Improving this aspect of information processing might, for example, improve memory for verbal instructions, or the ability to operate machines in which controls have to be moved in some prescribed order.

(iv) Speed of Information Processing. Speed of response is not in itself an attentional strategy, but it is important for efficient processing (see Ben-Yishay *et al.*, 1979). The speed with which we are able to respond to events within our environment is critical to our safety or the kind of job we are able to do. Driving a car safely requires fast, reliable processing of many aspects of information. An element of controlled information processing is always present, and there are a number of critical decision points which must be observed. Clearly, in determining an individual's functional level, it is not only the efficiency of attentional control which is important, but also the speed at which a response can be executed, acting on available information. This is an important variable in attentional training since speed of information processing is often significantly affected by brain injury.

Methods of Retraining

Vigilance Training. Vigilance is a procedure which requires a person to monitor a stimulus array and respond to changes that have a predetermined significance. It is a function which involves selective and sustained attention, and is therefore important to many occupational skills, and one which appears to be particularly vulnerable to severe brain injury.

Auditory Vigilance. The task used by Claridge (1967) to study attention in schizophrenia is a useful procedure which can be adopted for vigilance training. It requires the patient to monitor, with the aid of earphones, a random series of numbers, recorded on cassette tape and presented at the rate of one per second. The 'target' is a sequence of three odd numbers. Patients are required to monitor the sequence of random numbers, and to make a response (tap the top of the table) each time a target sequence occurs. The procedure differs from that used by Claridge in that the number sequence lasts for only 15 minutes during the early stages of training, whereas Claridge's original task lasted at least one hour. Also, the number of targets in any sequence can be varied to provide a high or low event target ratio as required. The duration of the task can be increased as the patient's level of performance improves, allowing the therapist to measure any decrement in performance over the time period of the task.

Variations on this theme are possible for patients who have language or intellectual problems and who would not be able to understand odd and even numbers. In such cases the task could be adapted to include a sequence of auditory tones. A series of tones could be presented which range from, for example, 20 to 30 Db. At random intervals, a target tone of 35 or 40 Db could be included, to which the patient has to respond. When training sustained attention in the visual modality, a sequence of light flashes could be used, with a target flash differing in the brightness level from the other flashes in the series. Task difficulty can be increased by altering the speed at which individual stimuli are presented, or by varying the similarity between the target and non-target stimuli.

Another vigilance procedure that can be applied is the dichotic listening task. This procedure presents two sets of information to an individual at the same time. The basic method is to present one set of information to the left ear and another set of information to the right ear. The subject is then asked to 'shadow' the information reaching one ear whilst ignoring whatever information is being fed into the other ear. During this procedure, the subject may be asked to switch attention from the left ear to the right, thereby inhibiting a previously established source of information in order to concentrate on new information. Various forms of this method have been developed to investigate different aspects of attentional functioning, and most are appropriate for retraining purposes. For a more detailed description, see Cherry (1953). Research with the dichotic listening procedure has established that the timing of the information presented to each ear is critical, and that the subject matter and relationship between the material presented to each ear are also important. It is therefore advisable to obtain a tape recording which has been carefully constructed, rather than attempt to make a recording using sophisticated equipment and materials. Suitable tape recordings could probably be obtained from university psychology departments.

Visual Vigilance. A particularly good piece of equipment for training visual aspects of vigilance and attention is the Possum Basic Skills Trainer. This was developed for use mainly as a teaching aid for mentally handicapped patients with problems of communication. The patient is required to sit in front of a panel on which is placed a transparency containing 32 symbols divided into two 16-cell matrices. The matrix on the left hand side of the panel contains a different symbol in each cell, while the matrix on the right hand side of the panel has the same 16 symbols, but distributed differently throughout the matrix. A reference symbol in one of the cells of the left hand matrix is illuminated, and the patient is required to move a scanning light along the rows or down columns of the right hand matrix until they locate a symbol which matches that illuminated on the left hand matrix. The patient records a hit by pressing a button as soon as the scanning light reaches the target symbol. The apparatus provides a tune if the response is correct, and a 'raspberry' if it is not. The stimulus on the left hand side of the screen will only advance after a correct match. If an incorrect match is made, then the same stimulus remains illuminated and the patient has to repeat the procedure.

Various errors can be made during this task. The patient can record a 'column miss' by allowing the scanning light to move past the column which contains a matching symbol. Alternatively, a 'symbol miss' could occur if the patient, having moved the scanning light into the correct column, fails to stop it over the matching symbol. Task complexity can be varied by speeding up or slowing down the movement of the scanning light, or by making the discrimination between the symbols on the left and right hand side of the matrix panels more difficult.

Although this piece of equipment was not designed to fulfil the purpose of attentional training, it does possess four important attentional training characteristics which are known to be impaired in some way following severe brain injury. These are:

(a) Visual Scanning. Monitoring the moving light and comparing the reference symbol to the target symbol requires an organised form of visual scanning and improves perception of the visual field.

(b) Perceptual Matching. This improves aspects of visual discrimination.

(c) Decision Making. Depending on the speed of movement of the scanning light, the patient has to anticipate the appropriate time to press the button to stop or redirect the movement of the scanning light. Speed of decision-making is directly related to the speed at which the scanning light moves across the matrix. Either a premature or a delayed response will result in a target miss and a lost opportunity to earn reinforcement.

(d) Motor Reaction Time. Once a decision has been made regarding the estimated speed of movement of the scanning light, the patient must still implement the motor response to complete the procedure successfully.

The above techniques can either be used singularly or in conjunction with each other. One of the auditory tasks described could be used concurrently with the predominantly visual processing task presented by the Possum Basic Skills Trainer. This means that the patient must respond to the visual and motor requirements of the Possum while maintaining auditory attention to the other vigilance task. This calls for divided attention and increases the amount of controlled processing necessary to avoid errors. The demands of this *combined* task are considerable for the brain-injured patient, but if used appropriately (for example, towards the end of a retraining programme to integrate the attentional cues and increase task difficulties), the technique could prove most effective and improve many attentional characteristics necessary on tasks where different sources or different kinds of information have to be monitored.

Maze Learning. Another task which has attentional characteristics and appears to be appropriate for training sequential attention is maze learning. Here, the individual is required to retain an idea of a route involving a number of changes of direction. The information must be remembered in an ordered way to achieve an error-free run through the maze. This means that the patient must retain in primary memory either a visual picture of the movement of a stylus along the maze pathway, or a series of verbal cues indicating the route — for example, 'second left, third right', etc. We have constructed an electrical maze which contains 100 studs in a 10 x 10 matrix. The correct points along the maze are attached to an electrical circuit. If the patient makes a correct response (for example, touching a live stud with the stylus), a circuit is completed and the patient receives feedback on his correct response by means of a buzzer. An error response is met with no auditory feedback. To complete the task successfully the patient is required to make two error-free runs through the maze. If an error is made, then the patient has to return to his previously correct point on the route and try again. The length of the route can be increased simply by including more points on the circuit. The route can be varied simply by altering the circuit connectors at the rear of each stud position.

Memory Span. Training in serial memory skills is a way of improving the verbal aspects of sequential attention. This effectively means attempting to increase the patient's span of attention, thus enabling more information to be held at any given time and thereby overcoming, to some extent, the limitations on information processing in the controlled attentional mode and allowing more effective 'chunking' of information (see Miller, 1956). To do this, one must first allow the patient to consolidate his information processing at some level. When this is achieved, another unit of information can be added, and so on until the patient's span increases to a level appropriate to the information processing requirement of the situation.

Memory span training could involve remembering numbers or letters in a prescribed order, progressing on to word span tasks, using words that can be arranged into sentences of varying lengths and complexity. Gradually the sentences could be arranged so that, if put together in the order presented, they form a short story. This might help with aspects of verbal information processing of a kind that is involved in the registration and recall of verbally presented instructions, or the content of lessons at school.

Computers and Training

Video games and home computers have begun to revolutionise many aspects of learning. Succesful performance on most of these games, whether space invaders or computer chess, requires many of the cognitive functions that are disrupted following a brain injury. Intense concentration, visual scanning, planning, judgement, anticipation and motor responses are obvious abilities necessary for good performance on most of these games. As such, they are a useful way of helping patients to improve decision-making strategies, sustaining attention and utilising information from short-term memory stores.

There are obvious advantages in the use of such games as a form of therapy in a controlled clinical situation. First, they are easy to administer and represent an available source of technological hardware to those therapists who do not have the resources or the aptitude for developing their own training technique. One does not have to think very hard to see how different games can be used to exercise different cognitive skills involving attention and memory. Secondly, the wide range of games available means that one can develop a cognitive training library, buying those games most appropriate for the major problems in cognitive rehabilitation. Thirdly, and most importantly, patients enjoy these games: this is a considerable advantage because it overcomes problems of motivation frequently found with this group of patients (Field, 1976) and helps to improve skills, often without the patient being aware of it.

There is a good supply of video computer programmes currently on the domestic market. The Atari programmes contain useful retraining techniques for clinical purposes; the 'brain games' cassette is particularly appropriate as this has a variety of games, one of which involves auditory and visual cueing of spatial and sequential memory. It has two levels of difficulty, using either six or nine empty rectangles. The game begins when the word 'touch' appears in one of the rectangles, paired with a tone of a certain pitch. The player must indicate correctly the corresponding location on the keyboard. As long as the player is correct, the computer will add an additional location-tone pair, up to a maximum of 32. The game can be played with or without the tone by turning down the sound on the TV receiver.

Another task on this cassette involves visuo-spatial memory for the location of different designs. Four designs are shown, arranged vertically, with or without auditory distraction (white noise). After viewing them briefly, the player is presented with the designs in a different position on the screen and in a mixed-up order. The player must then recall the correct order and reproduce it.

This cassette also includes an addition task and a digit span task, again at different levels of complexity, which are valuable information processing exercises. The other, more popular, target games like space invaders, asteroids, etc. all involve co-ordination of visual and motor input as well as spatial and temporal estimations. These games are useful for training eye-hand co-ordination, motor reaction time, decision time, impulsivity, judgement, and an appreciation of consequences.

The problems surrounding these procedures are not insignificant, and their use in cognitive retraining is not clear. The main problem is that these games are designed for entertainment, not therapy. They are not always easy to score in a way that is meaningful to the therapist, who may wish to know the kind of progress a patient is making. Normal individuals may more than treble their score after a few hours playing space invaders, but as yet there is little hard evidence that such performance generalises to other behavioural or cognitive areas. Work being carried out in America does suggest that this is occurring (Lynch, 1982; Trexler, 1982), but results from a carefully controlled study using outcome measures are yet to be obtained. There is also a problem in knowing what particular cognitive function one is trying to train. Most games involve a multiplicity of skills, making it impossible to state with any confidence that a particular task is having a specific effect on any individual cognitive process. There is also the problem of establishing task difficulty when isolating and training a particular skill.

For a more varied approach and the opportunity to learn how to design one's own training programme, it is better to obtain a mini computer rather than opting for video games. A wide range of home computers are currently available, and most have a range of useful games and educational programmes which are likely to benefit patients with concentration problems. They allow therapists to develop their own programmes to suit specific treatment problems, and accommodate patients who have physical and psychological handicaps.

We are currently developing programmes that fulfil most requirements for effective attention and serial memory training, and anticipate that before long we will have a catalogue of computer tasks that will fulfil the requirements of most forms of neuropsychological training. Home-made programmes are usually more effective in that they incorporate automatic scoring techniques and allow task difficulty to be varied in several different ways (for example, altering the speed of presentation; variety of stimuli; different response options, etc.). As such, these tasks suit nearly all patients because they can be set at a level which accommodates their particular ability. There is some evidence that such procedures are improving cognitive skills in patients who are well out of the period when spontaneous improvement could be expected (Bracy, 1983).

Behaviour Training

Possibly the most effective, least technological and therefore easiest attentional training procedure is that offered by behaviour learning. Since the early 1960s psychologists have been using behavioural methods to increase attention span in normal and hyperkinetic children. Staats *et al.* (1964) and Staats (1965) showed how failing to provide adequate incentives often leads to the erroneous conclusion that some children have basic deficits in cognitive ability, such as short attention span or low frustration thresholds. Wood and Eames (1981) and Oakley (1983) also pointed out the importance of attentional variables in behavioural learning and rehabilitation because those patients who were seen to make a poor response to rehabilitation were generally found to have important attention deficits which prevented them from giving adequate co-operation in therapy sessions. The studies by Staats and his colleagues on four-year-old children who were having difficulty in learning to read due to short attention span and poor co-operation showed that their attention span could be increased from 15 to 45 minutes simply by linking their performance to some form of meaningful reward. They suggest that, if given the right sort of incentive, even very young children will engage in complex learning activities with sustained interest and attention.

Levin and Simmonds (1962) and Martin and Powers (1967) showed that the attention span of brain damaged and retarded children could be significantly increased by creating favourable incentive conditions. The same results have been obtained with brain-injured adults (Wood, 1983a). Patients who show short attention span respond to reinforcement procedures where rewards are given in proportion to the amount of time spent attending to task. The graph below illustrates this point in a patient whose level of co-operation and potential for rehabilitation increased in proportion to the amount of time he was able to attend to rehabilitative training.

Attention is very important to most aspects of learning. One of the most influential forms of learning is observational learning (Bandura, 1969). This teaches us most of our social behaviour, helps in the development of language and is the process by which many people

Figure 8.1: Attention to Task Programme

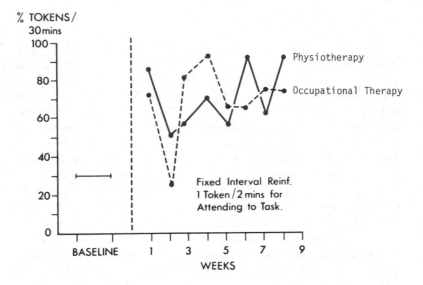

learn manual skills or crafts by seeing them demonstrated. As Bandura stated, however, the individual's capacity for observational learning depends on the ability to receive the stimuli on which to model behaviour. Simply exposing individuals to different kinds of stimuli does not, in itself, guarantee attention to the correct cues or the selection of the most relevant events from the stimulus complex. Bandura regards the use of appropriate reinforcement as important to observational learning, because it allows the therapist to direct the patient's attention to relevant aspects of a learning task, and then reward attention which successfully identified the correct stimulus. He suggests that this will improve not only selective attention, but also aid retention of information by activating deliberate coding and rehearsal strategies of modelled responses that have some general value.

One effective application of behavioural methods in rehabilitation has been via 'Conductive Education' (Cotton, 1965, 1974). This uses a technique developed in Hungary by Professor Andras Peto, based on the work of Pavlov and Luria. It assumes that the optimum conditions for learning include opportunity for a patient to concentrate on a task which is capable of being repeated many times until learning is achieved. So far, it has been applied to children with congenital brain damage who have learning problems because they are unable to focus their concentration in an ordinary classroom environment, often because there are too many distractions. We have found it a very useful procedure in adults with acquired brain damage as a result of trauma or intracranial haemorrhage.

A procedure described as 'Rhythmical Intention' is used, whereby speech is employed both to focus attention and to determine the pattern and speed of various movements involved during activities of daily living. By *verbally* controlling their movements, the patient is able to exclude other (distracting) stimuli and concentrate on the task in hand. It parallels a behavioural procedure because in addition to the emphasis placed on attentional factors in learning, it employs two other important training characteristics:

(i) Shaping behaviours, by breaking each task down into its component parts, which are individually practised until learning has been achieved and the parts can be sequenced together to form a useful behaviour pattern.

(ii) Knowledge of results, which allows the patient to obtain useful feedback about performance in a particular situation.

Summary

This chapter has attempted to introduce a method of cognitive training within the framework of an established theory of information processing, which can be adapted to suit various rehabilitation activities affected by attentional disorders. Recent experience of such training methods (Ben-Yishay *et al.* 1979; Wood, 1983b) suggests that brain-injured patients are able to improve their information processing skills, leading to faster responses, longer periods of concentration, and better selective attention. Such improvements have shown signs of generalising to other aspects of attention-related behaviour not directly included in the training task.

'Attention' tends to be used as an umbrella term, covering many aspects of behaviour and ability. Attention training, however, is likely to use quite specific procedures directed at particular kinds of information processing difficulties. This means that potential therapists should be able to identify different kinds of attention disorder, and apply the type of training programme that is likely to obtain the best results. Eames and Wood (1983) describe how various problems of memory and attention can be construed as information processing deficits or disorders of consciousness. Details of this kind are potentially important to 'cognitive-therapists', who need to expand their knowledge and understanding of the neuropsychological basis of cognitive-behaviour relationships.

Another problem is the lack of correspondence between a patient's complaints of poor concentration and their performance on various psychometric tasks which are assumed to have a large attentional component. So far, few research studies investigating this area have produced hard evidence of attention deficits which can clearly be associated with descriptions given by patients of attention difficulties. As Miller and Cruzat (1981) point out, this is almost certainly a failure of the tests to be sensitive to the kind of problems experienced by patients. This does not mean, however, that because such psychological tests fail to record significant deficits, they are unlikely to be of use in a training capacity: quite the opposite. For example, our experience shows that dichotic listening techniques, while not particularly good for measuring selective attention in the brain injured, are quite useful when applied as training tasks.

Attention, by definition, is a control function which ensures that cognitive processing is directed towards significant features of the environment. This means that attention must utilise information pertinent to our past experience, as well as our motivational and emotional state (Stevens, 1981). A disturbance of attention may have a profound effect on many cognitive functions. It is a central feature of the neuropsychological impairment following severe head injury, and interferes with many aspects of rehabilitative training. The nature of this attentional deficit remains as vague and diffuse as the explanations offered regarding its mechanisms. There is little doubt, however, that an efficient information processing system is an essential prerequisite for many kinds of cognitive retraining. This provides a common-sense argument for improving a patient's ability to cope with the attentional requirements of a task before trying to develop various cognitive strategies that may be important for the implementation of a particular skill.

9 RUNNING A MEMORY GROUP

Barbara Wilson and Nick Moffat

Therapists are invariably short of time and one way of dealing with this situation is to treat people in groups rather than on a one-to-one basis. A more important reason for working with groups rather than individuals is the possibility that memory impaired people may benefit from interaction with others having similar disabilities. Many such people believe they are losing their sanity and this fear may be alleviated by observing that there are others with similar difficulties. Participants in the group may also give advice to each other and may be more likely to use aids or strategies if their peers are doing so. The influence of the peer group on the individual's behaviour is likely to be stronger than the exhortations of the therapist, however well intentioned these may be. It is also true to say that memory groups have face validity: the participants (and their relatives) *believe* such treatment to be effective; and this in itself may have indirect therapeutic value. Furthermore, it is nearly always possible to ensure that each member of the group succeeds at something during a meeting because group therapy provides such a wide range of tasks of varying degrees of difficulty. For people used to failure it is no bad thing to provide some element of success. Finally, memory groups are probably important for the education of the therapists running them — at least in our current state of knowledge. Considerable information can be gained by observing different patients' responses to different strategies: we can note, for instance, which tasks are enjoyed by the group and which are not; and we can record the occurrence of particular problems and subsequently adopt alternative approaches.

This chapter will first describe the two very different memory groups that are run by each of the authors for patients with acquired brain damage. It will then go on to discuss memory therapy groups for the elderly and, in particular, consideration will be given to classroom reality orientation as a possibly effective approach to the problems of the confused elderly. The chapter concludes with a description of the organisation of a memory group and a discussion of ways of evaluating the effectiveness of such a group.

171

The Rivermead Memory Group

This group meets for 45 minutes each day, five days a week for three weeks at a time. Approximately five groups are held each year depending on the numbers of memory impaired patients attending the unit, the needs of these patients, and what competing groups are in operation. It is possible, for example, for a memory impaired patient to be recommended for the wheelchair manoeuvring group, the hydrotherapy group, the hand activities group and the memory group — all running at the same time! Obviously, some sharing out of group activities has to be organised within the unit as a whole.

There are between four and six patients in each memory group, all of whom will have different memory problems, varying degrees of memory impairment and possibly physical and perceptual difficulties too. Those with marked language deficits, however, do not attend. At the end of three weeks the group may continue for a further three weeks but usually there is a break for a post-treatment assessment of each participant. The next group may recommence three or four weeks later or there may be a much longer interval before the next group starts.

Normally each group consists of entirely new members but occasionally one patient may attend more than one memory group. There are always two organisers, the clinical psychologist and a therapist from another discipline, usually from occupational therapy or physiotherapy. On most days both organisers are present although it is not uncommon for one to run the group alone. Visitors are frequent and include students and other staff from the unit, relatives, and professionals from other organisations.

A three-week syllabus from one group is presented for readers to follow or adapt if they wish. There were five members in the group at the time: two men and three women. Four of them had received severe head injuries and one had suffered a sub-arachnoid haemorrhage. The ages ranged from 18 to 53 years. Two were in wheelchairs and two had marked perceptual difficulties. The aim each day was to cover at least one exercise from each of the following categories:

(a)   Memory games, tests, and general stimulation.
(b)   External aids (e.g. notebooks).
(c)   Internal strategies (e.g. visual imagery and first letter cueing).

The equipment used throughout the three-week period comprised: a blackboard, chalk, notebooks, paper, pencils, a piece of card, kitchen timer, electronic aid (a Toshiba memo-note 60), stopwatch, daily newspapers, pictures from magazines, poems, English comprehension exercises, photographs of unfamiliar faces and playing cards.

Day One

(See Chapter 4 for a description of the mnemonic techniques described.)

1. Introductions. The group leader introduces herself and each person in the room.

2. Explanations. The members of the group are informed of the frequency of memory problems after stroke or head injury and it is explained to them that their biggest difficulty is likely to be in learning new things. Such information is felt to be necessary because memory impaired people tend not to realise the extent of their problems, and they commonly make an error of judgement by thinking that their biggest problem is going to be the gap that will exist in their *past* memory.

3. Descriptions. The goals we hope to achieve in the next three weeks are outlined. These are:

(a) improving memory through games and exercises;

(b) finding ways round their problems through external aids and techniques to make remembering easier;

(c) practice in using the aids and techniques;

(d) finding the best ways for each person to learn new information.

4. Memory Problems Questionnaire. Each person is asked whether or not they have problems remembering certain tasks. The ten-item questionnaire is based on the work of Kapur and Pearson (1982). The group leader fills in the answers.

5. Use of Aids Questionnaire. Each person is asked whether or not they use certain aids. This is based on the work of Harris (1980b).

6. Reality Orientation Techniques. (a)

(a) Questions about the year, month, day, date and approximate time are asked of individual group members.

(b) Each person is asked to tell us the names of all the people in the group. If they do not know, the initial lettering of the name is provided as a clue. If this fails some other clue is given (e.g. a word that rhymes with the name). If this fails the correct name is supplied.

7. Hiding a Belonging. Each member supplies a belonging which the leader puts somewhere in the room. Each person is asked to watch

carefully and to ask for their belonging before going over to tea.

8. Alarm. A kitchen timer is set to ring after ten minutes. Each person is given a job to do when the alarm sounds (e.g. water the plant or open the window).

9. Attention Training/Trick Sentences. Cards are held up (one for each person) with a 'trick' sentence written on it (e.g. 'Paris in the the Spring'). After two seconds the card is removed and the person asked to say what is written on the card. This procedure is repeated until the error is spotted.

10. Attention Training/Covering Symbols (based on the work of Gross, Ben-Nahum, Murk and Kohn, 1980). Symbols are drawn on a sheet of plain paper, one at a time in full view of all participants. Once the group has identified each symbol it is covered up with a piece of card. When the fourth symbol is drawn the therapist says: 'When I cover up this symbol the first symbol will reappear.' (The card is just big enough to cover three symbols.) 'What will it be?' This procedure is repeated until the sheet of paper is full.

11. 'Mrs Brown Went to Town.' In this familiar game the first person says, 'Mrs Brown went to town and bought a loaf of bread' (or some other item). The second person repeats this and adds an item of his or her choice. Each successive person repeats the previous items in the original order and adds one more. (Two or three times round the group is probably sufficient.)

12. Retrieving Belongings. Each person is asked what has been hidden and where it has been hidden. Clues are given as necessary.

Day Two

1. Revision. The group is reminded of what we hope to accomplish in the next three weeks.

2. The use of Aids and Strategies. The group leaders describe how certain aids and strategies are used in their everyday lives.

3. Orientation.
(a) Dates etc. (as on Day One).
(b) Names (as on Day One).

4. Visual Imagery for Names. The group is given an explanation of imagery as 'remembering by pictures'. Two names are selected from those in the group to illustrate the technique. Drawings of the names are made on the blackboard then rubbed out. Tests for remembering the two names are made at random intervals during the rest of the session.

5. Hiding a Belonging (as in Day One).

6. Alarm (as in Day One).

7. Homework. Each person is asked to bring a paper and pencil to the group tomorrow. Each one is also asked *how* he or she is going to remember to do this. A discussion follows on the advantages and disadvantages of each person's method.

8. News. The group is asked if they can relate a recent item of news. Three current newspapers are produced and various articles discussed.

9. General Discussion Time and Questions. Each member speaks about their own particular problems, fears and anxieties. Various solutions are suggested and advice given, both by the leaders and the participants.

10. Retrieving Belongings (as in Day One).

Day Three

1. Visitor. A visitor arrives from the Applied Psychology Unit, Cambridge. He is introduced.

2. Orientation. (a) and (b) (as in Day One). The visitor's name is also requested.

3. Visual Imagery. The names and images (from Day Two) are requested and another name is 'drawn' on the blackboard.

4. News. The group is asked what news items were discussed the previous day. Current items are then requested and elaborated upon.

5. Homework. Each person is asked whether or not they have brought a paper and pencil. Methods for remembering are discussed and alternative methods suggested.

6. Summaries in Notebooks. Notebooks are distributed to those people in the group who have not already received them. Everyone is asked to write a brief summary of the goals of the memory group (item 3 from Day One). Reminders of these goals are provided.

7. New Homework. All members of the group are asked to bring a newspaper to the group tomorrow. Methods for remembering to do this are discussed.

8. Visual-Peg Method. The 'one-bun' strategy (see Chapter 4) is explained, illustrated and practised. The 'pegs' are written on the blackboard and the images (in this case ten objects) are drawn, one beside each 'peg'. The images are then erased and the group tested.

9. Electronic Aid. The group is shown the Toshiba memo-note 60 and a demonstration given on how to write and store messages. This is followed by a lengthy discussion on the applications of the machine for everyday problems, its advantages and disadvantages.

Day Four

1. Orientation (a) and (b) (as in Day One).
2. Homework (as in Day Three).
3. Alarm (as in Day One).
4. Hiding a Belonging (as in Day One).
5. First Letter Cueing (see Chapter 4). The group is asked if any of them have learned to read music and if so how they remembered the notes. The 'Thirty days hath September' rhyme is discussed together with other mnemonics. First letter cueing is then demonstrated and practised.
6. Face-name Associations. This method of remembering names is described, demonstrated and practised using five photographs of unknown people. The group members are told each name and then asked to select a distinctive feature of the face. Next they are asked to transform the name and imagine it interacting with the feature. Finally, one photograph is shown to each participant who has to say what the distinctive feature is and then supply the name. If one or other of the steps is not successfully completed other group members are asked to supply the answer.
7. Summaries. A summary of the day's activities is written down by each member of the group.
8. Retrieving Belongings (as in Day One).

Day Five

1. Revision. The group is asked what we did yesterday.
2. Orientation (as in Day One).
3. First Letter Cueing. (a) Yesterday's items are tested. (b) A new set of items is practised. (c) A discussion is held on the practical applications of this method. (d) Each group member provides one item which is written on the board. The group then decides how a word or a sentence can be devised from the initial letters.
4. Alphabetic Cueing. Ten animal names are read out and the group are asked to recall as many as possible. The leader then tells the group that each animal name begins with one of the first ten letters of the alphabet. The letters A–J are written on the blackboard and the group asked to write in the rest of the names. A discussion follows on the organisation of material to be remembered. Finally, the group speaks about the use of alphabetic searching for retrieving a word which is on the tip of the tongue.
5. Notebook Summaries (as in Day Three).

Day Six

1. Notebook Check. As the group have not met for two days over the weekend each person is asked to produce his or her notebook.
2. Weekend Activities. People are asked to tell the group what they did at the weekend and write one piece of information in their notebooks.
3. Alarm. The alarm is set to sound after 15 minutes. The group is asked to write one piece of information in their notebooks and today's activities when the alarm sounds.
4. Orientation (as in Day One).
5. Corsi Blocks (adapted from Corsi, see Milner, 1971). Nine wooden blocks attached to a board are placed in front of each individual. The group leader taps a sequence of 4, 5, 6 or 7 blocks (depending on the ability of the testee) for immediate reproduction. Each individual tries to improve on his or her previous span.
6. Visual-Peg Method (One = Bun). The procedure used is the same as on Day Three but on this occasion members of the group try the method in order to remember things they have to do. First a list is drawn up of everyday tasks they might have to carry out. For example, pay for their newspapers or phone the dentist. Secondly, the group is asked to recall the 'pegs', i.e. the rhymes, and describe how to use the method. The first task in the list is then considered. People are asked how this can be linked with a bun. In our example the newspaper deliverer, carrying a pile of newspapers and holding out her hand, is sketched sitting on a bun. Everyone is asked to look carefully before it is rubbed out. They are then asked to imagine the sketch as vividly as possible before the next activity on the list is dealt with in the same way.
7. Face-name Association. The names from Day Four are tested and revised. Three more names are added.

Day Seven

1. Orientation (as in Day One).
2. News (as in Day Two).
3. Face-name Associations. The names from yesterday are tested. A clinical psychology student is visiting so the procedure is tried out with her face and name too.
4. PQRST (described in Chapter 4). This method is explained and practised using a short passage from today's newspaper. The letters PQRST are written on the blackboard together with the word each letter represents. The group leader then reads the newspaper passage

and explains that the 'P is for Preview stage'. One key question is then requested from each person. For example, 'What was the man's name?' 'What job did he do?' The questions are written on the blackboard and the group is reminded it now has completed the 'Q for Question stage'. The leader reads the passage again after asking the group to call out whenever one of the questions is answered. This is the 'R for Read Stage'. Next the group states the answers (the 'S for State stage') and finally the members are tested on the answers (the 'T for Test stage').

5. Method of Loci. (a) By way of introducing this method, objects are placed, one at a time, in various locations in the room. The group is informed that the objects will be removed and that they should try to remember where each objects has been positioned. The objects are removed by the leader. Individuals are asked either where a particular object had been placed or what object had been in a certain location. (b) The group is told how a variation of this method has been used both by the ancient Greeks and by famous mnemonists who remembered vast numbers of things by imaging them in certain places. It is suggested that some memory impaired people could benefit from this practice. The group then tries to remember common objects by imaging them in rooms in their own homes.

6. Recording the Day's Activities in the Notebooks.

7. Delayed Testing of the PQRST Passage practised earlier.

Day Eight

1. Orientation (as in Day One).

2. Revision of Face-name Association.

3. Revision of PQRST. What the letters stand for and remembering the news item.

3. Method of Loci. Revision of procedure and objects from the previous day.

5. Poem. The first verse of 'The Eagle' by Alfred Lord Tennyson is learned on the blackboard. The group is told that this poem can be lerned by some of them in a few minutes. All members read the verse aloud before being asked to close their eyes. The leader rubs out four words. The group open their eyes and individuals are asked to fill in the missing words. Prompts and cues are given to those who experience difficulties. The procedure is repeated and a few more words rubbed out. This continues until the whole poem is erased.

6. Pelmanism (pairs). This familiar card game requires each player to select two cards of the same numerical value from an array on the table. If a 'pair' is obtained the player keeps that pair and has an extra turn.

The winner is the person with most pairs at the end. (A whole pack of 52 cards is not used as these have been proved to be too difficult for the Rivermead groups. Usually, eight or ten pairs are sufficient. Picture cards such as 'Snap' or 'Kan-U-Go' letter cards are useful variations. Some people find the pictures easier than the numbers and some find them more difficult.)

7. Recording the Day's Activities in Notebooks.

Day Nine

1. Three visitors from Reading University are introduced and the face-name association procedure is used to learn their names.
2. Method of Loci. The group try to remember yesterday's list. The method is then tried for remembering which people to invite to a party, and also for remembering song titles.
3. PQRST. A new newspaper article is selected and the procedure used on Day Seven is followed.
4. Summarising the Day's Events and Recording in Notebooks.
5. Trick Sentences (as in Day One).

Day Ten

1. Visitors' Names from Yesterday. The group is asked to name yesterday's visitors.
2. The Airplane List (from Crovitz, 1979). Ten words are inserted into a bizarre story. After listing the words and then reading out the story the group is asked to recall the words.
3. Kim's Game. This is another familiar game. Several objects are placed on a tray for a short period of time. The tray is removed from sight and the group have to remember as many items as possible.
4. Revision of Alphabetic Cueing (as in Day Five). The words used are items of food.
5. Poem on the Blackboard. Revision of verse one of 'The Eagle' and the introduction of the second verse.
6. Return to Kim's Game. How many objects can the group still remember?

Day Eleven

1. Discussion of Weekend Activities. Recording activities in notebooks.
2. Orientation (as in Day One).
3. Jobs to Remember Without the Alarm. Each person is asked to remember to do one job before going to tea. Unlike previous days

no alarm will be sounded.

4. Autobiographies. Two fictitious people are described and their autobiographical details summarised on the blackboard. One is Mr Green, aged 37, an electrician with three children living in Kidlington. The other is Mrs White, aged 41, a radiographer, with two children living in Wheatley. The drawings and details are erased and the group asked to fill in the information about the two people on a prepared sheet of paper.

5. Spatial Memory (adapted from Diller *et al.*, 1980). The group is shown a card with an arrangement of dots. After ten seconds the card is removed and each person is given a blank card and asked to draw in the same number and placement of dots. These are then compared with the original.

6. Art Picture. A reproduction of a well-known painting is shown for 15 seconds. Individuals are then asked questions. For example, 'How many people are in the picture?' 'What was the colour of the woman's dress?'

7. Visual Imagery for Surnames. Most people in the group have by now learned all the first names but surnames are less familiar. We discuss how we could use imagery to remember surnames.

8. Recording in Notebooks.

Day Twelve

1. Orientation (as in Day One).
2. News (as in Day Two).
3. Remembering to do things Without the Alarm (as in Day Eleven).
4. Story Recall. A list of ten words is read to the group. Members are then told that all the words will be heard in a story to be read to them. The story is read and as each word from the list is identified the members call out.
5. Memory for Movement. (a) One person in the group acts out a story as it is read aloud by the group leader. First the actor and then other members of the group are asked to recall as much of the story as possible. Other stories are then acted by different members. (b) Sequences of hand movements are demonstrated to the group by the group leader. Sometimes the group merely watch the movements and sometimes the movements are copied. A discussion follows on whether participation leads to better recall than passive observation.
6. Word Lotto (adapted from Huppert, personal communication). Each person has a sheet with 15 words printed on it. (All sheets contain the same words but in different orders.) The group leader reads out a

list of 30 words, 15 of which are on the printed sheets. Members cross out the words on the sheets as they are called. When the sheets have been completed, the lists are collected. Members are given blank paper and pencils and asked to write down as many words from the original list as they can remember.

7. Attention Training (as in Day One). This time letters are used instead of symbols. The group discusses how the letters might be made into a sentence (first letter cueing) to aid recall. This procedure is then tried with a new set of letters.

8. Recording in Notebooks.

Day Thirteen

1. Levels of Processing (adapted from Craik and Lockhart, 1972). The leader reads out a word and asks a question. For example, 'jumper. Does this have more or less than four letters?' or 'Cloud. Is this a fruit?' or 'Yellow. Does this rhyme with mellow?' or 'Pony. Would this fit into the sentence "in the garden I met a . . ."?' Twenty words and questions are read in this way. The questions are designed to cover four levels of mental processing, from superficial to relatively profound. (The examples above illustrate these levels.) Afterwards group members are asked to write down as many words as they can remember from the list. The purpose of this test is to demonstrate to members of the group that deeper levels of processing usually result in improved recall.

2. PQRST. First, the group revises what the letters stand for and what has to be done at each stage. Then the group discusses how PQRST can be applied in everyday settings. Finally, the procedure is practised using a new extract.

3. Alarm. The group is asked to remember to summarise the day's proceedings in their notebooks when the alarm is sounded.

4. Discussion of yesterday's work.

5. Writing in Notebooks.

Day Fourteen

1. Walk. The whole group goes for a walk around the grounds of the unit. On returning they are asked questions such as 'What building did we pass first?' 'How many people did we meet on the way?'

2. Mrs Brown (as on Day One).

3. Alarm (as on Day One).

4. Revision of Levels of Processing from yesterday.

5. Summarising in Notebooks.

Day Fifteen

1. Discussion of yesterday's work.
2. Alarm — jobs (as on Day One).
3. Overview of all the Strategies and Aids we have used and discussed over the past three weeks and others we might have considered using.
4. A General Discussion. What people think of the group and which strategies and aids individuals prefer.
5. Repeat of Questionnaire administered on Day One.

The Birmingham Memory Group

The idea for running a memory group began in the summer of 1980, whilst working in a sheltered workshop/rehabilitation centre for the severely head-injured. In line with studies of the prevalence of memory problems among the survivors of severe head injuries, 12 of the 28 regular attenders experienced memory problems. Half of these amnesic patients were randomly selected for the memory group, with the others forming a control group.

The original memory group ran for a total of 15 weeks, with weekly meetings lasting for one and a half hours. The staff involved in the group included the clinical psychologist and one or more members of the rehabilitation staff — who were mainly occupational therapists.

The content of the session resembles that of the Rivermead Memory Group in many respects. Therefore, only a brief outline of the group proceedings will be offered, together with examples of ways in which the groups do in fact differ.

Composition of Each Session

Each session consists of four stages, beginning with the members reporting back on homework assignments which had been agreed the week before. Then the patients and also the therapists describe any practical memory problems they have experienced during the past week, together with any notable achievements in remembering. Thirdly, a new memory strategy is taught. In order to gain some idea about the efficacy of each strategy, the group members are given a task before the strategy is introduced and again afterwards. This provides valuable feedback to the therapists and patients about the benefits of particular strategies. Furthermore, the members of the group are asked to provide an estimate of how well they think they will do on the pre-training tasks, and also on the equivalent tasks once the strategy has been taught. This provides an additional exercise in making judgements about the level of memory ability and means that patients who do poorly on a given task might also have predicted this, and therefore can be rewarded for accurate self-judgement. This system sometimes uncovers self-fulfilling prophecies of poor performance, but often emphasises the benefits of the strategy compared with the group member's estimate of its worth.

Finally, new homework assignments are agreed and these usually involve practical applications of the memory strategy which has been taught during the session. A handout is provided giving information about the strategy and space is supplied for the homework assignment to be written down. A pairing system is used in which two patients are paired together to remind one another about homework tasks.

Outline of Activities in Each Session

Week One. Introduction and Exernal Aids. This includes the making and wearing of name badges. Focus is maintained on personal information, including remote memory such as family names, addresses and birthdays, since many of the members can recall this information. This provides a relatively non-threatening start to the course. A range of external memory aids are demonstrated and notebooks provided, with a homework assignment requiring the use of a wall calendar and forward planning diary.

Week Two. External Aids. External aids such as shopping lists and writing on the back of the hand are encouraged.

Week Three. A–Z Searching. A variety of tasks involving recalling information are used in a game-like fashion with the aim of eliciting a 'feeling of knowing' without the person being able to freely recall the word. The material used includes maps to recall town names, or names of relatives. Additional items use the methodology developed by Brown and McNeil (1966) in which the definitions of rare words are provided and the group members are asked to supply the word defined. Examples include the name for a male deer, or the measure of the depth of water in six-foot units (Moffat, 1983).

If a group member experiences a 'tip of the tongue' phenomenon the person is encouraged to think what the first letter of the word might be, together with any other attributes of the word (for example, the number of syllables). If this does not prove sufficient the first letter of the word is provided, and then additional letters added until the word is recalled.

For items which could be common knowledge, such as place names, the members are encouraged to work individually and quietly, which proves difficult for some of the more disinhibited head-injured patients. Interruptions or spoiling the exercise by supplying the answers are strongly discouraged in this and other sessions, with the result that there appears to be increasing conformity across the sessions.

Where the information will not be common knowledge, such as the name of a member's second cousin, a group approach is encouraged to try various means, particularly the use of different first letters, to help the person recall the name.

Week Four. First Letter Mnemonics. Popular mnemonics, such as BBC, are used to illustrate the principles of first letter mnemonics. The emphasis is changed to the encoding of information, initially using well-known mnemonics and progressing to newly constructed ones, such as encoding the names of the group members.

Week Five. Organisation. Group members are asked to organise pictures of objects into different categories, so that no items are left over. Efficient and inefficient strategies are noted, and further attempts at producing the former are encouraged. Other exercises are used, including triads such as 'hide-ride-conceal', with the task of finding the 'odd word out'. A semantic selection is encouraged (e.g. 'ride') rather than an accoustic-visual strategy (e.g. 'conceal'). No attempt is made to test memory during this session because if a patient has a problem with both organisation and memory, only one deficit is dealt with at a time.

Week Six. Organisation and Memory. The remembering of items of shopping by organising them into categories is practised. Attempts are made to even out the number of categories used and the number of items in each category. Recall of the list is tested, and further practice offered.

Week Seven. Verbal Strategies. A number of passages are constructed which contain salient information such as the time and place to meet someone. The task is to telegram this information by extracting the relevant information and restating it in as few words as possible. More elaborate use of verbal strategies involve use of the PQRST techniques described earlier.

Week Eight. Attention Training. A range of exercises is used, including that developed by Gross *et al.* (1980) as described earlier. A digit distraction task is also used in which a series of digits is read out with a male voice randomly interspersed with a female voice: the aim being to repeat back only the series of digits spoken by the male voice. The game of Round Robin as an attentional exercise has been included in more recent training. It involves each member in turn saying the next consecutive number, except when there is a seven, a number containing a seven, or a multiple of seven, whereupon the person says 'Buzz', and the order in which the group members take turns is reversed. Simplified versions of this game can be devised if necessary.

Weeks Nine and Ten. Visual Imagery. The principles and practice of visual imagery are taught, with an emphasis on the learning of people's names, particularly those of members of the group. Details of this form of training are given earlier in this chapter and in Chapter 4.

Week Eleven. Peg Method. Examples of the use of this technique have been provided already (see above). As with many of the other strategies which are taught, the group members are first asked to estimate how many words they can recall immediately after being presented with a list of ten words. Following this the peg method is taught and a further ten words associated with the peg words. An estimate is obtained of the number of these words likely to be recalled.

As mentioned elsewhere (Wilson and Moffat, 1984) some patients experience problems learning the pegs (for example, 'One is a bun'), whilst others have difficulty associating the words with the pegs. However, as a general impression, the patients overestimate their ability prior to training and underestimate it after learning the peg method.

Week Twelve. Loci Method. This is used in the same way as that described in Chapter 4 and as practised by the Rivermead Memory Group.

Weeks Thirteen, Fourteen and Fifteen. Practical Problems. The final three sessions provide additional time to deal with specific practical problems. Among these are the forgetting of items involved in a construction task, resulting in vital stages being omitted. The relevant stages are listed for the client and this form of external aid is gradually phased out as learning occurs.

Memory Therapy Groups with the Elderly

An additional feature of the Birmingham Memory Group was that all the participants were head-injured patients. The Rivermead Memory Group included a wider range of patients with acquired brain damage, but neither group was intended to include the confused elderly. It is important to distinguish between the type of memory therapy group that is appropriate for the confused elderly suffering from some form of dementia, and the treatment required by the elderly who complain of memory loss but who have no major cognitive impairment. This latter group may be helped by a memory therapy group similar to that described above, whilst the confused elderly may be more appropriately treated by 24-hour or classroom reality orientation.

There appear to be two main reasons why memory therapy groups might be considered for the non-confused elderly. Firstly, older people often complain of poor memory (Kahn, Zarit, Hilbert and Niederehe, 1975). For some individuals this might be a consequence of reduced abilities, but for many others depression, or the stereotype of memory loss with ageing, may result in memory complaints in the absence of impairment on memory tests. Therefore, group counselling might help to reduce these memory complaints. Secondly, a variety of memory strategies have been successfully applied with the elderly (see Chapter 4), and might be incorporated into a memory therapy group, as already described at Rivermead and Birmingham.

With a cognitively impaired group of subjects, in which there is scope for improvement in memory test performance, the benefits of memory therapy might be demonstrated. One of the authors (N. Moffat) is currently investigating the value of selected aspects of memory therapy with the elderly who show mild memory impairment. This is being conducted with individuals, and a pilot memory therapy group is being operated. However, there is probably only a narrow range of elderly subjects who might be helped in this way, since Zarit *et al.* (1981) suggest from their experience that this form of direct training 'may not benefit persons with a severe disfunction'. For those who are known to suffer from a more severe impairment of memory, or additional cognitive disfunction (perhaps as a result of some form of dementia) the various types of reality orientation training outlined below may be more appropriate.

Reality Orientation

Reality Orientation (RO) is concerned with the maintenance or relearning of current information such as time, place, names of others and current events. The main methods of teaching this information to the confused elderly are by verbal repetition, the use of visual aids such as weatherboards, and stimulation of the senses.

The principles of reality orientation may be carried out during every interaction with a patient throughout a 24-hour period. This may be supplemented, and in some cases replaced, by sessions which specifically practise current information. These sessions may involve one member of staff working with a selected patient for perhaps ten minutes (Johnson, 1979); although the more common practice is to hold group sessions which last for between half an hour and one hour, and typically include two therapists and three to six patients, depending on the level of concentration and ability of the participating patients.

An important feature of these RO sessions is the emphasis on a relaxed atmosphere in which success is encouraged. In this country a mock pub has been created in one ward in Leeds' Hospital, and in another unit an old-fashioned living room has been used for the group sessions. In the USA the term 'classroom' is often used to refer to the sessions, perhaps reflecting a more competitive atmosphere in which members graduate from one level to another. A special environment is not essential for the group sessions but a friendly and supportive approach is desirable.

As general guidelines for appropriate interaction with the confused elderly during RO, Holden and Woods (1982) suggest that conversation is kept specific and reality-based, often using objects to help focus and maintain concentration. The use of short, simple sentences by the therapist is recommended and the group members encouraged to repeat the information or respond to it appropriately. Reference to the past may be used to relate to the present but confused talk is not accepted and is dealt with by distraction, tactful disagreement or by acknowledging the feeling of what is being said whilst ignoring the actual content.

It is suggested that the members of a group should be approximately similar in both level of orientation and mental ability so that group activities can be planned to involve all the participants. This may necessitate the formation of up to three levels of group, with a member transferring to a different group if there is sufficient change in the level of ability.

Holden and Woods (1982) describe a Basic group for the most disorientated and withdrawn (Holden Communication Score; HCS above

25); and a Standard group catering for the moderately disorientated (HCS between 15 and 25); and an Advanced group catering for those with mild disorientation (HCS of less than 15). The Basic group might focus mainly on information about time, place, weather and names of group members. Considerable use may be made of visual aids such as a weather orientation board (see Appendix I for suppliers of materials). The Standard group may incorporate the basic information described above, but could also include discussion and activities relating the past to the present, the stimulation of the senses, and the building up of interaction between group members. In the Advanced group the members would have considerable responsibility for determining the activities, which may include discussions, planning and participating in leisure activities and arranging visits. Such a group might encourage the maintenance of activities, thus forming part of the wider rehabilitation or care plan.

Ideas for running appropriate and flexible sessions can be found in Hanley (1982), Holden and Woods (1982) and Rimmer (1982), together with other training resources which are mentioned in Appendix I. There are also a number of journal articles which describe the running of reality orientation programmes. These include Degun (1976), Drummond, Kirchoff and Scarbrough (1978), Hahn (1980), Holden (1979), and Hanley, Cleary, Oates and Walker (1981). A brief review of the literature on reality orientation is provided in Chapter 4, with a more comprehensive review being available in Holden and Woods (1982) and Woods and Holden (1982).

The research evidence clearly supports the inclusion of reality orientation as a form of memory therapy, since patients often improve in verbal orientation. However, as with other forms of memory therapy, the benefits are often confined to the information which is taught, with little or no generalisation. Therefore, the careful selection of appropriate behaviours as targets for the therapy is essential.

As we have observed at Rivermead, reality orientation need not be confined to work with the confused elderly. Unfortunately, the reverse is not likely to be true in that the confused elderly may not benefit to any large extent from new developments in memory therapy; although there may be scope for the use of certain strategies and external aids with those who retain some insight and cognitive ability in the early stages of Alzheimer's disease (Kurlychek, 1983).

It would seem, then, given the current state of our knowledge, and the variety of potential candidates for the different memory groups, that it would be premature to establish strict selection criteria or a rigid prescription for the contents of a memory group with a given patient population. The present situation suggests that the running of a diversity of memory groups with varied populations is required. Such practice will enrich our understanding of ways of enhancing memory and will also provide us with a valuable field for research.

Organising and Evaluating a Memory Group

Some of the difficulties encountered in running a memory group will be similar to those found in organising any kind of group: finding a suitable time and place for meetings; uncertainty about how much leadership to provide; concern about how best to organise the activities and how much general discussion to encourage and control. Neither the Rivermead group nor the Birmingham group are intended to be psychotherapeutic. It would be wrong to think of them as a means by which discussion exercises are facilitated. For these reasons the stages of group development described, for example, by Bion (1959), and others who are interested in ways discussion develops within groups, are not directly relevant to the purposes and strategies of our groups. Instead we shall concentrate on issues specifically related to memory groups, which seem to us to have a particular set of problems that are in many ways different from those experienced by other kinds of groups involved in rehabilitation.

Membership

Before staring a new group it is necessary to consider the particular needs of each individual in order to ensure that the final grouping has a reasonable chance of achieving a degree of success. At this stage it is quite possible that some individuals will be excluded because their problems are not only different from the majority of the group but they may also cause a conflict of interests within the group. Others will be saved embarrassment by being excluded from the group. An intelligent person with a classic amnesic syndrome and no other deficits may be unwilling to co-operate in a group which contains a confused, disturbed, physically handicapped, head-injured person and a disinhibited frontally damaged patient. People who have right hemisphere damage and non-verbal memory problems but whose verbal memory is above average may not believe there is anything the matter with them. Furthermore, they may feel affronted by being placed in a group with people who cannot remember anything that was said to them two minutes earlier. Ideally, some degree of homogeneity is desirable.

The most successful group at Rivermead contained five young people all under 28 years, all of whom had a verbal IQ in the above-average range, and all but one of whom had no other cognitive deficits apart from memory impairment. In reality, however, this situation rarely arises and it is much more common to work with a more disparate group. We exclude people who have severe speech or language problems, partly because we feel they will be embarrassed at not being able to communicate freely in our groups and partly because most of the group exercises involve speaking and comprehending. Nevertheless, mild aphasics have been included at times and they have participated fully and with obvious enjoyment. One young woman with a nearly total acquired alexia was included in one of the Rivermead groups. Potentially this could have caused much difficulty as recording information and using written aids are integral processes within the group. However, the young woman had no other language disturbances and in fact she benefited from some of the tasks. Others excluded from the group are those with severe behaviour problems because they are so disruptive. This is not to say that such people should not be included in a group at all but to simply point out that their disruptive behaviour makes progress within a memory group impossible. Patients who are severely and generally intellectually impaired are also excluded. To participate in the group it is necessary to have reasonable comprehension and motivation. Most of the group members are able to read and write – at least to an eight- or nine-year-old level.

Even with these exclusions the range within a group is wide. The current Rivermead group consists of one 59-year-old man with a classic amnesic syndrome resulting from meningitis (KJ described in Chapter 5); one 27-year-old head-injured man in a wheelchair suffering from perceptual problems (MC also described in Chapter 5); a 13-year-old head-injured girl, also in a wheelchair, who in fact has some behaviour problems but these are usually apparent only during physical exercises when she experiences difficulty and some pain. There is a 27-year-old head-injured man who appears to be on the brink of coming out of Post-traumatic Amnesia but who is still disoriented and confused, and talks at greath length. Finally, there is a 43-year-old man with marked frontal lobe damage who confabulates a great deal. He also perseveres in his speech, his writing and his motor movements. His behaviour ranges from apathy to agitation and verbal aggression. Despite the wide range of problems exhibited by these patients there is, nevertheless, a sufficient degree of homogeneity to enable the memory group to operate quite successfully.

There is little point in running the memory group if fewer than four patients are present. On certain days, of course, there will be absentees through sickness or other pressing appointments within the unit. There are always two members of staff available to run the group session. This ensures that memory group sessions can be run continuously even though one or other of the leaders may not be available on certain days. However, it would be undesirable to have too broad a spectrum of staff members involved in the organisation of the memory group as continuity and cohesion might suffer. In both the Rivermead and the Birmingham units physiotherapists, occupational therapists and trainee clinical psychologists have taken on the role of supporting group leader.

Management

In managing a memory group the leader has to be aware of the wide variety of needs of individual patients. Inevitably, mistakes and misjudgements will be made and these will be manifested at times in prolonged work on certain areas which do not meet the real needs of a patient. However, as mentioned earlier, ensuring some degree of success is one of the principles of a memory group, and working on a problem-free area is one way of achieving this. Other ways of obtaining success may involve some engineering of the time interval. Most participants will have an adequate immediate memory span so asking one of them to do something immediately will increase the chances of success. Those with a less severe impairment can be asked after a longer delay. Similarly, in the reality orientation exercises the easiest question for most people is 'What year is it now?' This question can be asked of the most disoriented person, at least on some occasions. For patients who find almost every task too difficult we include some motor memory activities, for example, mirror-writing or reaction-time tasks. Improvements on these can almost be guaranteed even though the patient may not remember having done them before. These improvements should, of course, be charted or recorded in some way so that feedback of success can be provided. Audio or video recordings are alternative ways of providing feedback of successful performance which would not normally be remembered by patients.

There will be other patients in the group who will spend too little time on their areas of greatest need. If possible, some individual memory therapy should be provided for these. Failing this, it may be necessary to set the rest of the group a task which they can do on their own whilst the group leader spends this time giving individual attention to such a patient. Alternatively, when both leaders are in attendance, one of them could work with an individual patient for some of the time.

Another potentially difficult area concerns the relationships that exist between patients. The behaviour of one patient may cause a disturbance among others. The group might include a person who will not stop talking (a fairly common difficulty after head injury) and who never gives anyone else a chance to answer a question or raise a point; or a person who quarrels incessantly with everyone; or who sees himself as superior to the group and consequently refuses to participate. There are no easy answers to the problems raised by such patients. In some cases ignoring the disruptive behaviour might be the wisest solution, while for others an explanation about the effects they have on the rest of the group could be effective. Possibly a formal behaviour modification programme to reduce the problems would lead to the most effective changes.

Evaluation

There have been few reports on the effects of memory training carried out in groups. The studies which have been reported have examined the effects of Reality Orientation Therapy, a procedure designed primarily for elderly dementing patients. The results of these studies have been promising (Brook, Degun and Mather, 1975; Harris and Ivory, 1976). However, no reports have been published using this technique with younger patients with non-progressive brain damage. Furthermore, ROT includes few *specific* strategies for improving memory. It does not include training in the use of those strategies which have been shown to be effective aids to memory such as visual imagery (Jones, 1974; Wilson, 1981); verbal techniques (Cermak, 1975; Wilson, 1982); or external aids (Fowler, Hart and Sheehan, 1972). All these strategies have been used to improve performance on particular tasks with younger people who have non-progressive brain damage. However, all of these have involved training patients as *individuals*. To date there have been no studies evaluating the effects on memory functioning of group training. A further point of interest is whether training in the use of memory strategies to improve performance on specific tasks also has a general effect on memory. The available evidence suggests that neither practice nor training in the use of specific strategies improves memory generally (Milner, Corkin and Teuber, 1968; Brooks and Baddeley, 1976; Wilson, 1982). However, all of these studies were on patients with severe global amnesia. There have been no investigations into whether patients with less severe amnesia, such as head-injured patients, benefit from such training.

There is little point in therapists running memory groups if they do not result in any change in memory functioning. So answers to the questions above are urgently required. Ideally, some kind of evaluation should be carried out for each and every group. This leads us into several problems associated with research and we will not go into great detail here.

The simplest way to evaluate is to administer some test/s of memory functioning prior to starting a group, and readminister the same test/s after the group sessions have been concluded. The main faults with this design are: (a) one does not know whether any changes are due to the effects of treatment or to spontaneous recovery or changes over time; (b) the tests may be sensitive to practice effects too, i.e. the testee may do better the second time round simply because he or she has taken them before; and (c) the tests may not be sensitive to the detection of real changes in everyday memory functioning, i.e. the testee may show no significant change in test scores but have fewer everyday problems.

Even if it is possible for the above-mentioned problems to be resolved other difficulties may arise. If participants do improve after attending the memory group sessions the evaluator will not know whether it is the treatment provided in the group or the effects of extra attention and general stimulation which has caused the change. If it is the memory group itself then questions arise as to whether all the elements of the group treatment are essential or whether the same degree of success be achieved by simply giving the group memory games or solely visual imagery strategies or practice in using external aids.

Further questions surround methods of analysing results. Usually in research the results for the whole group are averaged out and a group mean is obtained. The pre- and post-treatment results are then subjected to a statistical test of significance. However, group means can be very confusing as they do not tell us about the responses of the individuals within the group. Some participants could do very well but this might be cancelled out by others doing very badly so that the overall group result implies that no change has taken place.

These and similar problems concern all people engaged in attempting to evaluate treatment. Solutions will be found to some problems and compromises may have to be made with regard to others (see Maxwell (1973) and Bolton (1974) for further discussion of this topic).

One possible way forward for therapists wishing to evaluate the effectiveness or otherwise of their groups is to adopt a multiple baseline across subjects design (see Hersen and Barlow, 1976; Yule and Hemsley, 1977 for a detailed discussion of this design). Essentially, subjects have differing baseline periods prior to the introduction of treatment. Improvement over time or spontaneous recovery and/or practice effects will be identified by better performances over the baseline period. If the treatment itself is effective then the patients will improve (or improve faster) after the introduction of the therapy. If it is ineffective then the results will be similar to those obtained during the baselines. If the treatment is detrimental the scores or performances will deteriorate after treatment. Let us take a hypothetical example. Suppose Anne, Betty, Charles and David are to be considered for a memory group and the therapist organising the group wishes to use a multiple baseline design. He or she first has to decide how to measure the memory impairment. The Rivermead Behavioural Memory Test described in Chapter 5 was devised precisely to answer such a question. Suppose the therapist chooses certain standardised tests, some items similar to those on the RBMT, and a rating scale – possibily similar to that devised by Sunderland, Harris and Gleave (in press), an adaptation of which is illustrated in Chapter 5. Anne is assessed on these various measures eight times in the four weeks prior to starting the group. Betty is assessed six times; Charles four times; and David twice. Providing no dramatic improvements have occurred over the baseline period then all can join the memory group. At weekly intervals thereafter the tests are readministered. Figure 9.1 illustrates the design and a possible outcome. Remember, the data used is hypothetical.

These data suggest that Anne and Charles benefit considerably from the group, Betty has not benefited at all and David has shown minimal improvement. It would be possible to subject these data to a statistical analysis although there is a controversy regarding the desirability of using statistics with multiple baseline designs (Hersen and Barlow, 1976). One school of thought believes that if statistics are necessary to establish the effectiveness of treatment and the data do not speak for themselves then the findings are not clinically significant. However, this is only one side of the argument and those who wish to consider the use of statistics should refer to Hersen and Barlow (1976) and Yule and Hemsley (1977). Articles on the use of statistics with single case or small group designs appear regularly in the journal *Behaviour Assessment* (for example, Edgington, 1982).

Problems remain, of course, even if this design is chosen. The practice effect, for example, may lead to an apparent but false improvement during the baseline period if the same tests are administered on

Figure 9.1: A Multiple Baseline Across Subjects Design to Investigate the Effects of Memory Therapy (hypothetical data)

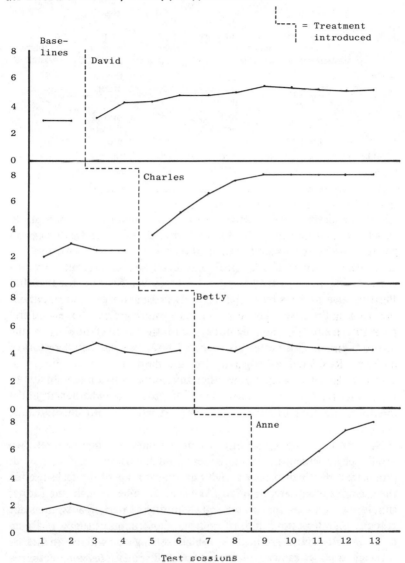

several occasions. Alternative forms of each test may be required, in which case it is necessary to establish that the different forms of the test are equally difficult.

Another possible solution to the evaluation of a memory group is to

Table 9.1: Design for Evaluating the Rivermead Memory Group

Patients	Weeks					
	1	2	3, 4, 5	6	7, 8, 9	10
1–5	pre-treatment assessment	pre-treatment assessment	memory group	inter-mediate assessment	non-memory group	post-treatment assessment
6–10	"	"	non-memory group	"	memory group	"
11–15	"	"	memory group	"	non-memory group	"
16–20	"	"	non-memory group	"	memory group	"

adopt the design used at Rivermead in an ongoing, long-term study which seeks to investigate (a) the effectiveness of group treatment and (b) the suitability of such treatment for certain groups of patients. This still does not solve all the problems described earlier but it goes a considerable way towards doing so. A crossover design is used so that the first five patients receive three weeks of memory group treatment followed by three weeks of treatment in another group. The second five patients receive the non-memory group treatment followed by the memory group. This pattern is repeated with each successive cohort of patients considered appropriate for the memory group. The cross-over design enables us to see whether any improvement is simply due to being in a group, that is, *any* kind of group; or whether it is the memory group in particular which is beneficial. Table 9.1 illustrates the design.

Any patient who shows improvement from week one to week two should be excluded as this indicates spontaneous recovery. The other group treatment can be any activity as long as none of the tasks used in the memory group are included. As far as possible, though, the format should be the same, that is, an equal number of participants, the same amount of interaction, and, of course, equal timing. Usually at Rivermead the alternative group is a problem-solving one where patients are set such tasks as games of logic, verbal and spatial reasoning activities and so forth. This kind of group can be run on very similar lines to the memory group.

Analyses of results can be made by using non-parametric statistics (see Siegel, 1956). For example, results from each group of patients and from all the groups combined can be subjected to a Wilcoxon 't' test to see whether any improvement over time is likely to be due to chance or to the effects of treatment. Secondly, the effects of memory group training can be compared with the effects of other group training by using a between groups comparison test (the Mann Whitney 'U' test). Thirdly, if memory training is shown to be effective in improving memory the persistence of such improvement can, for those patients who received memory group training, be examined by comparing results in the intermediate assessment with those in the post-treatment assessment. Finally, patients can be divided into two groups: those who benefit from training and those who do not. The two groups can be compared in an attempt to identify predictors of outcome.

Appendix I

Materials for Staff and Patient Training in Reality Orientation: General Guidelines and Manuals

Hanley, I. (1982) *A Manual for the Modification of Confused Behaviour.* Lothian Regional Council, Department of Social Work, Shrubhill House, Shrub Place, Edinburgh.

Henneman, L. and Moffat, N. (1983) *Training Package on Reality Orientation* (In preparation). Details from Nick Moffat, Branksome Clinic, Layton Road, Poole, Dorset.

Holden, U.P. *et al.* (1980) *24-hour Approach to the Problems of Confusion in Elderly People.* Dr U.P. Holden, Psychology Department, Moorhaven Hospital, Bittadon, Ivybridge, nr. Plymouth, Devon.

Holden, U.P. and Woods, R.T. (1982) *Reality Orientation: Psychological Approaches to the Confused Elderly.* Churchill Livingstone, Edinburgh.

Rimmer, L. (1982) *Reality Orientation: Principles and Practice.* PTM Publications, Winslow Press, 23 Horn Street, Winslow, Buckingham, MK18 3AP.

Rush, J. and McAusland, T. (1982) *A Guide to Training Resources for Staff Working with 'Confused' Elderly People.* King's Fund Centre, 126 Albert Street, London NW1 7NF.

Video Tapes

Hanley, I.G. and Oates, A. (1980) *Group Reality Orientation.* 32 minute colour video, Audio-Visual Services Department of Psychiatry, University of Edinburgh, Morningside Park, Edinburgh EH10.

Hanley, I. *Introduction to Classroom Reality Orientation in Residential*

Settings for the Elderly. Umatic Colour, 25 minutes. (Address as immediately above.)

Holden, U.P. *Six Week Study in Reality Orientation.* Videotape, 30 minutes. TV Medical Department, University of Leeds, Leeds.

Tape and Tape/Slide Programmes

Drummond, L., Brians, L. and Scarborough, D. (1981) *Leading Reality Orientation Classes: Basic and Advanced.* Manual and Tape available from Intercraft Associates, Arlington Heights, Illinois, USA.

Woods, R.T. (1982) *Reality Orientation – An Approach to working with Confused Elderly People. Part I – 24-hour Reality Orientation.* 30 minute Tape, handout, slides. *Part II – Reality Orientation Sessions.* 30 minute Tape, handout, slides. Graves Audiovisual Library, 220 New London Rd, Chelsmford, Essex.

Visual Aids

Memory Board, Information Packs, Permacal, and Pictorial Signposts. Orientation Aids, Dalebank, Glencaple, Dumfries, Scotland.

10 FUTURE DEVELOPMENTS

Nadina B. Lincoln

The recent expansion of memory training techniques seems likely to continue, at least in the near future. The problems of memory impairment are common and even if there are no significant advances in the range of techniques available, implementation of what is known so far would take some time. However, ideas do not stand still and there are many aspects yet to be developed. The range of training techniques, the selection of appropriate methods according to the nature of the problem, the generalisation of training from specific tasks to daily life and the evaluation of procedures used in different settings and with different client groups all offer plenty of scope for further investigations. The aim of this chapter is to summarise the state of the art and to consider the questions which remain to be answered and the developments which are needed.

Normal Memory Theories

The link between theories of normal memory functioning and clinical management of patients has always been rather tenuous. The series of contacts between the experimental psychologist, the experimental neuropsychologist, the clinical neuropsychologist and the rehabilitation team has allowed a slow trickle of information to percolate through to those in direct daily contact with the patient rather than a direct interchange of ideas. This total separation of professionals who would otherwise learn from each other seems to be breaking down. Conferences on applied and practical aspects of memory such as the one on which this book is based have brought together the pure and applied scientists. This seems likely to make the experimentalists incorporate practical considerations into their theoretical models and the clinicians take account of what is normal memory in their evaluation and treatment of patients with impaired functioning. This can only be to the benefit of all of us.

It has already been pointed out (Chapter 1) that some of the concepts used by experimental psychologists are regarded in a different way by clinicians. If nothing else we hope to have at least highlighted some of the problems in using the same term for different concepts. This may avoid some confusion and breakdown in communication between the theorists and clinicians. This clarification of ideas may also enable clinicians to identify patients who have practical memory problems which either support or refute the ideas proposed by the theorist.

The distinction between semantic and episodic memory is one which is rarely considered in clinical practice. Most of the memory complaints made by patients relate to episodic memory, so the patients report being unable to remember events that have happened, such as going home for the weekend, and their daily activities. Assessments are also usually designed to investigate loss of episodic memory. Yet there are exceptions which may get ignored because they do not fit into the usual pattern. For example, discrepancies arise between results of mental status questionnaires given by medical staff and psychologists' assessments of dementia (Hare, 1978). The patients who fail to give information about past Prime Ministers, the present Sovereign and the name of the hospital are not always the same people as those identified on psychological testing as having acquired intellectual deficits. While psychologists often dismiss these short ratings as inappropriate and over-simplified, it may be that we are failing to identify the different aspects of memory tested in the different tasks.

Another example of the possible misinterpretation of clinical data through lack of awareness of theoretical models is illustrated in the case of Mr NH. Mr NH was a 59-year-old man who had received a head injury one month before being seen by a clinical psychologist. At first he had slight weakness of his left side, but this soon recovered and he was left with no physical signs. He was unable to recall anything that had happened before his accident. He could not give his date of birth, occupation, previous interests or the names of his children. When naming objects he was able to name items seen since the accident and often reported the occasion of learning the name, so, for example, when shown a picture of scissors, he named them and said he had been given some by his wife to use for cutting his nails. But he was unable to name other equally common objects, such as matches, key and paint-brush, which he had not seen since the accident. On episodic memory tasks, such as the Wechsler story recall (Wechsler, 1945) and Benton Visual Retention Test (Benton, 1974) his performance was within the average range.

The pattern of psychological test results was inconsistent with the usual pattern of deficits observed following a head injury. He had lost all his knowledge of the world yet was well able to acquire and retain new information. As a result, he was considered probably to have a hysterical amnesia, even though there was nothing in his previous history to suggest this was likely. In retrospect, what seems more likely is that there was some loss of semantic memory with relatively intact episodic memory. Because of his intact episodic memory he was able to relearn his knowledge about the world and thus reacquire much of the lost information.

The importance of the presentation of input in order for things to be remembered gives clues as to what may help patients remember. The need to attend to the learning task and to organise material in such a way that it is easier to remember can be helped by providing appropriate environmental clues. Mrs SC was a woman of 68 with dementia as a result of vascular disease. Her various complaints included not knowing which day it was and forgetting to take her tablets, three times a day. On a home visit it was apparent there were no visible reminders of the day, date or time of day. She and her husband wore watches, but had no clock or calendar visible in the house. Her tablets were in a cupboard in the kitchen and her husband kept a list of the times that she took them beside the telephone in the living room. He frequently forgot to tick his list and when I visited had difficulty in finding it because it had been put in a drawer with the telephone directories. In order to increase the chances that Mrs SC at least knew the day of the week and the month of the year she was given a large wall calendar. The woman was supervised by her husband as she crossed off each day on the calendar using a thick red felt pen. This meant that at least once a day she had her attention drawn to the day of the week and there was a visible reminder facing her every time she went into the kitchen of how far through the month it was. The tablets were moved into a visible place on the kitchen shelf and a large chart was hung from the shelf beside the tablets. Mrs SC was instructed to tick off the chart each time she took a tablet and her husband kept a check on whether she had done so. The timing of the tablets was also changed from after breakfast, mid-afternoon, and after supper, to being always after a meal, so that mid-afternoon became after lunch instead. This simple reorganisation of the material to be remembered was sufficient to enable her to cope with these tasks.

The importance of the context in which learning takes place also has implications for clinical practice. Much of the work described in the preceding chapters has been carried out with in-patients. While this has obvious practical advantages for the therapist, a more efficient approach might be to treat the patients in the place where the problems arise – their own home. Domiciliary treatment is rarely used in the rehabilitation of any cognitive deficits, yet since the problems of generalisation are so great it would seem worth trying in at least those cases where the deficits may be directly related to the environment.

Assessment of Memory Problems

The clinical assessment of memory up till now has been mainly by brief mental examination or by psychometric tests. The former sample very limited aspects of the dimensions of memory, since most of them only evaluate the person's awareness of general, personal (birth-date, address, etc.) information and limited general knowledge (Queen, Prime Minister, etc.). While they may be used as a quick screening device for the detection of gross deficits they are of little value in assessing milder or more specific problems. The psychometric methods generally consist of presenting information, either aurally or visually, and requiring the subject to select or recall the information after a specific delay. While useful for identifying difficulties on a standard task, they do not tell us much that is important in the rehabilitation process. They do not indicate what effect the problem is causing in daily life, how the person is coping with the difficulty and the factors that affect a person's performance on the task. Discrepancies between test results and everyday performance are common in clinical observations. Some patients will perform poorly on tests yet report no difficulties in daily life; others present with a multitude of problems yet are able to complete the tests with no significant deficits. The factors which account for these discrepancies may provide important clues to developments needed in our assessment techniques.

One possible reason for the discrepancy is that tests are measuring something very different from daily life memory. This has been suggested in previous chapters (Chapters 2, 5) and there is some evidence to support the idea. The implications of this are twofold. One is to develop assessments of memory in daily life. Some questionnaires have been developed to do this (Bennett-Levy and Powell, 1980; Sunderland, Harris and Baddeley, 1983) but as has been pointed out, these rely on self report and patients with severe memory problems might not be the most reliable observers of their own difficulties. The relatives may also need to rate the practical difficulties. The second implication is to make memory tests more similar in content to the type of activities performed in daily life. It seems that the closest relation between tests and daily life performance are obtained when the tasks are similar (Sunderland, Harris and Baddeley, 1983). This could be further developed by producing more assessments associated with common problems. For example, a face-name recall test, face recognition test, date-event association, shopping list recall and route recognition could be standardised in such a way as to have the advantages of a test and be meaningful from the patient's viewpoint.

A further development would be to introduce behavioural memory tasks into the routine clinical assessment of memory problems. Poon (1980) describes a test being developed at the Boston VA out-patient clinic. The patient is told that he is going to a 'get together' and will meet new acquaintances. A booklet is given to the subject depicting sequential scenes from the party in which names, addresses, faces and general information are presented in a story-related manner and then recall is tested at intervals up to one week following the presentation. A more practical measure is being developed by Wilson (see Chapter 5) in which she incorporates a series of memory tasks into the routine assessment of memory. These include activities such as reporting on a text read in the newspaper, remembering a route between two parts of a hospital and requesting an appointment card. This has the advantage of being observed by the clinician and therefore not limited by the inaccuracies of self-report. It also involves many activities of daily life, which makes it acceptable to the patient, and likely to be useful as a means of monitoring the effects of treatment.

Subjective memory questionnaires and behavioural memory tests may benefit from a detailed analysis of what memory tasks are required in daily life. Some tasks are obviously fairly regular occurrences, like face recognition, route finding and remembering to do domestic chores, such as putting out the milk bottles. Others, which are less obvious but seem to produce more complaints when they go wrong, are keeping track of time and recalling events that have happened throughout the day.

The discrepancies between memory test performance and daily life activities may also depend on whether people have developed their own strategies for remembering without specific training. Many people will compensate for difficulties by making lists but this may not become apparent during routine interviews and testing. Some strategies may become apparent during formal testing yet not be reflected in the scores obtained and consequently not given full consideration in the interpretation of test results. For example, the standard administration of the Wechsler Logical Memory subtest (Wechsler, 1945) is to read two short stories and ask patients to recall as much as they remember. These are scored according to the number of items in the story correctly recalled. However, some people will reiterate word for word certain phrases while others will describe a scene based on the story presented. Although the scores obtained may be the same the techniques being used to recall the information are different.

A patient using an auditory matching strategy may recall: 'Anna . . . Police Station . . . She had been robbed of . . . I forget how many pounds . . . they were touched by her story and made a collection for her', whereas one using a visual image strategy may recall: 'There's a woman . . . she's walking down the road . . . and she goes into a large building . . . there's a policeman there . . . and she tells him something . . . maybe she had something stolen . . . and then they give her some money . . . which she then takes and goes to buy some food.'

The strategies used by these two people are clearly different and techniques which identify what strategies people use and how success-ful they are may give valuable guidelines as to techniques which a person will find helpful in treatment. The ability of some people to develop their own strategies may enable them to cope with daily life and yet have quite marked deficits on tests where the strategies cannot be readily used.

Another factor associated with the relationship between test per-formance and daily life, is mood. Kahn's (Kahn *et al.*, 1975) work on elderly demented patients suggests that depression is an important factor in memory complaints. Those who complain of memory diffi-culties, and presumably who are also experiencing more problems in daily life, are more likely to be depressed than to present deficits on testing. The assessment of the significance of memory problems may require consideration of mood and personality factors as well as identifying the nature of the cognitive deficit.

Strategies of Memory Training

The range of strategies for use in training patients ideally needs to be extended. While this seems feasible for external aids, the scope of internal strategies is more difficult to imagine. Electronic external aids, although available, are not easy to obtain and the selection is limited. It would seem that there is no technical difficulty in producing the aids required but as demand is unlikely to be great, the manufacturers will not produce them unless their scope can be extended. It becomes a vicious circle that the development of memory training is hindered by the lack of appropriate external aids, but these are unlikely to be produced until the demand increases. As described in Chapter 3 the important considerations are portability, the range of functions provided and the simplicity of operation. Most therapists using electronic external aids usually have only one available for patients to see and try out. It would be useful, both for therapists and patients, if there was at least one centre where all the aids currently provided were available. Patients and therapists could try out the different aids and examine their relative advantages and disadvantages without incurring any unnecessary cost by ordering an inappropriate aid. Such centres already exist for communication aids and domestic appliances, so perhaps it would be quite feasible for a memory aid centre to be created.

Internal aids can be used to help recall events that people want to remember. At the moment it seems that the use of imagery is the most powerful strategy. This is particularly useful in patients with verbal memory deficits and relatively less impaired visual memory. The use of verbal mnemonics for those with predominantly visual deficits seems less successful. Although useful for lists and numbers they are not such effective cues for associations between names and faces and things to be done. However, this is based on subjective impressions rather than systematic observation. An evaluation of the relative effectiveness of different types of cue for different problems would provide a valuable guideline as to what strategy to suggest in clinical practice. It would also indicate the problems for which, as yet, no effective strategies have been found. At present, relatively little use has been made of either auditory cues or motor cues. For example the problem of route finding might be cued by having different sounds associated with right and left turns. A patient with predominantly visual spatial memory problems might be able to learn a sequence of tones to cue correct turns. On the other hand they might be able to learn a sequence of hand movements to act as prompts for the different turns. Names might also be converted into motor cues. For instance, the name 'Lincoln' could be converted into an action of *linking* fingers and then putting them *on* to the table.

An outline of how to match the strategy to the problem in relation to the person's abilities and deficits is described in Chapter 5. There is plenty of scope for further investigation of factors to be incorporated into this plan. The role of mood has already been mentioned, and factors such as depression may affect the choice of strategy. Similarly, most patients with memory problems also have other intellectual deficits. Aphasia, disorders of visual perception and impaired concentration could also determine the choice of strategies to be used. Further investigation of memory training in the presence of associated deficits or generalised intellectual impairment is clearly needed.

The problems, however, are not just confined to identifying the difficulty and finding the strategy to deal with it. The acceptability to the patient and the compliance with suggested strategies need greater emphasis. It is no good being able to demonstrate that a patient's recall can be improved by a particular strategy if he fails to use it in daily life. There are often difficulties in persuading a patient to accept what appears to be a rather cumbersome method of dealing with memory tasks. Although demonstration of its effectiveness is the best method of convincing patients, perhaps greater acceptance of the idea that memory training is possible will enhance this process. The medical profession has a generally pessimistic approach to the amelioration of memory deficits and a change in this may lead to greater acceptance by patients.

It is not unusual for a patient to have been told that nothing can be done about the problem and he will just have to live with it. Keeping a notebook or diary and writing lists may have been suggested but with little specific advice about what sort of information to record. A diary of regular daily events, such as meals, activities in physiotherapy and occupational therapy seems more likely to help that patient keep track of time and recall what he has done than a diary of distanced events, such as shopping trips, which may only happen occasionally. It is also far more likely that patients will get in the habit of writing things down if they have to record events that occur every day. By the time the infrequent shopping trip happens, the notebook will probably have been either lost or forgotten. Patients who are told to write lists for shopping and succeeded may then be recommended to try to do the shopping without a list. This seems to be based on the principle of exercising the mental muscle described in Chapter 3. It seems that if the person is coping by using lists then there is no point trying to do without and if they are not coping, it is unlikely that repeated practice and failures will be much help. Perhaps when planning future meetings concerned with the management of memory problems it is of paramount importance that members of the medical profession are present. The GP and the neurologist are likely to see a patient long before any memory training is considered: it is at this stage that a more positive approach might help with patient's acceptance of the idea that they can be shown ways to help themselves.

Practical Considerations

Memory training requires patients to play a very active part in their own rehabilitation and in this respect it is the antithesis of drug treatment. As rehabilitation in general becomes more client directed and patient, rather than staff, monitored, then the idea of the patient taking this active role may become more acceptable. The use of behavioural principles in rehabilitation, such as goal setting, self-reinforcement and feedback of progress, should help this process.

Most of the clinical work reported has been with head injury patients. For these people, who are often young, the memory difficulty may pose the single most limiting factor in their recovery and therefore it is appropriate that considerable efforts should be put into dealing with their difficulties. However, there are other diagnostic groups in whom memory deficits may affect their ability to cope with daily life and increase the handicap imposed by physical disability. For instance, it has long been recognised that patients with advanced multiple sclerosis have memory deficits recordable on standard psychological testing (Jambor, 1969; Staples and Lincoln, 1981). This seems to have some impact on their daily life, in that those with memory difficulties do less than their estimated capabilities and inaccurately report their capabilities (Lincoln, 1979). The question arises as to whether, by improving their memory performance, they could then make better use of their physical capabilities. While this might be appropriate for dealing with the reliability of self-report of behaviours, improvement in performance might be better achieved by the use of behaviour modification techniques. This is purely speculative, but since memory problems and poor performance may account for the hospitalisation of many patients with multiple sclerosis, it would seem worthy of further investigation. For example, Miss PB is a woman who is looked after at home by her mother. She has had multiple sclerosis for seven years and as a result has poor eyesight, poor co-ordination and memory problems. She is able to get about on foot with difficulty but needs supervision in all activities of daily living. She was catheterised because of urinary incontinence but still insists that her mother should help her on to the toilet even when this is not necessary. Although she is repeatedly told that she has a catheter which is on continuous drainage, she repeatedly asks to be taken to the toilet. In this instance it is the memory problem that makes her management at home more difficult for her mother and increases the disability imposed by her urinary incontinence.

The elderly are probably the single largest group with memory problems, yet the training techniques used with them are rather dissimilar to those mentioned in the preceding chapters. Reality orientation is the single most widely used memory training with the elderly and provided certain conditions are met seems to be relatively successful (Brook, Degun and Mather, 1975; Greene, Nicol and Jamieson, 1979; Woods, 1979). However, its aims are relatively limited and while appropriate for the type of patient usually given reality orientation training (in-patients on psycho-geriatric wards) it may be insufficient in its scope for the less impaired but nevertheless significantly handicapped patients. These people may be well orientated in time and place and able to cope with a simple daily routine yet be unable to return to live independently at home because of forgetting where they have put things, forgetting to turn the gas or electric cooker or fire off, leaving doors unlocked and handbags where they can be taken.

There is no reason why the methods described in this book should not be attempted. However, it should be remembered that if there is generalised intellectual impairment a wide range of abilities may be affected. The most likely techniques are the provision of environmental cues and external aids. These at least do not require the patient to learn new strategies for remembering.

The setting in which the treatment is conducted may affect the procedures which can be used and the problems which can be tackled. On an out-patient basis one is very dependent on the problems reported by the patient or observed by a friend or relative. If a patient reports no difficulties and the relatives say he remembers all he needs to remember, yet he fails to hold a job and performs poorly on testing, it is difficult to devise a memory training programme realistically. It may not be necessary, but the person's failure to return to work may be a sufficient indication that there are difficulties, and only direct observation of the person in a work environment may enable the problems to be identified.

Memory training may be carried out more easily in a rehabilitation department than in an out-patient clinic. Most of the training programmes described have begun on an in-patient basis. This enables the therapist to identify the difficulties in conjunction with the full rehabilitation team. Strategies may be developed and evaluated to deal with the difficulties observed while in hospital. Once the most effective strategies have been identified and the patient trained in their use, then both the patient and therapist can more readily identify how problems in daily life outside the hospital environment may be tackled. This increases the chance of success in the situation where it really matters. It is not going to be as important to a patient that he learns the names of staff in the unit as that he learns the names of work colleagues once leaving hospital. On a ward in-patient basis, one additional complication may arise if there is a lack of consistency in the approach of different members of staff. If all members of the rehabilitation team are aware of strategies which may be used then it is important that the advice given about which strategy a patient uses should be consistently given, so that if visual imagery is appropriate then all staff should prompt the use of that strategy and not suggest others which might confuse rather than assist.

This leads to the question of who should carry out memory training. It is tempting to conclude that all staff should for all of the time. However, not only is this an inefficient use of staff time but it also makes evaluation of treatment effects well nigh impossible. It seems that someone has to be responsible for evaluating the deficits. This may be by test performance or by simply collating information recorded by different members of staff. The next stage would be to identify appropriate strategies and try them on a selected range of tasks. Once the effective strategies have been selected then general encouragement in the use of those particular strategies for those particular problems may be necessary. Traditionally it has been clinical psychologists who have been involved in assessing memory deficits. With increasing emphasis on behavioural observation and less on tests, it may be equally appropriate for other professions to be involved in the assessment stage. The training and evaluation of the effectiveness of training has also traditionally been carried out by clinical psychologists, but given the shortage of clinical psychologists, this may not be feasible when one considers the potential number of patients to be treated. The clinical psychologist is likely to retain a key role in developing strategies, designing training methods and evaluating the effectiveness of treatment methods. However, for much of the implementation of training programmes, the occupational therapists, speech therapists and nurses, given the necessary training, should carry out a major part of the treatment.

Evaluation of Management Techniques

Evaluation has been emphasised throughout the discussion of treatment techniques. Single case experimental designs have been used to investigate whether a particular strategy has enabled a patient to recall more information than without the strategy. This initial stage is vital and needs to continue as part of all patient management programmes. It enables us to assess the value of what we are doing for each person. It also provides comparisons of the usefulness of different strategies for different problems. Once a series of single case experimental designs has been carried out it then becomes possible to identify similarities and consistencies between them. At this stage it becomes possible to design group studies to assess the generality of the findings. For example, if several case studies show that patients with severe verbal memory deficits and milder visual deficits can use imagery to learn people's names but those with visual memory problems do not benefit, one can then design a group study to check on the consistency of these findings for a wide range of problems. Although the single case designs enable us to identify for each patient what is effective, they do not necessarily provide guidelines about what is most likely to be most effective with what type of patient or help in selection of appropriate patients for training. Some patients fail the required skill and it is helpful to be able to identify these before embarking on a lengthy training programme so that alternative approaches may be used. Some group studies have been carried out but these have generally been on the effects of training on laboratory-type tasks rather than daily life skills.

The generalisation of training on specific tasks to other daily life skills needs further investigation. The clinical impression is that some patients, once having understood the principles behind the strategies used, can apply them to a variety of situations and develop new strategies of their own. Others need to be given a specific technique for each task and only apply it to that task unless given training in its use for other tasks. The means that may be used to promote generalisation of use of strategies is therefore crucial to the effectiveness of training as a whole. Further investigation of means of promoting generalisation across tasks, and across settings would provide valuable clinical information. One means of promoting the generalisation of the use of particular strategies is in the type of group activities described in Chapter 9. The tasks introduced can be either those in which a person has been specifically trained or an unfamiliar task for which there are strategies available but it is the responsibility of the patient to select the appropriate one. The value of group treatment seems likely to be that it provides a more efficient use of therapist time, it encourages generalisation of learned skills and it promotes the acceptability of using strategies. Whether this is really the case has not been investigated, nor has research been carried out to find the optimum balance between individual and group treatment.

Memory training is in its infancy. Techniques are available and could contribute to the rehabilitation of a large number of patients with deficits. The main aim of this book has been to describe what can be done by a variety of professions. Even if it only achieves the dissemination of this information it will represent a significant contribution to clinical practice. By presenting the limitations, and demonstrating the enormous scope for development that exists, we hope it will also provide a stimulus for further development of techniques of memory training. Many of the developments suggested here are likely to be a direct result of further use of memory training in clinical practice. Clinicians will gain experience of applying the techniques in different settings, in-patient and out-patient, with different client groups, patients with strokes, multiple sclerosis and dementia, and in conjunction with other handicaps, both physical and cognitive. This will inevitably lead to trying new strategies to aid recall and to developing appropriate means of assessing progress. However, the success of this is largely going to depend on convincing both patients and the medical professions that memory impairment is not an unavoidable handicap but, given appropriate management, some of the problems it causes can be reduced.

REFERENCES

Acker, W. (1980) In support of the microcomputer based automated testing: a description of the Maudsley automated psychological screening tests (MAPS) *British Journal of Alcohol and Alcoholism, 15,* 144–7.

Alzheimer, A. (1907) Uber eine eigenartige Erkranskung der Hirnrinde, *Allg. Z. Psychiatrie Psychoisch-Gerichtlich Med., 64,* 146–8.

Andrews, K. and Stewart, J. (1979) Stroke recovery: he can but does he? *Rheumatology and Rehabilitation, 18,* 43–8.

Atkinson, R.C. and Shiffrin, R.M. (1968) Human Memory: a proposed system and its control processes; in K.W. Spence and J.T. Spence (eds.), *The Psychology of Learning and Motivation,* vol. II, Academic Press, New York.

Atkinson, R.C. and Shiffrin, R.M. (1971) The control of short-term memory, *Scientific American, 225,* 82–90.

Baddeley, A.D. (1966a) Short-term memory for word sequences as a function of acoustic, semantic and formal similarity, *Quarterly Journal of Experimental Psychology, 18,* 362–5.

Baddeley, A.D. (1966b) The influence of acoustic and semantic similarity on long-term memory for word sequences, *Quarterly Journal of Experimental Psychology, 18,* 302–9.

Baddeley, A.D. (1982a) *Your Memory: A User's Guide,* Penguin Books, Harmondsworth, Middlesex.

Baddeley, A.D. (1982b) Amnesia: a minimal model and an interpretation; in L. Cermak (ed.), *Human Memory and Amnesia,* Lawrence Erlbaum Associates, Hillsdale, NJ.

Baddeley, A.D. (1982c) Implications of neuropsychological evidence for theories of normal memory, *Philosophical Transactions of the Royal Society London, B, 298,* 59–72.

Baddeley, A.D. and Hitch, G.J. (1974) Working Memory; in G.A. Bower (ed.), *The Psychology of Learning and Motivation,* vol. 8, Academic Press, New York.

Baddeley, A.D. and Warrington, E.K. (1970) Amnesia and the distinction between long and short-term memory, *Journal of Verbal Learning and Verbal Behaviour, 9,* 176–89.

Baddeley, A.D. and Warrington, E.K. (1973) Memory coding and amnesia, *Neuropsychologia, ii,* 159–65.

Baddeley, A.D. and Wilson, B. (in press) Differences among amnesias and between amnesics: the role of single case methodology in theoretical analysis and practical treatment; in W. Hirst (ed.), *Proceedings of the Princeton Amnesia Conference,* Lawrence Erlbaum Associates, Hillsdale, NJ.

Bandura, A. (1969) *Principles of Behaviour Modification,* Holt, Rinehart and Winston, New York.

Bennett-Levy, J. and Powell, G.E. (1980) The subjective memory questionnaire (SMQ): an investigation into the self-reporting of 'real-life' memory skills, *British Journal of Social and Clinical Psychology, 19,* 177–83.

Benton, A.L. (1950) A multiple choice type of the visual retention test, *Archives Neurology and Psychiatry, 64*, 699–707.

Benton, A.L. (1974) *The Revised Visual Retention Test*, Psychological Corporation, New York.

Ben-Yishay, Y., Rattok, J. and Diller, L. (1979) A clinical strategy for the systematic amelioration of attentional disturbances in severe head trauma patients, *Institute of Rehabilitation Medicine Monograph*, New York University Medical Centre, New York.

Bion, W.R. (1959) *Experiences in Groups*, Basic Books, New York.

Black, P., Markowitz, R.S. and Cianci, S. (1975) Recovery of motor function after lesions in motor cortex of monkey; in R. Porter and D.W. Fitzsimons (eds.), *Outcome of Severe Damage to the Central Nervous System*, Ciba Foundation Symposium 34, Elsevier, Amsterdam.

Bolton, B. (1974) *Introduction to Rehabilitation Research*, C. Thomas, USA.

Bowen, D.M., Smith, C.B., White, P. and Davison, A.N. (1976) Neurotransmitter-related enzymes and indices of hypoxia in senile dementia and other abiotrophies, *Brain, 99*, 459–95.

Bower, G.M. and Clark, M.C. (1969) Narrative stories as mediators for serial learning, *Psychonomic Science, 14*, 181–2.

Bower, G.H. and Bolton, L.S. (1969) Why are rhymes easy to learn? *Journal of Experimental Psychology, 82*, 453–61.

Bower, G.H. and Reitman, J.S. (1972) Mnemonic elaboration in multilist learning, *Journal of Verbal Learning and Visual Behaviour, 11*, 478–85.

Bowen, D.M., Smith, C.B., White, P. and Davison, A.N. (1976) Neuro-transmitter-related enzymes and indices of hypoxia in senile dementia and other abiotrophies, *Brain, 99*, 459–95.

Boyd, W.D., Graham-White, J., Blackwood, G., Glen, I. and McQueen, J. (1977) Clinical effects of choline in Alzheimer senile dementia, *Lancet, 2*, 711.

Bracy, O.L. (1983) Computer based cognitive rehabilitation, *Cognitive Rehabilitation, 1*, 7–8.

Brook, P., Degun, G. and Mather, M. (1975) Reality orientation, a therapy for psychogeriatric patients: a controlled study, *British Journal of Psychiatry, 127*, 42–5.

Brooks, D.N. (1972) Memory and head injury, *Journal of Nervous Mental Diseases, 155*, 350–5.

Brooks, D.N. (1975) Long and short-term memory in head injured patients, *Cortex, ii*, 329–40.

Brooks, D.N. (1976) Wechsler Memory Scale performance and its relationship to brain damage after severe closed head injury, *Journal of Neurology, Neurosurgery and Psychiatry, 39*, 593–601.

Brooks, D.N. (1979) Psychological deficits after severe blunt head injury: their significance and rehabilitation; in Oborne, D.J., Gruneberg, M.M. and Eiser, J.R., *Research in Psychology in Medicine, 2*, Academic Press, London, 469–76.

Brooks, D.N. (1983) Disorders of memory; in Rosenthal, M., Griffith, E.R., Bond, M.R. and Miller, G.D. (eds.), *Rehabilitation of the Head Injured Patient*, F.A. Davis Company, Philadelphia.

Brooks, D.N. and Aughton, M.E. (1979) Cognitive recovery during the first year after severe blunt head injury, *International Rehabilitation Medicine, 1*, 166–72.

214   *References*

Brooks, D.N., Aughton, M.E., Bond, M.R., James, P. and Rizvi, S. (1980) Cognitive sequalae in relationship to early indices of severity of brain damage after severe blunt head injury, *Journal of Neurology, Neurosurgery and Psychiatry*, *43*, 529–34.

Brooks, D.N. and Baddeley, A. (1976) What can amnesics learn? *Neuropsychologia*, *14*, 111–22.

Brooks, D.N. and McKinlay, W.W. (1983) Personality and behaviour change after severe blunt head injury: a relative's view, *Journal of Neurology, Neurosurgery and Psychiatry*, *46*, 336–44.

Brown, R. and McNeil, D. (1966) The 'tip of the tongue' phenomenon, *Journal of Verbal Learning and Verbal Behaviour*, *5*, 325–37.

Buzan, A. (1977) *Speed Memory*, David and Charles, Newton Abbot.

Carr, A.C., Ghosh, A. and Ancill, R.J. (1983) Can a computer take a psychiatric history? *Psychological Medicine*, *13*, 151–8.

Carr, J. (1980) Imitation, discrimination and generalisation; in Yule, W. and Carr, J. (eds.), *Behaviour Modification for the Mentally Handicapped*, Croom Helm, London.

Castro-Caldas, A. and Botelho, M.A.S. (1980) Dichotic listening in the recovery of aphasia after stroke, *Brain and Language*, *10*, 145–51.

Cermak, L.S. (1975) Imagery as an aid to retrieval for Korsakoff patients, *Quarterly Journal of Studies of Alcoholism*, *34*, 1110–32.

Cermak, L.S. (1976) The encoding capacity of a patient with amnesia due to encephalitis, *Neuropsychologia*, *14*, 311–26.

Cermak, L.S. (1980) Comments on imagery as a therapeutic mnemonic; in Poon, L.W., Fozard, J.L., Cermak, L.S., Arenberg, D. and Thompson, L.W. (eds.), *New Directions in Memory and Aging*, Lawrence Erlbaum Associates, Hillsdale, NJ.

Chadwick, O., Rutter, M., Schaffer, D. and Shrout, P.E. (1981) A prospective study of children with head injuries. IV: specific cognitive defects, *Journal of Clinical Neuropsychology*, *3*, 101–20.

Cherry, C. (1953) Some experiments on the reception of speech with one and with two ears, *Journal Acoustic Society American*, *25*, 975–9.

Christie, J.E., Glen, A.I.M., Yates, C.M., Blackburn, I.M., Shering, A., Jellinek, E.H. and Zeisel, S. (1979) Choline and lecithin effects on CSF choline levels and on cognitive function in Alzheimer pre-senile dementia; in A.I.M. Glen and L.J. Whalley (eds.), *Alzheimer's Disease*, Churchill Livingstone, Edinburgh, pp. 163–8.

Citrin, R.S. and Dixon, D.N. (1977) Reality orientation: a milieu therapy used in an institution for the aged, *Gerontologist*, *17*, 39–43.

Claridge, G.S. (1967) *Personality and Arousal. A Psychophysiological Study of Psychiatric Disorder*, Pergamon Press, Oxford.

Conkey, R.C. (1938) Psychological changes associated with head injuries, *Archives Psychology*, no. 232 (ed. R.S. Woodworth), New York.

Cornbleth, T. and Cornbleth, C. (1979) Evaluation of the effectiveness of reality orientation classes in a nursing home unit, *Journal of American Geriatrics Society*, *27*, 522–4.

Corser, C.M., Baikie, E. and Brown, E. (1979) Effect of lecithin in senile dementia: a report of four cases; in A.I.M. Glen and L.J. Whalley (eds.), *Alzheimer's Disease*, Churchill Livingstone, Edinburgh, pp. 169–78.

Cotton, E. (1965) The Institute of movement therapy and school for conductors in Budapest, Hungary, *Developmental Medicine and Child Neurology, 7*, 437–46.

Cotton, E. (1974) Improvement of motor function with the use of conductive education, *Developmental Medicine and Child Neurology, 16*, 637–43.

Craik, F.I.M. and Lockhart, R.S. (1972) Levels of processing: a framework for memory research, *Journal of Verbal Learning and Verbal Behaviour, 11*, 671–84.

Craik, F.I.M. and Watkins, M.J. (1973) The role of rehearsal in short-term memory, *Journal of Verbal Learning and Verbal Behaviour, 2*, 599–607.

Crovitz, H. (1979) Memory retraining in brain damaged patients: the airplane list, *Cortex, 15*, 131–4.

Crovitz, H., Harvey, M. and Horn, R. (1979) Problems in the acquisition of imagery mnemonics: three brain damaged cases, *Cortex, 15*, 225–34.

Crow, T.J. and Grove-White, I.G. (1973) An analysis of the learning deficit following hyoscine administration to man, *British Journal of Pharmacology, 49*, 322–7.

Crow, T.J., Grove-White, I. and Ross, D.G. (1976) The specificity of the action of hyoscine on human learning, *British Journal of Clinical Pharmacology, 2*, 367–8.

Cummings, J.L., Benson, D.F., Walsh, M.J. and Levine, H.L. (1979) Left-to-right transfer of language dominance: a case study, *Neurology, 29*, 1547–50.

Davies, A.D.M. and Binks, M.G. (1983) Supporting the residual memory of a Korsakoff patient, *Behavioural Psychotherapy, 11*, 62–74.

Davies, P. (1979) Neurotransmitter-related enzymes in senile dementia of the Alzheimer type, *Brain Research, 171*, 319–27.

Davies, P. and Maloney, A.J.R. (1976) Selective loss of central cholinergic neurons in Alzheimer's disease, *Lancet, 2*, 1403.

Davis, K.L., Mohs, R.C., Tinklenberg, J.R., Pfefferbaum, A., Hollister, L.E. and Kopell, B.S. (1978) Physostigmine: an improvement of long-term memory processes in normal humans, *Science, 201*, 272–4.

De Dombal, F.T. and Gremy, F. (eds.) (1981) *Decision Making and Medical Care*, North Holland, Amsterdam.

Degun, G. (1976) Reality orientation: a multidisciplinary therapeutic approach, *Nursing Times, 72*, 117–20.

Dencker, S.J. and Lofving, B. (1958) A psychometric study of identical twins discordant for closed head injury, *Acta Psychiatrica Neurologica Scandinavia, 33*, Suppl. 122.

Deutsch, J.A. (1971) The cholinergic synapse and the site of memory, *Science, 174*, 788–94.

Deutsch, J.A. and Rogers, J.R. (1979) Cholinergic excitability and memory: animal studies and their clinical implications; in K.L. Davis and P.A. Berger (eds.), *Brain Acetylcholine and Neuropsychiatric Disease*, Plenum Press, New York, pp. 175–204.

Devor, M. (1982) Plasticity in the adult nervous system; in L.S. Illis, E.M. Sedgwick and H.T. Glanville (eds.), *Rehabilitation of the Neurological Patient*, Blackwell Scientific Publications, Oxford.

Dictionary of Mnemonics (1972), Eyre Methuen, London.

Diller, L., Weinberg, J., Piasetsky, E., Ruckdeschel–Hibbard, M., Egelko, S., Scotzin, M., Couniotakis, J. and Gordon, W. (1980) Methods for the evaluation and treatment of the visual perceptual difficulties of right brain damaged individuals (*Monograph*), *Institute of Rehabilitation Medicine*, University Medical Center, New York.

Diller, L. and Weinberg, J. (1977) Hemi-inattention in rehabilitation: the evolution of a rational remediation program; in Weinstein, E.A. and Friedland, R.P. (eds.), *Advances in Neurology*, vol. 18, Raven Press, New York.

Dimond, S.J. and Brouwers, E.Y.M. (1976) Increase in the power of human memory in normal man through the use of drugs, *Psychopharmacology, 49*, 307–9.

Drachman, D.A. and Leavitt, J. (1974) Human memory and the cholinergic system, *Achives Neurology, 30*, 113–21.

Drummond, L., Kirchoff, L. and Scarbrough, D.R. (1978) A practical guide to reality orientation: a treatment approach for confusion and disorientation, *Gerontologist, 18*, 568–73.

Eames, P.G. and Wood, R. Ll. (1983) Consciousness in the brain damaged adult; in R. Stevens (ed.), *Aspects of Consciousness*, vol. 4, Academic Press, London.

Edgington, E.S. (1982) Nonparametric tests for single-subject multiple schedule experiments, *Behavioural Assessment, 4*, 83–91.

Eich, J.E. (1980) The cue-dependent nature of state-dependent retrieval, *Memory and Cognition, 8*, 157–73.

Elithorn, A. and Telford, A. (1969) Computer analysis of intellectual skills, *International Journal of Man-Machine Studies, 1*, 189–209.

Elliot, R. (1969) Tonic heart rate, *Journal Personality and Social Psychology, 12*, 211–28.

Ericsson, K.A., Chase, W.G. and Falcon, S. (1980) Acquisition of a memory skill, *Science, 208*, 1181–2.

Erickson, R.C. and Scott, M.I. (1977) Clinical memory testing: a review, *Psychological Bulletin, 84*, 1130–49.

Etienne, P., Gauthier, S., Dastoor, D., Collier, B. and Ratner, J. (1979) Alzheimer's disease: clinical effect of lecithin treatment; in A.I.M. Glen and L.J. Whalley (eds.), *Alzheimer's Disease*, Churchill Livingstone, Edinburgh, pp. 173–8.

Etienne, P., Gauthier, S., Johnson, G., Collier, B., Mendis, T., Dastoor, D., Cole, M. and Muller, H.F. (1978) Clinical effects of choline in Alzheimer's disease, *Lancet, 1*, 508–9.

Evans, C.D. (1981) *Rehabilitation of the Head Injured*, Churchill Livingstone, London.

Evans, C.R. (1975) Chatting with computers, *Electronics and Power, 21*, 430–2.

Field, J.H. (1976) *Epidemiology of Head Injuries in England and Wales*, HMSO, London.

Folsom, J.C. (1968) Reality orientation for the elderly mental patient, *Journal of Geriatric Psychiatry, 1*, 291–307.

Fordyce, W.E. (1976) *Behavioural Methods for Chronic Pain and Illness*, Mosby, St Louis, Mo.

Fowler, R., Hart, J. and Sheehan, M. (1972) A prosthetic memory: an application of the prosthetic environment concept, *Rehabilitation Counselling Bulletin, 15*, 80–5.

Funkenstein, H.H., Hicks, R., Dysken, M.W. and Davis, J.M. (1981) Drug treatment of cognitive impairment in Alzheimer's disease and the late life dementia; in N.E. Miller and G.D. Cohen (eds.), *Clinical Aspects of Alzheimer's Disease and Senile Dementia*, Raven Press, New York, pp. 139–58.

Furst, B. (1972) *Number Dictionary*, revised and enlarged by Furst, L. and Storm, G., Memory and Concentration Studies, Mundelein, Illinois.

Gardner, H. (1977) *The Shattered Mind: The Person after Brain Damage*, Routledge & Kegan Paul, London.

Gazzaniga, M.S. (1978) Is seeing believing: notes on clinical recovery; in Finger, S. (ed.), *Recovery from Brain Damage*, Plenum Press, New York.

Gedye, J.L. and Miller, E. (1970) Developments in automated testing systems; in P. Mittler (ed.), *The Psychological Assessment of Mental and Physical Handicaps*, Methuen & Co., London, pp. 735–60.

Ghoneim, M.M. and Mewaldt, S.O. (1975) Effects of diazepam and scopolamine on storage, retrieval and organisational processes in memory, *Psychopharmacologia, 44*, 257–62.

Ghoneim, M.M. and Mewaldt, S.O. (1977) Studies on human memory: the interactions of diazepam, scopolamine and physostigmine, *Psychopharmacology, 52*, 1–6.

Gianutsos, R. and Gianutsos, J. (1979) Rehabilitating the verbal recall of brain injured patients by mnemonic training: an experimental demonstration using single case methodology, *Journal Clinical Neuropsychology, 1*, 117–35.

Glasgow, R.E., Zeiss, R.A., Barrera, M. and Lewinsohn, P.M. (1977) Case studies on remediating memory deficits in brain damaged individuals, *Journal Clinical Psychology, 33*, 1049–54.

Glees, P. and Cole, J. (1950) Recovery of skilled motor functions after small repeated lesions of motor cortex in macaque, *Journal of Neurophysiology, 13*, 137–48.

Glick, S.D. and Greenstein, S. (1973) Possible modulating influence of frontal cortex on nigrostriatal function, *British Journal of Pharmacology, 49*, 316–21.

Godden, D. and Baddeley, A.D. (1975) Context-dependent memory in two natural environments: on land and under water, *British Journal of Psychology, 66*, 325–31.

Godden, D. and Baddeley, A.D. (1980) When does context influence recognition memory? *British Journal of Psychology, 71*, 99–104.

Golden, C.J. (1978) *Diagnosis and Rehabilitation in Clinical Neuropsychology*, Charles C. Thomas, Illinois.

Goldstein, G., Turner, S.M., Holzman, A., Kanagy, M., Elmore, S. and Barry, K. (1982) An evaluation of reality orientation theory, *Journal of Behavioural Assessment, 4*, 165–78.

Goldstein, K. (1939) *The Organism*, American Book Co., New York.

Gollin, E.S. (1960) Developmental studies of visual recognition of incomplete objects, *Perceptual and Motor Skills, 2*, 289–98.

Goodwin, D.W., Powell, B., Bremer, D., Hoine, H. and Stern, J. (1969) Alcohol and recall: state dependent effects in man, *Science, 163*, 1358.

Greene, J.G., Nicol, R. and Jamieson, H. (1979) Reality orientation with psychogeriatric patients, *Behavioural Research and Therapy, 17*, 615–18.

Greene, J.G., Smith, R. and Gardiner, M. (1980) Reality orientation with psychogeriatric day hospital patients – an empirical evaluation. Paper presented at *British Psychological Society Annual Conference*, Aberdeen.

Groninger, L.D. (1971) Mnemonic imagery and forgetting, *Psychonomic Science, 23*, 161–3.

Gronwall, D. and Sampson, H. (1974) *Psychological Effects of Concussion*, Auckland University Press.

Gross, Y., Ben-Nahum, F., Murk, G. and Kohn, H. (1980) A rehabilitation algorithm theory and practice. Paper presented at the *Third European Conference of the International Neuropsychological Society*, Chianciano, Italy.

Gustafson, L., Risberg, J., Johanson, M., Fransson, M. and Maximilian, V.A. (1978) Effects of piracetam on regional cerebral blood flow and mental functions in patients with organic dementia, *Psychopharmacology, 56*, 115–17.

Haffey, W.J. (1983) A demonstration of Luria's qualitative neuropsychological method of cognitive remediation. Paper presented at the *Annual Meeting of the International Neuropsychological Society*, Mexico.

Hahn, K. (1980) Using 24 hour reality orientation, *Journal of Gerontological Nursing, 6*, 130–5.

Hanley, I.G. (1980) Optimism or pessimism: an examination of reality orientation procedures in the management of dementia. Paper presented at the *British Psychological Society Annual Conference*, Aberdeen.

Hanley, I.G. (1981) The use of signposts and active training to modify ward disorientation in elderly patients, *Journal of Behaviour Therapy and Experimental Psychiatry, 12*, 241–7.

Hanley, I.G. (1982) *A Manual for the Modification of Confused Behaviour*, Lothian Regional Council, Edinburgh.

Hanley, I.G., McGuire, R.J. and Boyd, W.D. (1981) Reality orientation and dementia: a controlled trial of two approaches, *British Journal of Psychiatry, 138*, 10–14.

Hanley, I.G., Cleary, E., Oates, M.G. and Walker, M. (1981) Diminishing elderly residents' confusion, *Social Work Today, 12*, 42, 8–10.

Hare, M. (1978) Clinical checklist for diagnosis of dementia, *British Medical Journal, 2*, 266–7.

Harris, C.S. and Ivory, P.B.C.B. (1976) An outcome evaluation of reality orientation therapy with geriatric patients in a state mental hospital, *Gerontologist, 16*, 496–503.

Harris, J.E. (1978) External memory aids; in Gruneberg, M.M., Morris, P. and Sykes, R. (eds.), *Practical Aspects of Memory*, London, Academic Press.

Harris, J.E. (1980a) Memory aids people use: two interview studies, *Memory and Cognition, 8*, 31–8.

Harris, J.E. (1980b) We have ways of helping you remember, *Concord. The Journal of the British Association for Service to the Elderly, no. 17*, 21–7.

Harris, J.E. (1984) Remembering to do things: a forgotten topic; in Harris, J.E. and Morris, P.E. (eds.), *Everyday Memory, Actions and Absent-mindedness*, Academic Press, London and New York.

Harris, J.E. and Sunderland, A. (1981) A brief survey of the management of memory disorders in rehabilitation units in Britain, *International Rehabilitation Medicine, 3*, 206–9.

Harris, J.E. and Wilkins, A.J. (1982) Remembering to do things: a theoretical framework and an illustrative experiment, *Human Learning, 1*, 123–36.

Hellebusch, S.J. (1976) *On improving learning and memory in the aged: the effects of mnemonics on strategy, transfer and generalisation*. Dissertation Abstract (1459-B Order No. 76–19, 496), University of Notre Dame.

Herrman, D. and Neisser, U. (1978) An inventory of everyday memory experiences; in Gruneberg, M.M., Morris, P. and Sykes, R. (eds.), *Practical Aspects of Memory*, Academic Press, London.

Hersen, M. and Barlow, D.H. (1976) *Single Case Experimental Designs: Strategy for Studying Behaviour Change*, Pergamon, Elmsford, New York.

Higbee, K.L. (1977) *Your Memory: How it Works and How to Improve it*, Prentice Hall, Englewood-Cliffs, NJ.

Holden, U.P. (1979) Return to reality, *Nursing Mirror, 149* (21), 26–30.

Holden, U.P. and Sinebruchow, A. (1979) Validation of reality orientation therapy for use with the elderly, unpublished manuscript.

Holden, U.P. and Woods, R.T. (1982) *Reality Orientation: Psychological apaproaches to the confused elderly*, Churchill Livingstone, London.

Holland, A.L. (1980) *Communicative Abilities in Daily Living*, University Park Press, Baltimore.

Honig, W.K. (1969) Fundamental issues in associated learning; in N.J. Mackintosh and W.K. Honig (eds.), *Fundamental Issues in Associational Learning*, Dalhousie University Press, Halifax, Nova Scotia.

Hunter, I.M.I. (1979) Memory in everyday life; in Gruneberg, M.M. and Morris, P.E. (eds.), *Applied Problems in Memory*, Academic Press, London.

Hussian, R.A. (1981) *Geriatric Psychology: A Behavioural Perspective*, Van Nostrand Reinhold, London.

Inglis, J. (1957) An experimental study of learning and memory function in elderly patients, *Journal Mental Science, 103*, 798–803.

Jackson, H. and Moffat, N.J. (1982) Training motor coding with the severely head injured, unpublished manuscript.

Jaffe, P.G. and Katz, A.N. (1975) Attenuating anterograde amnesia, *Journal of Abnormal Psychology, 84*, 559–62.

Jambor, K. (1969) Cognitive functioning in multiple sclerosis, *British Journal of Psychiatry, 115*, 765–75.

James, W. (1890) *Principles of Psychology*, Henry Holt & Co., New York.

Jennett, B. (1976) Post-traumatic epilepsy; in Vinken, P.J. and Bruyn, G.W. (eds.), *Handbook of Clinical Neurology*, vol. 24, Elsevier/North Holland Publishing Company, Amsterdam.

Johnson, C.H. (1979) *Reality Orientation: an Evaluation Study*, dissertation for British Psychology Society Diploma in Clinical Psychology.

Jones, M. (1974) Imagery as a mnemonic aid after left temporary lobectomy: contrast between material specific and generalized memory disorders, *Neuropsychologia, 12*, 21–30.

Jones, G. and Adam, J. (1979) Towards a prosthetic memory, *Bulletin of the British Psychological Society, 32*, 165–7.

Jones, D.M., Jones, M.E.L., Lewis, M.J. and Spriggs, T.L.B. (1979) Drugs and human memory: effects of low doses of nitrazepam and hyoscine on retention, *British Journal of Clinical Pharmacology, 7*, 479–83.

Kahn, R.L., Zarit, S.H., Hilbert, N.M. and Niederehe, G. (1975) Memory complaint and impairment of the aged: the effects of depression and altered brain function, *Archives of General Psychiatry, 32*, 1569–73.

Kapur, N. and Pearson, D. (1982) Memory symptoms and memory performance of neurological patients. Paper presented at the *Fifth European Conference of the International Neuropsychological Society*, Deauville, France.

Kazdin, A.E. (1982) *Single Case Research Designs*, Oxford University Press, New York.

Keefe, F.J., Kopel, S.A. and Gordon, S.B. (1978) *A Practical Guide to Behavioural Assessment*, Springer Publishing Co., New York.

Kimura, D. (1963) Right temporal lobe damage, *Archives Neurology, 8*, 254–71.

Klein, R.M. and Fowler, R.S. (1981) Pressure relief training device: the microcalculator, *Archives of Physical and Medical Rehabilitation, 62*, 500–1.

Krebs, E.W., Snowman, J. and Smith, S.H. (1978) Teaching new dogs old tricks:

facilitating prose learning through mnemonic training, *Journal of Instructional Psychology, 5*, 33–9.

Kreutzer, M.A., Leonard, C. and Flavell, J.H. (1975) An interview study of children's knowledge about memory, *Monographs of the Society for Research in Child Development, 40* (1, Serial No. 159).

Kurlychek, R.T. (1983) Use of a digital alarm chronograph as a memory aid in early dementia, *Clinical Gerontologist, 1*, 93–4.

Lacey, J.I. and Lacey, B.C. (1970) Some autonomic nervous system interrelationships; in P. Black (ed.), *Physiological Correlates of Emotion,* Academic Press, New York.

Lally, M. (1981) Computer-assisted teaching of sight-word recognition for mentally retarded school children, *American Journal of Mental Deficiency, 85*, 383–8.

Landauer, T.K. and Bjork, R.A. (1978) Optimum rehearsal patterns and name learning; in M.M. Gruneberg, P.E. Morris and R.N. Sykes (eds.), *Practical Aspects of Memory,* Academic Press, London.

Langer, E.J., Rodin, J., Beck, P., Weinman, C. and Spitzer, L. (1979) Environmental determinants of memory improvement in late adulthood, *Journal of Personality and Social Psychology, 37*, 11, 2003–13.

Levin, G.R. and Simmonds, S.S. (1962) Response to food and praise by emotionally disturbed boys, *Psychological Reports, 11*, 539–46.

Levin, H.S., Grossman, R.G., Sarwar, M. and Meyers, C.A. (1981) Linguistic recovery after closed head injury, *Brain and Language, 12*, 360–74.

Lewinsohn, P.M. and Graf, M. (1973) A follow-up study of persons referred for vocational rehabilitation who have suffered brain injury, *Journal of Community Psychology, 1*, 57–62.

Lezak, M.D. (1976) *Neuropsychological Assessment,* Oxford University Press, New York.

Lezak, M.D. (1979) Recovery of memory and learning functions following traumatic brain injury, *Cortex, 15*, 63–72.

Lincoln, N.B. (1981) Discrepancies between capabilities and performance of activities of daily living in multiple sclerosis patients, *International Rehabilitation Medicine, 3*, 84–8.

Lincoln, N.B. (1982) The Speech Questionnaire: an assessment of functional language ability, *International Rehabilitation Medicine, 4*, 114–17.

Locke, J. (1690) *Everyman's Library Edition* (1961), vol. I, 339–40.

Lorayne, H. (1979) *How to Develop a Super Power Memory,* A. Thomas and Co., Wellingborough.

Lorayne, H. and Lucas, J. (1975) *The Memory Book,* W.H. Allen, London.

Lucas, R.W. (1977) A study of patients' attitudes to computer interrogation, *International Journal of Man-machine Studies, 9*, 69–86.

Lynch, W. (1982) The use of computer games in cognitive rehabilitation; in L. Trexler (ed.), *Cognitive Rehabilitation: Conceptualization and Intervention,* Plenum Press, New York.

MacDonald, M.L. and Settin, J.M. (1978) Reality orientation versus sheltered workshops as treatment for the institutionalised ageing, *Journal of Gerontology, 33*, 416–21.

Martin, G.L. and Powers, R.B. (1967) Attention span: an operant conditioning analysis, *Exceptional Children, 33*, 565–70.

Mason, S.E. and Smith, A.D. (1977) Imagery in the aged, *Experimental Aging*

Research, 3, 17-32.

Masur, E.F., McIntyre, C.W. and Flavell, J.H. (1973) Developmental changes in apportionment of study time in a multitrial free recall task, *Journal of Experimental Child Psychology, 15*, 237-46.

Maxwell, C. (1973) *Clinical Research for All*, Cambridge Medical Publications.

McCarty, D. (1980) Investigation of a visual imagery mnemonic device for acquiring face-name associations, *Journal of Experimental Psychology, Human Learning Memory, 6*, 145-55.

McCough, G.P., Austin, G.M., Liu, C.N. and Liu, C.Y. (1958) Sprouting as a cause of spasticity, *Journal of Neurophysiology, 21*, 205-16.

McDonald, R.J. (1982) Drug treatment of senile dementia; in D. Wheatley (ed.), *Psychopharmacology of Old Age*, Oxford University Press, Oxford, pp. 113-38.

McMenemey, W.H. (1970) Alois Alzheimer and his disease; in G.E.W. Wolstenholme and M. O'Connor (eds.), *Alzheimer's Disease and Related Conditions*, Churchill, London, pp. 5-9.

McGhie, A. (1969) *Pathology of Attention*, Penguin Books, London.

McGuinness, D. and Pribram, K. (1980) The neuropsychology of attention: emotional and motivational controls; in M. Whitlock (ed.), *The Brain and Psychology*, New York, Academic Press.

McKinlay, W.W., Brooks, D.N., Bond, M.R., Martinage, D.P. and Marshall, M.M. (1981) The short term outcome of severe blunt head injured as reported by relatives of the injured person, *Journal of Neurology, Neurosurgery, and Psychiatry, 44*, 527-33.

McKinlay, W.W. and Brooks, D.N. (in press) Methodological problems in assessing psycho-social recovery following severe head injury, *Journal of Clinical Neuropsychology*.

Merchant, M. and Saxby, P. (1981) Reality orientation: a way forward, *Nursing Times, 77*, 33, 1442-5.

Mewaldt, S.P. and Ghoneim, M.M. (1979) The effects and interactions of scopolamine, physostigmine and methamphetamine on human memory, *Pharmacology, Biochemistry and Behaviour, 10*, 205-10.

Meyer, A. (1904) The anatomical facts and clinical varieties of traumatic insanity, *American Journal of Insanity, 60*, 373-441.

Miller, E. (1970) Simple and choice reaction time following head injury, *Cortex, 6*, 121-7.

Miller, E. (1975) Impaired recall and the memory disturbance in pre-senile dementia, *British Journal of Social and Clinical Psychology, 14*, 73-9.

Miller, E. and Cruzat, A.C. (1981) The effects of irrelevant information on task performance after mild and severe head injury, *British Journal of Social and Clinical Psychology, 20*, 1, 69-71.

Miller, G.A. (1956) The magical number seven, plus or minus two; some limits on our capacity for processing information, *Psychological Review, 63*, 81-97.

Milner, B. (1971) Interhemispheric differences in the localisation of psychological processes in man, *British Medical Bulletin: Cognitive Psychology, 27*, 272-7.

Milner, B., Corkin, S. and Tueber, J.L. (1968) Further analysis of the hippocampal amnesic syndrome: a 14-year follow-up study of HM, *Neuropsychologia, 6*, 215, 234.

Mindus, P., Cronholm, B., Levander, S.E. and Schalling, D. (1976) Piracetam-induced improvement of mental performance, *Acta. Psychiatrica Scandanavica*,

54, 150–160.

Moffat, N.J. (1983) The 'feeling of knowing' phenomenon amongst severely head injured (in preparation).

Moffat, N.J. and Coward, A. (1983) Training visual imagery for names with the head injured (in preparation).

Moray, N. (1969) *Attention: Selective Processes in Vision and Hearing*, Academic Press, London.

Morris, P.E. (1977) Practical strageies for human learning and remembering; in M.J.A. Howe (ed.), *Adult Learning*, Wiley, Chichester and New York.

Morris, P.E. and Reid, R.L. (1970) The repeated use of mnemonic imagery, *Psychonomic Science, 20*, 337–8.

Morris, R., Wheatley, J. and Britton, P. (1983) Retrieval from long-term memory in senile dementia: cued recall revisited, *British Journal of Clinical Psychology, 22*, 141–2.

Nelson, H.E. and O'Connell, A. (1978) Dementia: the estimation of premorbid intelligence levels using the new adult reading test, *Cortex, 14*, 234–44.

Newcombe, F. (1982) The psychological consequences of closed head injury: assessment and rehabilitation, *Injury, 14*, 111–36.

Newcombe, F. and Artiola i Fortuny, L. (1979) Problems and perspectives in the evaluation of psychological deficits after cerebral lesions, *International Rehabilitation Medicine, 1*, 4 182–92.

Nielsen, J., Homma, A. and Biorn-Henriksen, T. (1977) Follow up 15 years after a geronto-psychiatric prevalence study, *Journal of Gerontology, 32*, 554–61.

Oakley, D.A. (1983) Learning capacity outside neocortex in animals and man; in G. Davey (ed.), *Animal Models of Human Behaviour*, Wiley, London.

Olpe, H.R. and Lynch, G.S. (1982) The action of piracetam on the electrical activity of the hippocampal slice preparation: a field potential analysis, *European Journal of Pharmacology, 80*, 415–19.

Paivio, A. and Desrochers, A. (1979) Effects of an imagery mnemonic on second language recall and comprehension, *Canadian Journal of Psychology, 33*, 17–28.

Parker, S.A. and Serrats, A.P. (1976) Memory recovery after traumatic coma, *Acta Neurochir, 34*, 71–7.

Patten, B.M. (1972) The ancient art of memory, *Archives of Neurology, 26*, 25–31.

Perry, E.K., Perry, R.H., Blessed, G. and Tomlinson, B.E. (1977) Necropsy evidence of central cholinergic deficits in senile dementia, *Lancet, 1*, 189.

Perry, E.K., Tomlinson, B.E., Blessed, G., Bergmann, K., Gibson, P.H. and Perry, R.H. (1978) Correlation of cholinergic abnormalities with senile plaques and mental test scores in senile dementia, *British Journal of Medicine, 2*, 1457–9.

Peterson, L.R. and Peterson, M.J. (1959) Short-term retention of individual verbal items, *Journal of Experimental Psychology, 58*, 193–8.

Platel, A. and Porsolt, R.D. (1982) Habituation of exploratory activity in mice: a screening test for memory enhancing drugs, *Psychopharmacology, 78*, 346–52.

Pollak, I.V. (1982) Microprocessor-based communications system for the non-verbal person with serious motor handicaps: a preliminary report, *Bulletin of Prosthetics Research, 19*, 7–17.

Poon, L.W. (1980) A systems approach for the assessment and treatment of memory problems; in J. Ferguson and C. Taylor (eds.), *Handbook of Behavioural Medicine; 1, Systems Intervention*, Spectrum Publishers Inc., NY, pp. 191–212.

Posner, M. (1975) Psychobiology of attention; in M. Gazzaniga and C. Blakemore (eds.), *Handbook of Psychobiology*, Academic Press, New York.

Postman, L. and Phillips, L.W. (1965) Short-term temporal changes in free recall, *Quarterly Journal of Experimental Psychology, 17*, 132–8.

Powell, G.E. (1981) *Brain Function Therapy*, Gower Publishing Co. Ltd, Aldershot.

Price, D.L., Whitehouse, P.J., Struble, R.G., Clark, A.W., Coyle, J.T., DeLong, M.R. and Hedreen, J.C. (1982) Basal forebrain cholinergic systems in Alzheimer's disease and related dementia, *Neurosciences Comment, 1*, 84–92.

Pugh, E. (1970) *A Dictionary of Acronyms and Abbreviations*, Clive Bingley Ltd. and Hamden Court; Anchor Books, London.

Rabbitt, P. (1981) Cognitive psychology needs models for changes in performance with old age; in J.B. Long and A.D. Baddeley (eds.), *Attention and Performance, IX*, Lawrence Erlbaum Associates, Hillsdale, NJ.

Ratcliff, G. (1970) *Aspects of disordered space perception*, doctoral thesis, University of Oxford.

Raven, J.C. (1958) *Mill Hill Vocabulary Scale* (2nd edn), Lewis & Co., London.

Raven, J.C. (1960) *Guide to the Standard Progressive Matrices*, Lewis & Co., London.

Raybould, E.C. and Solity, J. (1982) Teaching with precision, *Special Education: Forward Trends, 9*, 9–13.

Reason, J. (1979) Actions not as planned; in G. Underwood and R. Stevens (eds.), *Aspects of Consciousness*, vol. 1, Academic Press, London.

Reason, J. and Mycielska, K. (1982) *Absent Minded?: The Psychology of Mental Lapses and Everyday Errors*, Prentice Hall, Englewood-Cliffs, NJ.

Reisberg, B., Ferris, S.H. and Gershon, S. (1981) An overview of pharmacologic treatment of cognitive decline in the aged, *American Journal of Psychiatry, 138*, 593–600.

Rey, A. (1959) *Le test de copie de figure complexe*, Editions Centre de Psychologie Appliquee, Paris.

Rimmer, L. (1982) *Reality Orientation: Principles and Practice*, PTM Publications, Buckingham.

Robertson-Tchabo, E.A., Hausman, C.P. and Arenberg, D. (1976) A classical mnemonic for older learners: a trip that works, *Educational Gerontologist, 1*, 215–26.

Ruesch, J. (1944) Intellectual impairment in head injuries, *American Journal of Psychiatry, 100*, 480–96.

Russell, W.R. and Smith, A. (1961) Post traumatic amnesia in closed head injuries, *Archives of Neurology, 5*, 4–17.

Sarno, M.T. (1969) *The Functional Communication Profile: Manual of Directions*, Institute of Rehabilitation Medicine, New York University Medical Centre.

Saunders, P. (1980) The use of microcomputers in the teaching of the mentally handicapped, *Apex, 8*, 87–9.

Schacter, D. and Crovitz, H. (1977) Memory function after closed head injury: a review of the quantitative research, *Cortex, 13*, 105–76.

Shallice, T. (1979) Neuropsychological research and the fractionation of memory systems; in L. Nilsson (ed.), *Perspectives in Memory Research*, Lawrence Erlbaum Associates, Hillsdale, NJ.

Shallice, T. and Warrington, E.K. (1970) Independent functioning of verbal memory stores: a neuropsychological study, *Quarterly Journal of Experimental*

Psychology, 22, 261–73.

Sheikh, K., Smith, D.S., Mead, T.W. and Brennan, P.J. (1978) Methods and problems of a stroke rehabilitation trial, *British Journal of Occupational Therapy, 41,* 262–5.

Shenton, R.K. (1975) The automatic memorandum clock, *Antiquarian Horology,* June, 337–9.

Shiffrin, R.M. and Schneider, W. (1977) Controlled and automatic human information processing. II, perceptual learning, automatic attending and a general theory, *Psychological Review, 84,* 127–90.

Siegal, S. (1956) *Nonparametric statistics for the behavioural sciences,* McGraw-Hill, New York.

Signoret, J.L., Whiteley, A. and Lhermitte, F. (1978) Influence of choline on amnesia in early Alzheimer's disease, *Lancet, 2,* 837.

Sitaram, N., Weingartner, H., Caine, E.D. and Gillin, J.C. (1978) Choline: selective enhancement of serial learning and encoding of low imagery words in man, *Life Science, 22,* 1555–60.

Sitaram, N., Weingartner, H. and Gillin, J.C. (1978) Human serial learning: enhancement with arecholine and choline and impairment with scopolamine, *Science, 201,* 274–6.

Skilbeck, C.E. and Woods, R.T. (1980) The factorial structure of the Wechsler memory scale: samples of neurological and psychogeriatric patients, *Journal of Clinical Neuropsychology, 2,* 293–300.

Smith, A.D. (1975) Interaction between human ageing and memory, *Georgia Institute of Technology Progress Report,* no. 2.

Smith, A.G. (1969) *Irving's Anatomy Mnemonics,* 4th edn, London, Churchill Livingstone.

Smith, B.J. and Barker, H.R. (1972) Influence of a reality orientation training programme on the attitudes of trainees towards the elderly, *Gerontologist, 12,* 262–4.

Smith, C.M. and Swash, M. (1979) Physostigmine in Alzheimer's disease, *Lancet, 1,* 42.

Smith, C.M., Swash, M., Exton-Smith, A.N., Phillips, M.J., Overstall, P.W., Piper, M.E. and Bailey, M.R. (1978) Choline in Alzheimer's disease, *Lancet, 2,* 318.

Sokolov, Y.N. (1963) *Perception and the Conditioned Reflex,* Macmillan, New York.

Squire, L.R. (1981) Two forms of human amnesia: an analysis of forgetting, *The Journal of Neuroscience, 1,* 625–30.

Squire, L.R. and Davis, H.P. (1981) The pharmacology of memory: a neurobiological perspective, *Annual Review of Pharmacology and Toxicology, 21,* 323–56.

Staats, A.W. (1965) A case in and a strategy for the extension of learning principles to problems of human behaviour; in L. Krasner and P. Ullman (eds.), *Research in Behavior Modification,* Holt, Rinehart & Winston, New York.

Staats, A.W., Staats, S.W., Ginley, J.R., Minke, K.A. and Wolf, M. (1964) Reinforcement variables in the control of unit reading responses, *Journal of Experimental Analysis of Behaviour, 7,* 139–49.

Staples, D. and Lincoln, N.B. (1979) Intellectual impairment in multiple sclerosis and its relation to functional abilities, *Rheumatology and Rehabilitation, 18,* 153–60.

Sternberg, S. (1975) Memory scanning: new findings and current controversies, *Quarterly Journal of Experimental Psychology, 27*, 1–32.

Stevens, R. (1981) Brain Mechanisms and Selective Attention; in G. Underwood and R. Stevens (eds.), *Aspects of Consciousness*, Academic Press, London.

Strub, R.L. and Black, F.W. (1981) *Organic Brain Syndromes*, Davis, Philadelphia.

Sunderland, A., Harris, J. and Baddeley, A.D. (1983) Do laboratory tests predict everyday memory? A neuropsychological study, *Journal of Verbal Learning and Verbal Behaviour, 22*, 341–57.

Sunderland, A., Harris, J. and Gleave, J. (in press) Memory failures in everyday life after severe head injury, *Journal of Clinical Neuropsychology*.

Terry, R.D. and Davies, P. (1980) Dementia of the Alzheimer type, *Annual Review of Neuroscience, 3*, 77–95.

Terry, R.D. and Wisniewski, H. (1970) The ultrastructure of the neuro-fibrillary tangle and the senile plaque; in G.E.W. Wolstenholme and M. O'Conner (eds.), *Alzheimer's Disease and Related Conditions*, Churchill, London, 145–65.

Thomsen, I.V. (1977) Verbal learning in aphasic and non-aphasic patients with severe head injuries, *Scandinavian Journal of Rehabilitation Medicine, 9*, 73–7.

Toong, H.D. and Gupta, A. (1982) Personal computers, *Scientific American*, December, 89–98.

Trabasso, T. and Bower, G. (1968) *Attention in Learning Theory and Research*, Wiley, New York.

Trexler, L. (1982) (ed.) *Cognitive Rehabilitation, Conceptualization and Intervention*, Plenum Press, New York.

Vallar, G. and Baddeley, A.D. (in press) Fractionation of working memory. Neuropsychological evidence for a phonological short-term store, *Journal of Verbal Learning and Verbal Behaviour*.

Vanderheiden, G.C. (1982) The practical use of microcomputers in rehabilitation, *Bulletin of Prosthetics Research, 19*, 1–5.

Van Zomeren, A.H. (1981) *Reaction Time and Attention after Closed Head Injury*, Srets and Zeitlinger BV, Lisse.

Van Zomeren, A.H., Brouwer, W.H. and Deelman, B.G. (1983) Attentional deficits: the riddles of selectivity, speed and alterness; in Brooks, D.N., *Closed Head Injury: Social, Psychological and Family Consequences*, Oxford University Press, Oxford.

Van Zomeren, A.H. and Deelman, B.G. (1976) Differential effects of simple and choice reaction after closed head injury, *Clinical Neurology and Neurosurgery, 79*, 81–90.

Van Zomeren, A.H. and Deelman, B. (1978) Long term recovery of visual reaction time after closed head injury, *Journal of Neurology, Neurosurgery and Psychiatry, 41*, 452–7.

Vigouroux, R.P., Baurand, C., Naquet, R. *et al.* (1971) A series of patients with cranio-cerebral injuries studied neurologically, psychometrically, electroencephalographically and socially, *International Symposium on Head Injuries*, Churchill Livingstone, Edinburgh.

Volans, P.J. and Levy, R. (1982) A re-evaluation of an automated tailored test of concept learning with elderly psychiatric patients, *British Journal of Clinical Psychology, 21*, 93–102.

Wall, P.D. (1975) Signs of plasticity and reconnection in spinal cord damage; in

Porter, R. and Fitzsimmons, D.W. (eds.), *Outcome of Severe Damage to the Central Nervous System, Ciba Foundation Symposium 34*, Elsevier, Amsterdam.

Wall, P.D. (1977) The presence of ineffective synapses and the circumstances which unmask them, *Philosophical Transactions of the Royal Society of London, Series B*, 378, 361–72.

Walsh, K. (1978) *Neuropsychology: A Clinical Approach*, Edinburgh, Churchill Livingstone.

Walton, D. and Black, D.A. (1957) The validity of a psychological test of brain damage, *British Journal of Medical Psychology*, 30, 270–9.

Warrington, E.K. (1971) Perception of naturalistic stimuli in patients with focal brain lesions, *Journal of Brain Research*, 31, 370.

Warrington, E.K. (1974) Deficient recognition memory in organic amnesia, *Cortex*, 10, 284–91.

Warrington, E.K. and James, M. (1967) Disorders of visual perception in patients with localised cerebral lesions, *Neuropsychologia*, 5, 1–13.

Warrington, E.K. and Taylor, A.M. (1973) The contribution of the right parietal lobe to object recognition, *Cortex*, 7, 152–64.

Waterfall, R.C. (1979) Automating standard intelligence tests, *Journal of Audiovisual Media in Medicine*, 2, 21–4.

Wechsler, D. (1945) A standardised memory scale for clinical use, *Journal of Psychology*, 19, 87–95.

Wechsler, D. (1955) *Wechsler Adult Intelligence Scale*, Psychological Corporation, New York.

Welford, A.T. (1980) Memory and age: a perspective view; in L.W. Poon, J.L. Fozard, L.S. Cermak, D. Arenberg and L.W. Thompson (eds.), *New Directions in Memory and Aging*, Lawrence Erlbaum Associates, Hillsdale, NJ, pp. 1–17.

White, D.R. (1971) *A Glossary of Acronyms, Abbreviations and Symbols*, Don White Consultants, Germantown, Md.

White, P., Goodhart, M.J., Keet, J.P., Hiley, C.R., Carrasco, L.H., Williams, I.E. and Bowen, D.M. (1977) Neocortical cholinergic neurones in elderly people, *Lancet*, 1, 668–71.

Whiting, S.E., Cockburn, J., Bhavnani, G. and Lincoln, N.B. (1984) *The Rivermead Perceptual Assessment*, NFER-Nelson.

Williams, M. (1968) The measurement of memory in clinical practice, *British Journal of Social and Clinical Psychology*, 7, 19–34.

Wilson, B. (1981) Teaching a patient to remember people's names after removal of a left temporal lobe tumour, *Behavioural Psychotherapy*, 9, 338–44.

Wilson, B. (1981a) A survey of behavioural treatments carried out at a rehabilitation centre for stroke and head injuries, in Powell, G. *Brain Function Therapy*, Gower Press, Aldershot.

Wilson, B. (1982) Success and failure in memory training following a cerebral vascular accident, *Cortex*, 18, 581–94.

Wilson, B. and Moffat, N. (1984) Rehabilitation of memory for everyday life; in Harris, J. and Morris, P. (eds.), *Everyday Memory: Actions and Absent Mindedness*, Academic Press, London.

Wilson, J.T.L., Brooks, D.N. and Phillips, W.A. (1982) Using a microcomputer to study perception, memory and attention after head injury. Paper presented at *Fifth Annual Conference of International Neuropsychological Society*, June 15–18, Deauville, France.

Wollen, K.A., Weber, A. and Lowry, D.H. (1972) Bizarreness versus interaction of mental images as a determinants of learning, *Cognitive Psychology, 3*, 518–23.

Wood, R.Ll. (1983a) Behaviour disorders: their presentation and management; in D.N. Brooks (ed.), *Outcome of Severe Blunt Head Injury*, Oxford University Press, Oxford.

Wood, R.Ll. (1983b) An attention training procedure during rehabilitation of severe brain injury; in G. Stanley (ed.), *Proceedings of the Sixth Brain Impairment Conference*, Melbourne, Australia.

Wood, R.Ll. and Eames, P.G. (1981) Application of behaviour modification in the rehabilitation of traumatically brain injured adults; in G. Davey (ed.), *Application of Conditioning Theory*, Methuen, London.

Woods, R.T. (1979) Reality orientation and staff attention: a controlled study, *British Journal of Psychology, 134*, 502–7.

Woods, R.T. (1983) Specificity of learning in reality orientation sessions: a single case study, *Behaviour Research and Therapy, 21*, 173–5.

Woods, R.T. and Holden, U.P. (1982) Reality Orientation; in B. Isaacs (ed.), *Recent Advances in Geriatric Medicine*, Churchill, Livingstone.

Woods, R.T., Simpson, S. and Nicol, R. (1980) Reality Orientation: the relative effects of 24 hour reality orientation and reality orientation sessions (unpublished manuscript).

Woodward, S. (1979) The effects of the reality orientation classroom on elderly confused people. Unpublished dissertation, University of Surrey.

Wurtman, R.J. and Growdon, J.H. (1979) Dietary control of central cholinergic activity; in K.L. Davis and P.A. Berger (eds.), *Brain Acetylcholine and Neuropsychiatric Disease*, Plenum Press, New York, 461–81.

Yates, F.A. (1966) *The art of memory*, Routledge & Kegan Paul, London.

Yule, W. and Carr, J. (eds.) (1980) *Behaviour Modification for the Mentally Handicapped*, Croom Helm, London.

Yule, W. and Hemsley, D. (1977) Single case methods in medical psychology; in S. Rachman (ed.), *Contributions to Medical Psychology, 1*, Pergamon Press, Oxford.

Zarit, S.H., Cole, K.D. and Guider, R.L. (1981) Memory training strategies and subjective complaints of memory in the aged, *Gerontologist, 21*, 158–64.

Zeaman, D. and House, B.J. (1963) The role of attention in retardate discrimination learning; in N.R. Ellis (ed.), *Handbook of Mental Deficiency*, McGraw-Hill, New York.

AUTHOR INDEX

SUBJECT INDEX

absent mindedness 64, 92
acoustic visual strategy 184
activities of daily living 30, 33,
    34, 42, 169, 203, 207
affective states 63
aide memoire 69
aims of treatment 31–2, 35, 66,
    84, 96–7, 107, 109, 173
airplane list 179
alphabetic cueing and searching
    79–80, 176, 179, 183
Alzheimer's disease *see* dementia
amnesia 6, 12, 17, 63–5, 89, 91,
    100–1, 106, 132–3 *passim*,
    192–3; amnesic patients 12–13,
    17–18, 64, 66–9, 76–8, 81, 88,
    106, 152, 182; amnesic syndrome
    42, 90–2, 97, 189
aneurysm 90–1, 104, 122
anterior communicating artery 90–1,
    104
anxiety 35, 64, 141
aphasia 42–3, 87, 89–90, 99, 101,
    103, 111, 120, 131, 141, 161–2,
    167, 190, 206
articulatory loop 12, 15, 19
assessment 2, 28–45, 66, 84, 96–7,
    116–23 *passim*, 131, 160, 202–4,
    209
attention 3, 20, 29, 35, 42, 148–70,
    201; alertness/arousal 149–50;
    disorders of 153–5; divided atten-
    tional deficit 154; effort 150–1;
    focused attentional deficit 154,
    and memory 151–3; selective
    attention 159, 161, 168–9;
    selectivity 149–50; sustained
    attention 158–9, 161; training
    4, 155–70, 174, 181, 185; vigil-
    ance training 160–3

baselines 36, 41, 82, 97, 107–8,
    123–4, 156–7, 168
behavioural: approach 3, 106, 110,
    207; assessment, analysis and
    observation 34–5, 40–2, 96–7,
    106–7, 146, 188, 209; change
    156–7; memory tests 97–8, 194,

203; methods 167–9; problems
    33, 35, 145, 155, 157, 190;
    programmes 3, 6, 8, 43, 107,
    167–9, 192, 207; psychology 150
Birmingham group 182, 186, 189,
    191
brain damage: 1, 3, 6–7, 27, 29–30,
    35, 43, 51, 63–4, 66, 70, 77,
    86–7, 91–3, 99, 103–4, 122,
    140–70 *passim*

calendars 201; *see also* external aids
case studies 89–92; KJ 89–90; DE
    90–1; MC 91–2, 106–8; Mr B 97;
    KW 122; NH 200; PB 207; TA
    124; SC 201; SO 125; RM 129
central executive 15, 19
central nervous system 86, 149
cerebral vascular accident *see* stroke
chaining 3, 108–9
chanting and recitation 52
checklists and rating scales 29, 31–5,
    40–1, 43, 94–5, 200
chunking 164
cholinergic neurotransmission and
    cholinergic activity 3, 51, 133–8,
    140, 142–3, 145–7
cholinergic receptors 133–5, 137–8
clinical psychologists *see* psycho-
    logists
coal gas poisoning 6
coding *see* encoding
cognitive: abilities 29, 43, 154, 159,
    167; change 124, 134; function
    27, 42–3, 140, 146, 165, 170;
    impairments and deficits 12, 29,
    35, 40, 43, 140–1, 143, 145, 202,
    204, 211; levels 155; recovery
    115; rehabilitation and training
    113, 156, 165, 169–70; skills 50,
    167; variables 63
coma 155
communication aids 205
computers *see also* microcomputers
    and training 53, 67, 111–31, 164–7
concentration 29, 65, 148, 154,
    156–8, 165, 168–70, 206
conductive education 168–9